ETHICS

ETHICS

VOLUME 2

Applications of an Ethical Theology

TRUTZ RENDTORFF

Translated by
Keith Crim

FORTRESS PRESS   **MINNEAPOLIS**

BJ
1253
.R4413
1986
v2
151059
mar.1991

ETHICS
Volume 2
Applications of an Ethical Theology

Translated from the German *Ethik: Grendelemente, Methodologie und Konkre-tionen einer ethischen Theologie*, Band 2 (Stuttgart: W. Kohlhammer Verlag, 1981).

Library of Congress Cataloging-in-Publication Data

(Revised for vol. 2)
Rendtorff, Trutz.
    Ethics
    Translation of: Ethik.
    Vol. 2 published in Minneapolis, Minn.
    Includes bibliographical references and indexes.
    Contents: v. 1. Basic elements and methodology in an ethical theology—v. 2. Applications of an ethical theology.
    1. Christian ethics.   I. Title.
BJ1253.R4413   1986   241   85–45484
ISBN 0–8006–0767–8 (v. 1)
ISBN 0–8006–0909–3 (v. 2)

The paper used in this publication meets the minimum requirements of American National Standard for Information Sciences—Permanence of Paper for Printed Library Materials, ANSI Z329.48–1984.   ∞™

Manufactured in the U.S.A.   AF 1-0909

93   92   91   90   89   1   2   3   4   5   6   7   8   9   10

Contents

Preface

The concrete applications of ethics are based on the basic elements of the ethical realities of life and on the methodology of ethics, and they follow the approach developed there. The Introduction explains this in greater detail. Anyone who deals with ethical questions in detail to any degree knows the obstacles that must be overcome in seeking to apply ethical principles and the risks that this involves. In my efforts to set forth the concrete applications of ethics I have always kept in mind Dietrich Bonhoeffer's advice and warning: "An ethic cannot be a book in which everything is written about how the world ought to be but unfortunately is not, and an ethicist cannot be a person who always knows better than anyone else what is to be done and how to do it. An ethic cannot be a reference work for moral actions which are guaranteed to be unobjectionable, and an ethicist cannot be the competent evaluator and judge of every human action. An ethic cannot be a testtube in which we can create ethical or Christian persons, and an ethicist cannot be the embodiment and the ideal type of a basically moral life" (*Ethics*, ed. Eberhard Bethge, 1975, p. 285).

This heartfelt comment of Bonhoeffer's anticipates the expectations that are attached in one way or another to the applications of ethics. It also makes good sense whenever someone sets out in the tradition of theological ethics to tread the path of a detailed development of ethical practice. It is in agreement with the basic convictions of ethical theology that ethics must be mediated, comprehended, and portrayed by means of the ethical realities of life of which it is speaking. Dignified reserve and exclusive and uninterrupted attention to basic principles may be the prerogative of philosophers, but here it would be out of place, even though concrete applications of ethical principles are particularly susceptible to criticism. Therefore this book is addressed to readers who are willing to engage in argumentation. The terrain where these applications are made is not a sort of Christian commando bridgehead or command post but is moral discourse both within and outside theology.

Apostles of duty pure and simple prefer to avoid the responsibility of showing us what the reality looks like that corresponds to the duty. But concrete applications can be required only when we can know and state the form of reality in which a demand can hold sway. Ethical applications must submit to this mediating task. They often prove to be occasions of strife because the concrete problems of the ethical reality of life are of concern to us in every instance. The future of ethics begins in the present wherever ethics seeks for mutual understanding and agreement concerning its task. To this extent the applications developed here are not intended to put an end to discourse but, in their own way, to promote it. Thus the content of the applications and the method by which they are arrived at follow logically from the task of theology to "lead the way by formulating the question in a manner that truly accords with reality" (vol. 1, p. 7).

Here at the conclusion of my work on these concrete applications, I wish to thank my wife, Margrit Rendtorff, and Dr. Friedrich W. Graf for their help and advice, and Herbert Will for his assistance in the preparation of the manuscript. Herbert Will also prepared the indexes found at the end of [the German edition]. Mrs. Editha Sauer has again demonstrated her abilities in preparing this work for the printer, and I wish to thank her, as well as the publishing house W. Kohlhammer and the editor of the series in which both volumes 1 and 2 appeared [in Germany].

TRUTZ RENDTORFF

PART FOUR

APPLICATIONS OF ETHICS

Introduction:
Approaching the Task

"Ethics is the theory of the conduct of human life" (vol. 1, p. 11). The practical applications do not turn their back on the theory. Rather, the theory is the backbone of the applications. An ethic that is consciously based on the ethical realities of life must in specific situations discover and set forth the features of those situations that qualify them as ethically relevant. That is the task to be performed in developing these applications. They lead the ethicist to differing places where life is being lived and to ever differing positions toward the issues. Ethical questions are life questions that are encountered in the living of life and toward which we must adopt positions amid the realities in which our lives are lived out. That is the starting point for the ethics developed here. The basic elements of the ethical reality of life were developed in volume 1, pages 31–82, in terms of an ethical theology. The methodology of ethics (vol. 1, pp. 85–188) exposed ethical theology to the various currents and directions of ethical argumentation. Now the applications of ethics take up both the basic elements and the methodology and carry their development forward along the paths and in the situations where examples are possible of how the meaning of ethics for life can be made clear. The multiplicity of individual themes with which the applications deal, in contrast to the discussion of the bases and the methodology, is at once new and both challenging and compelling. At the same time, the discussion of the individual issues is determined throughout by the points of view that were developed and for which supporting arguments were given in volume 1. It is in reference to them that the concrete applications have been arranged and developed. Thus the applications stand in a theoretical frame of reference that serves to identify the specifically ethical significance of the problems arising in the actual living of our lives.

The first way the applications are developed is with reference to the basic element of life termed the "givenness of life" (vol. 1, pp. 33–49). The ethical applications here involve life situations that demand our

3

taking a position in regard to the elementary prerequisites for life. Such a position is then placed in relation to the three methodological aspects of the question, What should we do? (vol. 1, pp. 88–94). In bringing one of the basic elements of ethical theology together in this way with methodological considerations, we are able, concerning the applications of the theory, to discuss what it means, first, to enter into obligations and to act by the rules; second, to take part in renewing the validity of these prerequisites and to exercise responsibility for leading our own life; and third, to attain clarity concerning the goals of our actions and to justify our actions.

The second way in which the applications are developed is with reference to the basic element of life termed the "giving of life" (vol. 1, pp. 51–73). Here the ethical applications involve the active life, the independent commitment of our life to the cause of building up the ethical reality of life. Once again, by taking methodological considerations into account we can find examples of appropriate positions for the tasks of, first of all, making life possible for others, as our duty; second, participating in the development of personal independence, as the handing-on of a sense of responsibility; and third, acknowledging that life is given to us as a trust.

The third way in which the applications are developed is with reference to the basic element of life termed "reflection on life" (vol. 1, pp. 75–82). Here the ethical applications deal with the conflicts growing out of the differences between humans involved in action, conflicts that become truly life threatening and that lead to the quest for orientation on the frontiers of life. With the help of the methodological aspects, the applications of ethical theory here take the form, first of all, of the inescapable necessity of acknowledging human differences; second, of our responsibility in life-threatening situations; and third, of ethical orientation on the frontiers of the actions that are open to us.

Thus we have in outline a sketch of the theoretical frame of reference of the concrete applications. In this framework, the examples examined of typical situations in life fall into five different categories. The examples are chosen from the realms of marriage and family, politics, economics, culture, and religion. In contrast to the approach often found in theological ethics, these realms are not reviewed in succession in and for themselves. Instead, the procedure will be to trace positions that cut across the various realms. Themes will thereby be defined in concrete examples. This procedure should protect the independence of ethics from being lost sight of in a mass of individual aspects and bits of information that no one can cope with. Hence, it is in terms of ethical arguments that the applications are structured. We have thus not an apparent sequence or hierarchy of realms of life but a discussion in which the specific structure of ethical argumentation can be perceived more clearly. The fundamental principles of ethical theology are equally relevant for all the applications, and in their relations to one another the whole reality of life entrusted to us becomes our theme.

The applications have no claim to completeness but are examples of ethical argumentation, so that the whole realm of the reality of ethical living can be identified which demands that we take a position on questions of how we should live. The descriptions of issues are therefore developed only to the extent necessary to clarify the ethically relevant relationships.

The applications follow the basic pattern of the theory of how to lead one's life. That pattern constitutes the content and the subject matter of an ethical theology, but the explicit question of what is theological in ethics is less important than the examination of the specific structure of the positions assumed in the various areas of experience. All the individual definitions are equivalent in the theological understanding of reality developed in volume 1, so that only by taking all the applications into account together can we speak of having produced an ethical theology. This mediated theological nature of the applications conforms with the insight that theology does not have any supernatural wisdom at its disposal but must find a constructive way to bring its understanding of reality into play indirectly. Thus the applications lead us back to the task of ethical theology, which was their starting point, and lets us see them in a new and specific light.

The bibliographies for the individual themes are in no sense exhaustive. Thus attention is called to sources in which additional lists of works may be found: A. Hertz et al., eds., *Handbuch der christlichen Ethik*, 2 vols., 1978; A. Utz, *Bibliographie der Sozialethik*, 1956–; H. Kunst et al., eds., *Evangelisches Staatslexicon*, 2d ed., 1975; Gorres-Gesellschaft, ed., *Staatslexikon: Recht, Wirtschaft, Gesellschaft*, 6th ed., 8 vols., 1957–70; G. Krause and G. Müller, eds., *Theologische-Realenzyklopädie*, 1977– *(TRE);* F. Karrenberg, ed., *Evangelisches Soziallexikon*, 7th ed., 1980; *Lexikon für Theologie und Kirche*, 2d ed., 11 vols., 1957–68 *(LThK²);* O. Brunner, W. Conze, and R. Koselleck, eds., *Geschichtliche Grundbegriffe: Historisches Lexikon zur politisch-sozialen Sprache in Deutschland*, 4 vols., 1973–79; *Zeitschrift für Evangelische Ethik*, index of articles and subjects from 1957 on *(ZEE); Die Religion in Geschichte und Gegenwart: Handwörterbuch für Theologie und Religionswissenschaft*, 3d ed., 6 vols., 1957–65 *(RGG³).*

1. The Basic Structures of Life: Applications of the Givenness of Life

When we begin to take seriously the question of where it is in the actual living of our lives that we encounter specific tasks that require us to take a stand, we come to realize that we live in a world that makes definite claims on us. We find ourselves in situations involving basic relationships and requiring us to accept certain presuppositions. Moral discourse begins in the reality of life as it is given to us. This does not mean that we can decide whether or not we want to be involved in the concrete situations of life. Moral discourse begins with basic structures of life that demand our taking a stand. That is the theme of this first investigation of the concrete issues of ethics. Examples will be drawn from five areas of life:

1. The relationship between wife and husband
2. The political community
3. The earning of our living
4. Culture as the shape given to our world
5. Religion as the expression of our relationship to God

In these basic structures we encounter elementary relationships that it is our duty to accept. This does not mean that we are to accept the relationships unconditionally and uncritically. First of all, a position we take is our answer to the question of what we can contribute to the renewed validity of the presuppositions on which we base our lives. Second, these basic structures demand personal responsibility. And third, out of the relationship between our duty and the responsibilities placed upon us we are confronted with the task of achieving clarity about the goals of our life, that is, the task of evaluating our actions. These three aspects must find concrete and specific application in the various basic structures of life. They can be brought together in a maxim to guide our actions: Act in such a way that your life is lived in the service of fundamental presuppositions, that it contributes to the renewed validity of those presuppositions, and that it is thus open to an evaluation of the goals of your actions.

a. Entering into Elementary Relationships: Acting by the Rules

To adopt a position in regard to the basic structures of human life means, first of all, to recognize the ethical task implicit in life's elementary situation. Here the discussion must be clearly related to the ethical dimensions of life. Actions based on duty must be defined in terms of our assuming elementary responsibilities that require specific applications in life situations.

1) Marriage as the Model for Life in Community

Being married means entering into the responsibilities involved in the marriage relationship and fulfilling those responsibilities in one's own life.

Marriage is taken here as the first paradigm of a life relationship, not in order to assign it importance of the first rank but for a different reason. It is to marriage as an ethically conditioned way of life that we owe our lives. For this reason, our accepting the presuppositions that are basic to life and entering into elementary relationships involves concrete significance. It is necessary to consider in general the importance of marriage for the structure of life before an individual can decide in connection with his or her own life and career whether or not to marry. Marriage as a way of life is much in dispute today, perhaps more than ever before. The debate about marriage and the conflicts in and around marriage presuppose the validity of marriage, even where doubts are raised. What constitutes this validity, what the reasons for it are that must be made specific in the ethics of marriage, and why marriage is in dispute are all issues that indicate the importance of defining our position with respect to the basic structures of the ethical realities of life, realities that specifically represent the givenness of life. We must first examine the ethical structure of marriage, in order to cast light on the positions we intend to adopt.

For relevant literature, see H. Ringeling, "Die biblische Begründung der Monogamie," ZEE 10 (1966): 81–102; Interkonfessioneller Arbeitskreis für Ehe- und Familienfragen, "Christliche Einheit in der Ehe," 1969; W. Kasper, Zur

Theologie der christlichen Ehe, 1977; H.-J. Thilo, *Ehe ohne Norm? Eine evangelische Eheethik in Theorie und Praxis,* 1978; G. Gassmann, ed., *Ehe—Institution im Wandel: Zum evangelischen Eheverständnis heute,* 1979; E. Bleske, *Konfliktfeld Ehe und christliche Ethik,* 1981.

In a basic ethical sense, marriage is a community in which, by means of the relationship of husband to wife and wife to husband, human beings come to share in the reality of a living relationship that no one has or can have alone and over which no one has sole authority. Marriage is the always new and elementary expression of the fact that all persons who have received life as male or female are destined for community, that is, for a reciprocal relationship. Marriage is an example of human community.

This perspective neither ignores nor minimizes the extraordinary variety of forms that marriage takes, as seen through the history of culture, sociology, religion, and law. These data can be used to explain changes and crises in marriage. They can also be used as evidence that marriage is not a natural way of life but always only a convention adopted by consensus. Such a theory requires us to identify those points of view that are to play a role in moral discourse and to develop them in such a way as to show how marriage lays claim to the lives of persons as a living community in the ultimate sense. Indeed any theory must come to grips with Margaret Mead's conclusion that "no society has ever developed a form of marriage of general validity which did not involve the requirement 'till death us do part'" (*Male and Female,* 1977, p. 195).

Ethics cannot ignore the history of the problems that it deals with. Neither can it escape the task of taking a systematic stand on those problems. See, e.g., H. Schelsky, *Soziologie der Sexualität,* 1967; D. S. Bailey, *Mann und Frau im christlichen Denken,* 1963.

Marriage is a form of community that, involving as it does husband and wife, has for them its own distinctive obligations. It is not a question of whom the marriage "belongs to," because neither partner has sole authority over the marriage, but each can participate in it only by accepting the relationship and entering into it. For this reason the marriage can and must make claims on those who have entered it. The biblical metaphor that says that in marriage husband and wife become "one flesh" (Gen. 2:24) clearly expresses this relationship. At the same time, the difference between the sexes is the basis for their fundamental dependence on each other. Thus the basic implication of marriage is that husband and wife are equal in their marriage relationship. Ethics must make this equality explicit. The community of marriage gives clear expression to the original social nature of the givenness of life. But it does so only for those who undertake the marriage relationship and affirm their readiness to acknowledge the responsibilities that marriage involves. It does not do so in any purely natural way or without that participation which involves one's entire manner of life. Thus the Christian understanding of marriage affirms in a decisive manner human personality and individuality. In the Christian tradition this has been overlooked and neglected whenever marriage has been subsumed under the claims of natural goals and ordinances. Personality and individuality are involved wherever it is a question of adopting specific positions or of responsibility for one's own actions and life in marriage. Thus it is also the occasion for the crisis in marriage. As far as the social form of marriage is concerned, the Christian understanding of the form of marriage is open to the forces of historical change, because its basic feature is respect for the personality of husband and wife and not some specific historical or economic configuration of society. For this reason the specifically Christian nature of marriage has become much clearer in the modern age. It is both the basis for and the occasion of the experience of crisis in marriage, because it constitutes an especially precarious level of demands on the fulfillment of marriage. This means that our contemporary task is to present an ethically relevant view of marriage, because the social conditions that have come down to us from the past are no longer an adequate basis for marriage. That task has as its goal a shared life in which husband and wife participate equally.

The view of marriage as a form of life in community means that marriage contains within itself its own "purpose." This statement involves a criticism of traditional teachings about marriage and touches on the heart of the contemporary debate. Again and again the attempt to define marriage in terms of specific goals has threatened marriage and brought it into crisis.

That the view of marriage as a community contains its goal within itself is beyond dispute, if we perceive the community encompassing the life of a husband and a wife, a community that cannot be separated out as one area or one part of their life, because it exists solely in their shared life together. A living marriage involves all the aspects of an individual's life, including the making of responsible decisions about conduct. Its reality encompasses the whole of human life, and therefore lays claim to, changes, and shapes in multiple ways the life of an individual. Therefore marriage involves the wholeness and permanence of the relationship, because it is not a specialized relationship involving only goals and commitments that can be separated from one's life history but involves the living persons who are partners in the marriage. Marriage as a continuing relationship involves the entire span of life and all its contents, because a person does not bring to the marriage specific goals that are to be realized with the help of marriage but brings himself or herself, that is, the reality of a life that is not at an individual's own disposal for the accomplishment of certain goals but is rather the totality of the individual's own personal life. A marriage that served only certain goals would be a marriage with reservations and not a living community. A marriage that was seen as the means to a goal or goals and was lived that way would not take seriously the life of either of the marriage partners. This line of argument leads us to affirm that the ethically responsible independence of a marriage can be recognized when it is defended against use as an instrument for achieving goals, that is to say, against use by either the husband or the wife of the other partner for private goals that can be separated and distinguished from the marriage itself. A utilitarian understanding is in reality a negation of the marriage as a living community.

Just as one's life as something given is not at one's own disposal, so too the community of marriage is not at the service of individual goals. Marriage cannot be regarded as something to be used apart from the community of the partners who have entered into it. For these two persons it constitutes the reality of life. The basic ethical meaning of marriage demands that we make a commitment to enter into a community. It would be the opposite of a marriage if either partner were unwilling to accept the claims of the marriage, to be formed by it, to submit to its responsibilities. Anyone who enters into a marriage undertakes to build and form a community that has not existed before in this distinctive and individual form. A marriage partner forms a new reality, not for or by himself or herself but in and through community, that is to say, through joining with another in a shared life. Marriage constitutes something that might be called a transindividual biography for the individuals who enter into it.

This approach explains how it is that although marriage has been made to serve various goals that have changed through the course of history, the ethical structure of marriage could not be made ultimately dependent on these goals. Only the autonomy of marriage understood in an ethical sense enables us to understand how and why marriage can involve such differing goals. It is not free of relationships to society and to the state. The same persons who are marriage partners are also citizens, workers, Christians, and participants in the cultural life of the community.

The traditional understanding of marriage, even in Christianity, has often been stated primarily in terms of its purposes. These include procreation, the continuation of an extended family, the amassing and preservation of property, and the formation of an economic unit. In the moral tradition, especially in the ascetic-sacramental tradition of confession, marriage was taught as an instrument for the regulation of sexual activity, the prevention of promiscuity, and the control of unchastity. The various doctrines of the purposes of marriage are extremely informative because they show that it is not possible to single out and establish any one purpose, or even any clear priority of purposes, that could serve as a basis for marriage as a living community. Rather, the opposite is the case. Any purpose that has been or could be mentioned can actually be established and achieved in some other way than through marriage.

The identification of goals, whatever form the goals may take, is not a sufficient basis for the meaning of marriage. Goals always presuppose that meaning. It is beyond question that marriage always serves goals and can be made to serve specific goals, but it is another matter to try to derive its ethical meaning and its true authority from such goals. The damage that is done by adopting a basis for marriage that is oriented to goals is that in every case in which the goals can be achieved by other means the reasons for marriage as a permanent, living community disappear. Thus marriage becomes merely a means to an end and not a living reality, and it should surprise no one if a goal-oriented concept of marriage contains the cause of its own crisis. A modern, quite subtle form of such a definition of goals holds that marriage serves and should serve the goal of self-fulfillment, the expression of one's own personality.

In the face of the modern challenge that makes marriage an instrument in the service of autonomous self-realization, ethical discourse must show that marriage as a living community is the way by which one comes to share in a reality of life that no one has or can have alone. Marriage opens the way to an extension of life of which no one is capable alone but which is given to persons as husband and wife only through this living community. Thus marriage is an intensification and enrichment of personality and individuality that cannot be achieved by oneself. It would be false idealism to accept and acknowledge this expansion and intensification of life only where it represented the fulfillment of desires and not where it also involved the intensification of complexity and the possibility of conflict, that is to say, the realities of life.

On the basis of these presuppositions we can establish more precisely that marriage is to be a lifelong relationship. It is not possible to designate a point in time when marriage would have fulfilled its purpose and thus come to an end before the living community itself was at an end.

In the history of the teachings about marriage, the binding nature of marriage for the duration of life has been primarily derived from the vow taken in the marriage ceremony. This is appropriate, because in the performance of the ceremony, the binding force of marriage as a living community is reinforced for the partners in their own specific case. Nonetheless it would not be sufficient to say that the basic ethical meaning of marriage as a permanent relationship is grounded in the wedding ceremony itself. Rather, the wedding has as its presupposition and its goal the autonomous reality of marriage as a living community. In terms of its ethical logic, a marriage is not entered into with the expectation that its permanence—and that always means its reality—is dependent on the force and reality of the marriage ceremony. The commitment involved in the act of marriage has its validity in the meaning that marriage has for the shared life that the bride and groom now affirm to each other and to the public.

What is the significance of the public act of marriage, which is also a legal and ecclesiastical act? The public nature of the wedding, like the legal form of marriage as a community of life, gives expression to the basic meaning of the marriage. The public performance of the marriage ceremony is always also the explicit and formal commitment to perform the duties involved in marriage and to enter into its basic responsibilities. The wedding reinforces the understanding that the future course of the marriage will not be dependent on just the intentions and expectations the marriage partners bring with them, but that the partners affirm the independence of the marriage as a living community and accept the claims that the marriage places on their individual lives. This is independent of the specific legal obligations that under the marriage laws play a role in one way or another. The public act of marriage "before God and this company" documents that the marriage is an institution in which the partners unite their lives and their destinies. In it the partners explicitly affirm the social nature of marriage as a community more important to them than their immediate self-fulfillment and as a basic commitment into which they are willing to enter, beyond their immediate intentions.

In sociological terms, every marriage is a social entity; that is, it does not remain hidden that two persons have chosen to live together as husband and wife, because in this act they are also entering into a form of relationship to the society in which they live. A desire to keep this relationship hidden is hard to reconcile with the existence of a marriage. The recognition a formally concluded wedding receives corresponds with the recognition that there is also a public realm outside the marriage, a society in relation to which the marriage exists and which has its own life. This moving beyond the purely private world is an element in the recognition of the social nature of the marriage to which the husband and wife are committing themselves. Today where a "marriage without a wedding" is discussed and practiced, the reason is usually a general distrust of institutions, basically because of reservations against the demand that we recognize social obligations that go beyond the individual. This shows a reluctance to live one's own life as an expression of social responsibility.

The public nature of the marriage ceremony and the legal form of marriage as an institution can and must be recognized, because they correspond to the ethical significance of marriage and support it.

Therefore there is an essential relationship between civil marriage and church marriage. The separation of the two has its basis in the historic distinction between church and state but not in any systematic, ethical separation between distinct realms of human life. From time to time there are those who argue for a church marriage without a prior formal civil marriage, but this would mean a conscious rejection of the public character of marriage and a return in modern form to the medieval state of a "clandestine marriage." But there no longer exist the hindrances to a marriage that once were the grounds for a secret, nonpublic marriage. Today it is no longer external factors that play a role but merely inner reservations. For this reason the question of the relation between civil and church marriage is not relevant. What are relevant are the reasons that lead the partners to the marriage or marriagelike arrangement to make such a request. They want to have only a part of the marriage—for example, the religious meaning as something private and inward but not the public and binding aspects with their implications for their lives. Such a separation would imply a rejection of the law, and this would mean also a rejection of a socially mature and responsible way of life, with all the problematic consequences that would result.

For a discussion of the rejection of law, see T. Koch, "Ehe und 'Nichteheliche Lebensgemeinschaft' als Thema der Ethik," in *Die nichteheliche Lebensge-*

meinschaft, ed. G. Landwehr, 1978. On the relationship between civil and church marriage law, see W. Müller-Freienfels, *Ehe und Recht,* 1962; P. Mikat, "Ehe," in *Handwörterbuch zur deutschen Rechtsgeschichte,* vol. 1, 1964, pp. 809–33; H. Dombois, *Kirche und Eherecht: Studien und Abhandlungen,* 1953–72; A. Dieckmann, "Eherecht," in *Evang. Soziallexikon,* 7th ed., 1980, pp. 270–94.

2) The Ethical Significance of the Political Task

To act politically means to enter into the task involved in the political order of our common life. Political power is derived from the ethical obligation to be a part of the community.

Human life is to be explicitly formed and shaped as life in community. It is from this reciprocal dependence that the political task derives its ethical dimension. In setting its specific goals, political activity enters into the elementary responsibility of striving to form and shape a political community and in so doing to comprehend its responsibility for the conduct of life in political terms. In this sense, the political task is to be understood as providing a concrete basic structure for the life that has been given. Ultimately, the problems of an ethics of politics require that the political task not be seen as something added to human life as an afterthought, something that constitutes only a special application of ethics. This task must be perceived in each specific situation and is unavoidable if we are to achieve a satisfying life. Therefore it is not possible to negate or suspend political activity in cases where it is misused or where there are conflicts about the way it is to be conducted. Every debate about the content of the political task must be seen in the light of the fact that the task is inescapably obligatory. Every explicitly political action involves this presupposition as the condition for its own possibility. It is therefore inappropriate to draw a contrast between politics and ethics or to postulate an insuperable difference between them.

Such a concept can arise only if political action is understood solely as carrying out one's own will in opposition to others, by force if necessary—an understanding that presupposes that the life of human beings in relationship to one another is open for exerting such influence as a feature of the task of forming and shaping a common life. The political task in its basic ethical significance must be related to the basic structure of given life from which all specific tasks proceed and from which they derive their specific ethical qualification.

The following titles illustrate the breadth of the discussions of political ethics: R. Niebuhr, *Christian Realism and Political Problems*, 1953; H. D. Wendland, and Th. Strohm, eds., *Politik und Ethik*, 1969; C. J. Friedrich, *Politik als Prozess der Gemeinschaftsbildung*, 1970; D. Hahn, *Der Begriff des Politischen und der Politischen Theologie*, 1975; T. Koch, "Kriterien einer Ethik des Politischen," in *Handbuch der christlichen Ethik*, vol. 2, 1978, pp. 244–52; H. P. Meyer, *Tagesordnungspunkt: Politik*, 1978.

In the foreground of the traditional understanding of the political task in Protestant theology we find the restraint and regulation of life-threatening physical force, or the responsibility for preserving life.

In the history of exegesis, this tradition is oriented to Romans 13 and reduces the concept of the political task largely to the use of the judicial power of the sword. In Lutheran theology this concept has at times been restricted to a theologically motivated one-sidedness that defined the political task solely as that of restraining the tendency of sinful human beings to engage in violence and as a "provisional ordinance of God necessitated by the Fall" (Thielicke). In contrast to this largely negative definition of politics, we find the position that "true Christians" do not need *this* political office, because they, having been freed from sin, do not need this threat of the sword and the law (Luther, *Von weltlicher Obrigkeit*). As a consequence of this distinction the content of the political task was determined solely by a coercive concept of political authority, based on external force and compulsion against sinners, so that politics was widely equated with police power and with punishment. Important and relevant though the task of protecting life may be, such a line of argument results in a total obscuring of the relationship of politics to the formation and development of wholesome public life. U. Wilckens has shown that in this traditional exegesis of Romans 13, only one statement has been singled out. The other, which affirms that those who do good do not need to fear the sword, has been neglected. He has shown that worldly authority in its fundamental significance stands in the service of a good life and makes it possible (U. Wilckens, "Römer 13:1–7," in *Rechtfertigung als Freiheit: Paulusstudien*, 1974, pp. 203–45; further literature is cited there).

Only insofar as we regard the basic community possible does it follow that we can lay claim to it in order to protect life. This task has its ethical criterion in the original political task. The "sword" does not constitute the basis of politics; it functions strictly in the service of politics.

For a discussion of Lutheran teachings about the state, see R. Hauser, *Autorität und Macht: Die staatliche Autorität in der neueren protestantischen Ethik und in der katholischen Gesellschaftslehre*, 1949; W. Schweitzer, *Der entmythologisierte Staat: Studien zur Revision der evangelischen Ethik des*

Politischen, 1968; H. Dombois and E. Wilkens, eds., *Macht und Recht: Beiträge zur lutherischen Staatslehre der Gegenwart*, 1956; M. Jacobs, ed., *Evangelische Staatslehre* (Textsammlung), 1971; K. G. Steck, "Revolution und Gegenrevolution in der theologischen Ethik des neunzehnten Jahrhunderts," in K. G. Steck and T. Rendtorff's *Protestantismus und Revolution*, 1969, pp. 27–62. For a work dealing specifically with the understanding of punishment, see H. Dombois, ed., *Die weltliche Strafe in der evangelischen Theologie*, 1959.

Just as the basic ethical significance of marriage would not be correctly expressed if, for example, it were understood only in terms of the prevention of sexual immorality, so too it would be inadequate to speak of the political task primarily in terms of punishment and the combating of crime. These restrictive elements of the political order are secondary in content to the constructive task of politics, which we must keep clearly in mind.

The function of the political order to provide for public safety indicates emphatically the starting point for this discussion: the responsibility that men and women have in their lives for building and shaping the political community in which they live. Thus it is appropriate to see in the task of protecting life a concrete application of the political task in an elementary sense. But this is a task related to those lives for whom one is responsible. Thus the preservation of public safety is not an adequate definition of the content of the political task. It is one element in a comprehensive task of preserving peace, if peace be taken as expressing the goal of politics. To understand peace as defining the content of political life is to formulate the goal of politics as seeking to bring about a satisfactory life for those who constitute the community. Only because the political task is necessary to the formation of a political community is this task required to include the protection of life. The recognition that human life involves the formation and shaping of a political community points up the ethical significance of political power. If we ask why politics is inseparable from power (and this is a fundamental question for ethics), we must answer that it is because the success of human life depends on being involved in a structure that transcends the individual and thus unavoidably requires the recognition of this task. The primary ethical issue is not who holds the power. It is that in every case power must be exercised in the continuous building-up and effective formation of the common life. Power as political power results from an elementary necessity of life and thus is to be understood as conferred power. The ethical justification of power is not the strength or competence of those who hold it; the justification is that power is conferred in the common interest. The ethical ambivalence of power is not found in a fundamental contrast between power and ethics arising because power always involves an element of control over the destiny of others, which in specific instances is exerted against the will of the governed. In a fundamental sense, it is possible to speak of the ethical ambivalence of power, because power is the function of a task undertaken in the common interest, and its use is unavoidable whenever and wherever there is no adequate agreement about how to use it, that is to say, about the actual form of the political community. The opposite of the unjust or disputed use of power, which is experienced as oppression, as abuse of force, is not the rejection of power altogether. Such anarchy would be the negation of any perception of the actual political task. The necessity of which we have spoken here means that there cannot be a power vacuum in the political community. Because the political task is essential to life in community, we cannot lay claim to ethics as a simple critique of power. On the contrary, the relevance of power for the basic ethical structure of the reality of life must be specifically brought to bear on the political task.

See M. Hengel, *Christus und die Macht*, 1974; N. Luhmann, *Macht*, 1975; P. Tillich, *Love, Power, and Justice*, 1954; H. Greifenstein, ed., *Macht und Gewalt*, 1978.

The concept formulated by Max Weber and others—that we are to understand power as the opportunity to assert one's will against an opponent and to succeed in doing so—is unsatisfactory. It does not deal with the elementary social character of power but thinks of power only in terms of exerting one's own will. That would involve either a direct use of power against others or a misuse of power. This understanding does not reflect the fact that the exercise of power by the will of an individual must take into account the dependence of the individual's life on an ordering of relationships in a way that transcends the individual and that thus can triumph only in the form of an expression of the common interest.

For Weber's point of view, see the often-quoted lecture in which he draws an antithetical distinction between an ethic of character (the Sermon on the Mount) and a responsibility ethic (*Politik als Beruf*, 1919; 6th ed., 1977).

In the traditional concepts of political order a major concern was to define political activity as an example of applying the basic structure of the ethical reality of life. The task of politics was presented in terms of a political "office," as an ordinance or an institution established by God. Present-day ethical discussion should once again take up the systematic concerns that were dominant in that point of view. The issue, in short, is to identify points of view for which political activity is not based on the arbitrary will of individuals or the unmediated will of whoever is in power but is derived from a preexisting, elementary ethical obligation. This position can be expressed by stating that there is no such thing as absolute power but that, rather, power as the realization of the political task always involves an order in which it has a limited function as servant. The traditional view spoke of political activity as having the character of a servant or the structure of a mandate, because it viewed political activity as the administration of a previously instituted order, the subject of which was not man but God. That order, in the most fundamental sense, was not at the disposition of those who hold political office or of those on whose behalf the offices are exercised. The problem of the modern political order is that the actions that lead to the establishment of a constitution often involve a revolutionary transformation of an older order, a transformation in which the homo politicus is the express subject of the actions. As a result, the formation of the new order is a major theme, and the order is not adopted as something given. It is not, however, the task of this ethical discussion to trace the historical development of the modern constitutional state. It is our task rather to investigate whether under modern presuppositions, and if so how, the ethical interests of tradition should play a formative role.

The connection between the traditional concept of political order and the modern understanding of politics is to be seen in the differing form of political order, that is, principally in the formation of community on the basis of a written and agreed-upon constitution. For it is the structuring of political action through constitutional constraints that distinguishes this action from purely arbitrary decisions or the imposition of an individual's political will. To this extent the modern constitutional state represents in its own way the orientation of the political task to already existing elementary responsibilities, even though it does so in a highly complex manner. This makes clear the ethical requirement that the political community not be allowed to become the means for the specific, self-determined goals and intentions of those in power at a given time but rather that the exercise of power be in the service of the community. The connection between the concept of the modern constitutional state and the concept of order in the ethical-theological tradition is seen with greatest clarity wherever specific and basic human rights are explicitly removed from the control of the political ruler and the constitution thus functions as a normative criterion calling all political actions to account.

The connection with the traditional concept of political office as a divine ordinance can be further seen when the content of the political task is to develop the common element in the current problems of community life and to identify them specifically as binding. This political task derives its authority by being a function of the community under law. The concept of a state governed by law expresses that elementary and binding authority which is a basic element of the political task and which is incorporated into that task.

For discussions of the history and theory of law, see R. Smend, "Verfassung und Verfassungsrecht" 1929, in *Staatsrechtliche Abhandlungen*, 2d ed., 1968; H. Heller, *Staatslehre*, 1934, reprinted 1974; W. Kaegi, *Die Verfassung als rechtliche Grundordnung des Staates: Untersuchungen über die Entwicklungstendenzen im modernen Verfassungsrecht*, 1945; C. J. Friedrich, *Der Verfassungsstaat der Neuzeit*, 1953; K. Loewenstein, *Verfassungslehre*, 3d ed., 1975; E. W. Böckenförde, *Staat, Gesellschaft, Freiheit*, 1976; K. Hesse, *Grundzüge des Verfassungsrechts der Bundesrepublik Deutschland*, 12th ed., 1980; W. Mager, *Zur Entstehung des modernen Staatsbegriffs*, 1968; D. Merten, *Rechtsstaat und Gewaltmonopol*, 1975; H. Quartitsch, *Staat und Souveränität*, 1970; R. Zippelius, *Geschichte der Staatsideen*, 3d ed., 1976.

In the everyday world the constructive character of political activity plays an extremely important role, far beyond the traditional concept of political order as merely administrative responsibility. "Order" here takes on the dynamic sense of "establishing order," the constantly changing definition of what constitutes the common good and public obligation in each specific situation. The political order assumes the form of a permanent political discourse and grows out of the social and political nature of humankind. Openness is an essential feature of political order, and the modern political order must be public in nature. Its concrete form is the permanent process of reformulating and redefining the common life, the updating and confirmation of the basis of shared and therefore responsible life in human community and the form that that life takes. Any refusal to act openly and publicly is an indication that those exercising political power are seeking to escape their dependence on the political community and to make their power absolute. It makes no real difference whether the rejection of openness occurs in the interest of the pure exercise of power or in the interest of imposing an ideological program. Later in this discussion we will consider the fact that opposing interests are at work and that the consideration of political order takes on the nature of a battle over the public definition of our shared life in community.

The decisive point for ethics is always that the political task arises out of an elementary necessity in human life to form and shape a common life in explicit terms, and that therefore all special interests, goals, and plans for action are to be subordinated to this essential task. The concrete form of political activity at any specific time is certainly not the reflection of an eternally established order. Still, public discussion of its contemporary form is not something arbitrary but is a consequence of an inescapable necessity confronting the conduct of human life in the service of the political realization of life in community.

3) Earning a Livelihood through Work

Human work means participating in earning the means to support life; productive work is our necessary way of sharing in the elementary responsibility of providing for our life in community.

Human beings must provide for themselves the necessities of life. The petition of the Lord's Prayer "Give us this day our daily bread" (Matt. 6:11) is related to this basic human dependence on the means of sustaining life. Thus in this third example of a basic ethical situation of human life, our task is to explore the way ethical responsibility finds concrete expression. It does not exhaust itself in the necessity of dealing with hunger so that physical existence can continue. The binding nature of the task is found rather in that the means of life are created and prepared through human labor.

Since life itself depends upon work for its preservation, human work is the place where this fundamental ethical situation of human life takes concrete form. Ethical discourse must, however, be kept free from any tendency to glorify work. It will soberly build on the fact that the work we must do is a part of the life that has been given to us, whether we see it in the perspective of the second creation account (Gen. 2:15) or in the interpretation of the human situation after the Fall according to which we are to earn our bread through the sweat of our brow (Gen. 3:19). In an elementary fashion, work lays claim to the way human life is to be lived if the life that has been given us is to be fully realized. Therefore we must discover in our work this human and ethical necessity as a condition for the way we live, and it may not be pushed far off from elementary concerns about the question of human self-realization, to a place remote from the givenness of life. The necessity of working for the sake of life establishes work in the most basic sense as a means of life. In work the presuppositions of the givenness of life are related to providing the means for life and are incorporated into the active responsibility of human beings.

The elementary dependence of life on work is not derived from any general concept of work—neither in terms of social history nor in the practical terms of how work is accomplished. On the contrary, human work is the starting point of a process of interactions and relationships. It is not directed exclusively toward the satisfaction of the physical requirements of life but it constitutes a structure basic to human society. If human life is given to us in such a way that we must provide the means of life through work, work is seen as another manifestation of the original social nature of life as it is given. We are attempting to do justice to this complexity of the ethical task of economics by dealing in this third approach with the community of life mediated through work.

An extensive literature on the subject is found in an article by H. D. Preuss et al., "Arbeit," *TRE* 3:613–69. For the social history of the concept, see W. Conze, "Arbeit," in *Geschichtliche Grundbegriffe,* vol. 1, 1972, pp. 154–215; G. Brakelmann and J. Moltmann, eds., *Recht auf Arbeit—Sinn der Arbeit,* 1979.

If the ethics of work is so intimately connected with the basic structure of the givenness of life, Christian ethics should adopt the perspective that human work is not something "prior to" or "beneath" our true humanity but that we are called by God to engage in work. Our ethical approach cannot be guided by the idea of a dignified superiority to work nor by the demand that work be overcome and eliminated so that we may attain to our true humanity. The elementary obligation to work must be taken seriously as an application of the basic structure of life. This ethical perspective is distinguished from the understanding of work that has found advocates since ancient times and is expressed in describing work as *negotium,* "nonleisure," that is, in negative terms and concepts. If *otium,* "leisure," is seen as the true situation for which we are to strive, then "nonwork" is the appropriate human state and there are no longer any grounds for endeavoring to establish the ethical obligation to provide the means for life. Such an elite ethos cannot be made a universal principle. Freedom from work is possible only through the work of others, because no one alone can be free from dependence on the means for supporting life. Wherever nonwork is in principle established as a privilege, there too the human community of life by means of work is in principle negated.

The view that the basic meaning of work is to be found in the life community it creates is thus not identical with the view that work has an immediate moral value for the individual, as for instance, through enabling the person to become moral through working. To be sure, it is important to ask what function the necessity of working has for an individual's life. The basic obligation involved here is that of sharing through work in the community given us by life, that is to say, the social nature of work. A person can escape this only at the expense of the work of others, and this constitutes only an exception and can never become the rule. Thus the private benefit work has for individual morality remains secondary to the function of work for the community.

We are hence arguing for an ethical understanding of work that is basically not defined by goals that lie outside the work itself but that understands work in terms of the fundamental structure of reality as it confronts us. Therefore the particular goals of work can be rightly evaluated only insofar as work as the means for life is of itself open to those goals. The contemporary debates about the ethical order of the economy center on the question of the productivity of human labor. This involves the historically developed capacity of human labor to produce more means for supporting life than are absolutely necessary for the preservation of human physical existence. Under the conditions of modern society, work has come to be seen in terms of productivity as a source of wealth, of an abundance of the means for supporting life, to a degree far exceeding that of previous times. That brings with it the problems and opportunities of prosperity. As a consequence, work itself has become the source of an increasing relative independence of various groups and classes from work, so that work becomes the means by which many can escape from work. This brings the problems and opportunities of leisure. Even so, it is by work that prosperity and leisure are made possible. Therefore the relative liberation from work does not release people from the community of life that work makes possible. It does, however, provide the opportunity in many cases for people to pursue a way of life as total self-interest, independent of the necessity of working. As a consequence of increased productivity, labor becomes the instrument for pursuing interests that are no longer related to any dependence on work, although without work they would not be attainable.

This brief statement of the problem raises the question of how basic ethical responsibility remains valid for the productivity that results from labor. The significance of the question is that the means for supporting life that are generated by the productivity of labor create the possibility of extensively transforming and reshaping the human community. As a consequence the productivity of human labor is seen as a leading factor in the ordering of human life in community, and the original social nature of work plays a powerful role in this ordering. Productivity is not only a source of human inequality in matters such as the division of labor and the unequal distribution of work tasks, including liberation from work. Beyond that it provides the means for an organization of the issues of human life by means of which the complex differentiation of developed societies has become possible. The sense of community produced by work is in this way greatly diminished in comparison with all other aspects of human community.

This gives rise to the precarious situation of moral discourse in the area of economics. The multiplicity of political, social, and individual problems touching on the organization and conduct of life which must be dealt with by moral discourse in the realm of economics makes it very difficult to clarify the necessary moral position in its basic structure. The ethical question must be phrased in economic terms and not in moral concepts that are formulated independently and only later applied to economic situations. Therefore it is methodologically important to be clear about how the provision of the means of life can be dealt with concretely in terms of basic ethical structures.

Recognizing the great complexity and heterogeneous nature of economic theories, we can identify in various ways elements of this basic structure as they relate to model economic theories.

Adam Smith, founder of modern classical economics, formulated the arguments that identify work as an element in a community that is both ethically grounded and politically structured. In the broader context of English eighteenth-century moral philosophy, he saw work as providing the necessary means for sustaining life. "Every individual is continually exerting himself to find out the most advantageous employment for whatever capital he can command. . . . But the study of his own advantage . . . necessarily leads him to prefer that employment which is most advantageous to the society" (*Wealth of Nations*, 1937, p. 421).

On Adam Smith, see Eli Ginzberg, *The House of Adam Smith*, 1934. This is a classic analysis of Smith's economics.

But the reliance on self-interest in Adam Smith is far removed from making pure egoism the principle for organizing society, because owing to the means necessary for bringing society to realization, such reliance is grounded in an elementary social partnership. Regardless of the extent to which self-interest may be the mainspring for the production of goods, each individual is still dependent on others and on their economic activity. The economic importance of this fact is expressed in the exchange of goods. Such exchange is the basic process in the interrelated pursuit of self-interest by interdependent individuals. The decisive structural precondition of exchange which must be drawn on to explain economic life in community is, according to Smith, the division of labor. It has the effect of allowing a much larger number of persons to satisfy their needs or their self-interest, because they can all now not only make use of their own productivity, which is always limited by their own life situation, but also take advantage of the work and productivity of others. The division of labor and the exchange of goods is the elementary economic principle making possible the existence of life in community. Smith endeavored to bring these briefly sketched principles of economics into a broad program of the political organization of nations and their well-being and was not speaking of a society that allowed the irresponsible pursuit of self-interests.

Smith assigned work a decisive role in the realization of the independence of human life and placed the social and political organization of the common life under the requirement of recognizing the productivity of labor as the condition for the political organization of that life. Seen historically, this theory moved beyond a traditional, hierarchical, or feudal social order. The problems that quickly arose concerning how the productivity that results from the division of labor, with its expansive potential, can be incorporated into the shared life of the community had their origin in this dynamic understanding of labor.

For Hegel's use of Smith's ideas, see his *Rechtsphilosophie*, no. 189, in *Werke*, ed. E. Moldenhauer and K. M. Michel, 7:346–47. For interpretations of Hegel, see H. Marcuse, *Reason and Revolution: Hegel and the Rise of Social Theory*, 2d ed., 1983; G. Lukács, *Der junge Hegel*, 1948, 1973. J. Ritter (*Hegel und die französische Revolution*, 2d ed., 1973) incorporates this insight into the social relevance of work in order to demonstrate that the satisfaction of needs, when understood as the satisfaction of self-interests, can never be directly successful; the division of labor must be viewed as "labor for others" (no. 192). Hegel's critique attempts to subsume the satisfaction of individual needs under the institutions of law and state.

In taking up the theories of the English utilitarians (Bentham, Mill, et al.) and setting forth his disagreements with them, Karl Marx stressed the social nature of work, in sharp contrast to subsuming work under the pursuit of private interest. In so doing he adopted an economic interpretation of utilitarianism by presenting the basic structure of the social nature of work as being in itself the basic structure of the social nature of humankind, of the essence of humanity itself. Because of the dependence on the means of life, human life is made possible through the existence of a society based on the exchange of goods and services. Marx rested his critique on the contradiction inherent in an economics of self-interest, in that it is dependent on private property. The social distribution of the means of life produced by labor is in sharp contrast to the "unsocial" use of this productivity as private property, which stands in contradiction to the social nature of humankind. Private property is formed in a process of exchange involving the whole of society, but it is in contradiction to the condition for its own existence, because it keeps back for private interests that for which it is indebted to the whole of society.

For the Marxist concept of work, see K. Marx, "Ökonomisch-philosophische Manuskripte," (1844), in *MEW* 1:465–588; A. Schmidt, *Der Begriff der Natur in der Lehre von Marx*, rev. and exp. ed., 1971; K. Hartmann, *Die Marxsche Theorie: Eine philosophische Untersuchung zu den Hauptschriften*, 1970; H. Fleischer, *Marx und Engels*, 1970; E. M. Lange, *Das Prinzip Arbeit*, 1980.

It is not possible to discuss here in detail the reception accorded to Marxist theory. Its relationship to classical national economics is found at the point that the productivity of human labor is what constitutes the social nature of labor. Because of its productivity, labor is able to contribute to the means of life beyond what is required for immediate personal needs. Thus the dispute over whether this productivity is a result of the social nature of labor or, on the contrary, whether labor is relevant for society only because of its productivity in a specifically economic sense is of interest for ethics primarily when labor is seen as required by our relationship to a typical basic structure of the reality of life.

This relationship is, however, clearly demanded only in that in every case it is the productivity of human labor that enables us to enter into the obligation that confronts us and by means of which we participate in a society formed through the production of the means of life. The social form in which work is organized must comply with this requirement, because the independent contribution of the workers can be realized only through productivity. Therefore the provision of the individual for his or

her own needs can neither be denied nor made into the sole principle for
the organization of work. Either would be contrary to the basic social
function of work. But as a structural feature for the accomplishment of
work, its social nature is closely tied to the active accomplishment of
work, that is, to its productivity.

Work as participation in the economically defined ethical obligation of
the common life is in a basic sense the solution to the demand that we
take a stand on this issue. The productivity of labor, which seen in
historical terms, expanded only in modern times, shows that it is possible
to mobilize the resources of the economy in such a way as to achieve a
previously unknown increase in the well-being of nations.

This is especially true of the gap between the rich and the poor nations.
Immediate moral concern points toward the demand that the means of life be
distributed in a more just manner; that is, the rich should share their wealth with
the poor. If we bring this question so pregnant with relevance for the future into
relationship with the basic ethical structure developed here, the question takes on
a different form. However pressing the question how we can satisfy the world's
hunger for the elementary needs for sustaining life is, the ethical responsibility
involved here points to more far-reaching issues. We must move in the direction
of seeing to it that throughout the world access to work as the means of sustaining
life and as the means of productivity (as well as of individual independence) is
increased and made accessible to all. This means that the ethical question must be
considered in terms of the economy itself and not in moral concepts divorced
from the economy. Between work and the provision of the means of life there is a
relationship that is not accidental but essential to the life that has been given us.

The community that is constituted by work is an area for the application of the ethical issues involved in the basic structure of the givenness
of life. The nature of the life given to us demands that we participate in
the transmitting of life through work and in so doing enter into this
community and its life. This establishes the superior claims of the social
nature of the preservation of life through work over the claims of
personal interests. The human community established by work on this
earth cannot be abandoned or canceled in the selfish interests of a part of
the earth's population. That would deny the basic ethical obligations
involved in work. It is precisely the productivity of human labor that calls
for a world view in which the ethical obligations of the economy are
applied to the life given to all human beings to share. In this basic sense,
work—both its necessity and its productivity—is the primary criterion of
any ethic for economics.

4) Culture as a Task of Life

Culture involves taking a point of view toward the task of giving the world a humane form, a task that must be taken seriously in every case. It involves an elementary obligation that cannot be restricted to any specific form of life but that lays claim to the whole of human life and all human capabilities.

Culture is not a product of free and arbitrary human activity but results from a specific demand placed upon us by the givenness of life. We understand culture as a concrete application of ethics, in that the realities of human life demand that we make commitments. We are dealing here with the reflective thought involved in every act of commitment, especially with the claims that human intellectual life makes upon us. It is only in exceptional cases that intellectual life is concerned with the purely philosophical and rational concepts of thought. It includes all the ways in which the human response to the demand to make specific commitments in the world takes on concrete form. Marriage, politics, work—the basic life situations already discussed—belong to it just as much as art, religion, and literature. It constitutes a distinctive theme for ethics when the concept of culture is taken to embrace the same obligation in the conduct of life as does whatever governs human beings in shaping and being shaped by the world in which they live.

Ethics is primarily concerned not with purposeful human activity in acquiring knowledge, in science and technology, for example, but with intellectual activity in general as it deals with all aspects of reality. In this respect it would be wrong to reduce ethics to instructions on how to act. Ethics must raise the question of the nature of reality; that is to say, in this case it must operate with the insight that for us all that exists has been formed and determined through consciousness. In all the experiences of reality that have been or can be formulated we encounter the activity of human consciousness. It should also be emphasized that this activity is structured as a point of view toward the givenness of human life and is renewed in relationship to that givenness. It takes concrete form through the task of establishing a point of view toward the reality that has been given to us. The theme of culture is that reality challenges us to the life we are to lead.

Such a definition goes beyond the distinction between theory and practice, science and life, thinking and acting. Culture is the totality of all activity formed out of the history of our human points of view toward the reality that has been given us and to which we must respond. In this basic sense of the ethical reality of life, we encounter culture in our living of human life in such a way that it demands that we take a stand, that is, it challenges us to engage in the reflective thought that is given to us with life itself. Seen in this way, culture is a concrete expression of the givenness of life. The elementary obligation involved here can confront us in the form of a demand to use our intellect and to take part in the formation or use of our consciousness—a basic demand placed upon us by life itself.

The elementary task of education is not exhausted in the formation of our own intellectual personality, as in the ideal of the wise man or woman, the philosopher, or even the "cultured" person. It is rather a component of a more comprehensive cultural task of observing and giving form to the world that has been entrusted to us.

A human being is thus not by nature already human. Life is given to us from the start in the form of a demand that we make commitments. Acknowledging the task involved sets in motion the process that brings about the cultural formation of the world as the human environment. To be sure, this cultural task takes on concrete form in each instance under very specific historical conditions. But the goal of ethics here is to identify the basic challenge. Through the necessity of making commitments, human beings show that they cannot be subsumed under what is already given.

In concrete terms, taking a stand involves the culturally determined nature of the life we lead and has nothing to do with the "essence" of humanity, either prior to or outside cultural activity.

It is characteristic of the present state of the problem that ethical interest is typically directed toward the question of how technology is an application of human reflective thought—that is, how it is an aspect of culture. We often hear the assertion that technology is ethically neutral. That assertion is erroneous. It calls attention, however, to a problem that must be discussed in our exploration of the basic ethical understanding of culture. The problem involved in such an assumption is that technology has its place only in the context of a culture created by human effort and for which humans are responsible, and that, moreover, it is used for the building up of that culture. Apart from that culture it has no ethical significance. But neither can it exist apart from that culture. Since, however, the cultural task in its basic sense is the condition that makes technology possible, it is not possible to speak of the ethical neutrality or the arbitrary nature of technology. It is possible for problems of a certain type to arise here because in the modern development of technology specific incongruences have become evident in the cultural task. Technology is of itself not necessarily connected with specific cultural purposes and intentions, but it can be made to serve a great variety of such purposes and intentions. In the broader sense this is true of culture in general. Thus within the realm of cultural activity we find a rivalry between views concerning the ethics of technology. Those who support the cause of a humane culture by means of technology oppose those who espouse a humane culture in opposition to technology and are critical of technology. In contrast to the optimism of those who are excited over the possibility of progress through technology there has always been a pessimism that is critical of technology, though it has been enunciated differently in different periods. Later in another context we will discuss some of the themes that are relevant here.

In this dispute ethics takes sides only insofar as it advocates the basic ethical significance of culture, including technology. Therefore ethics cannot accord to the criticism of technology any automatic rights. Instead it considers that criticism as one expression of the critical consciousness vital to the cultural task which does not regard culture in any of its concrete expressions as essential by its very nature. If we recognize that the criticism of technology in the name of humane culture is based on the concern that technology might overpower humans or assert its independence from culture, this concern should still not lead us to make the erroneous assumption that culture is the original state of human nature, to be defended against the assaults of technology, and that technology is by nature hostile to humanity. It is not this assumption that is relevant here but only the reminder it contains that humans are challenged to take a stand toward their own cultural activities—and this culture can be no means lay claim to being our natural environment. Thus the specific problems created by modern technology are never technological problems purely and simply but are the consequences of cultural activity in general and therefore challenge us to transform or renew our participation in the concrete aspects of our cultural task. This eliminates in principle any contradiction between ethics and technology. Technology is one of the concrete expressions of humane culture and can therefore be dealt with only in the context of its own range of ethical problems. This has always been the case with the relationship of the various dimensions of cultural activity to one another and is not a specific contrast between ethics and technology.

Certainly theological ethics cannot be pressed into the service of such a contrast. To regard, in the name of the doctrine of creation, a green meadow with cows grazing on it as essentially more in harmony with creation than a high-tech installation on the same spot would be to avoid our ethical responsibility to culture precisely at the point where it involves human participation in the most elementary sense. And it cannot be otherwise. Humane culture is not in competition with God's work of creation but is a response to the demands placed upon us by creation, because culture belongs to the structure of the life that has been given us.

Basic to the present discussion are the writings of M. Scheler and H. Plessner, and especially, A. Gehlen's *Der Mensch: Seine Natur und seine Stellung in der Welt*, 12th ed., 1978. See also W. Pannenberg, *Anthropology in Theological Perspective*, 1985. Also relevant is Paul Tillich's theory of culture, for a discussion of which see E. Amelung, *Die Gestalt der Liebe: Paul Tillichs Theologie der Kultur*, 1972. For the problems of technological culture, see the detailed bibliography in *Technik und Gesellschaft*, ed. H. Sachsse, vol. 1, *Ein Literaturführer*, 1974. See also H. Freyer, *Über das Dominantwerden technischer Kategorien in der Lebenswelt der industriellen Gesellschaft*, 1960; H. Stork, *Einführung in die Philosophie der Technik*, 1977; H. Sachsse, *Anthropologie der Technik*, 1978; H. Beck, *Kulturphilosophie der Technik: Perspektiven zu Technik–Menschheit–Zukunft*, 2d ed., 1979; H. Jonas, *Das Prinzip Verantwortung: Versuch einer Ethik für die technologische Zivilisation*, 1979; J. B. Cobb, *The Price of Progress*, 1972.

5) Religion as the Expression of Our Relationship to God

Religion is the human activity that is totally based on the givenness of life and that has as its theme our community in life with God, as part of that givenness. Religion involves an elementary obligation, because human activities require for their specific expression that we acknowledge the distinction between what lies within human power and what is possible only in a life in community with God.

Religion is the concrete expression of the basic ethical obligations of the life that has been given to us, and in religion we are obliged to take a stand in regard to the givenness of life in general. In this sense all humans have an elementary obligation to religion, an obligation that precedes and is developed in all the specific forms of religious expression. This basic ethical significance of religion is distorted wherever people inquire into the ethical consequences religion has for the conduct of human life, the ethical motifs religion evokes and develops, or the way it contributes to an ethically desirable life. Such questions place religion in relation to a goal that lies outside religion, and they are inadequate for establishing the basic ethical significance of religion as a human activity.

In the conduct of human life, religion is the activity in which men and women explicitly acknowledge that life, in all its aspects and in all the relationships that involve obligations, is given by God and therefore lays claim to them. The responsibilities of life require that we make commitments that are totally related, beyond all specific challenges, to God as the ground of our life. Therefore religion is distinct from all other institutions of human life, even though all of life's basic situations derive their right to our compliance from the givenness of life. The ethical significance of religion takes concrete form for the living of our lives in the shaping and forming of our relationship to God, and in this way in our engaging in the practice of religion. The ethics of religion therefore functions as the realm in which we explicitly honor God.

In this way the ethical understanding of religion forms a clear contrast to a dogmatic concept of religion, which undermines religion as a human activity because it limits the sovereign activity of God. Here ethics must raise these questions: What activity of human life corresponds to theology? And how can the distinction between God's activity and the human activity of which God makes use be expressed in concrete form so that the distinction can play a role in human life?

Thus far we have been speaking of religion as an independent area of life confronting us with obligations. Religion is thus no substitute for God's actions but is the way human beings relate to God. Accordingly, the belief that the external forms of human religious life are shaped and formed by human beings loses its sting and we no longer find a threat in the application of the methods of religious criticism. The need to take a stand is not eliminated by a critical approach. Where the modern criticism of religion has sought to meet this need through a program of human activities and self-realization that would make religion unnecessary, the result has regularly been the establishment of substitutes for religion that obscure the basic meaning of religion's distinction between God and man and replace it with a system in which human beings lord it over one another. Religion is a realm of its own, because none of the institutions we have been speaking of can at any time or in any of their concrete expressions describe or bring fully and exhaustively to realization our relationship to the whole of the life that has been given us. This does not mean that they are incomplete or inadequate and must be completed by the activity that is defined as religious. They are concrete expressions of the basic obligations of human life because and insofar as they make possible in concrete and specific ways the life that has been given to us. Therefore they cannot be expected to enable us to bring the whole of life to full realization.

It is only in relationship to the concrete situations of life that the specific ethical task of religion finds expression. Religion is made up of institutions whose form expresses our basic relationship to the givenness of life in such a way as to make permanently clear the distinction between what we can receive only in and through our actions and what we are obligated to do throughout life. To put it concisely, religion is the institution that maintains the distinction between God and humankind in the realities of life. This distinction is essential and beneficial because it makes us aware of the true and appropriate distinction in importance between the presuppositions for human conduct and the concrete expression of these presuppositions in our activities themselves. Religion helps clarify the ethical responsibilities that are inherent in the reality of life. This is successful, however, only if our relationship to God becomes explicit in our lives, and thus in this way the distinction between God and humanity is able to play a role in human life. Even the interdependence and convergence of all aspects of life, which cannot be integrated in any specific activity or any single institution because they involve the relationship of all human activity to the reality that has been given to us, are perceived in religion as the unity of human activity that transcends all specific activities. The historical fact that religion becomes concrete only in the plurality of religions does not negate this basic ethical significance but serves to underline it. The explicit religious institutions are not themselves identical with the reality of God but are only the forms that our relationships to God take.

The ethics of religion becomes concrete therefore in the specific form of religion, distinguishable from all other concrete expressions. Consequently religion cannot replace or delimit the other institutions of human life. To be sure it is involved in the other human institutions, because its range of interest includes the realities of life present in all human relationships. For this reason the relevant tasks and experiences of life also play a role in preaching and prayer, in worship and religious formation. But they play this role in respect of our basic orientation to our relationship to God. The specific nature of religious institutions should be regarded not as a handicap but as a concrete feature of their proper task. The universal relevance of religion can find concrete expression only in and through specific religious institutions. It is through the practice of religion that the distinction between God and humanity is made real in the context of human life.

There is another, closely connected consequence. Religion cannot make life in other human institutions dependent on it. It would be drawing a false conclusion from the universality of the relationship to God through religion if we were to make participation in the religious community an absolute condition for participation in political life or in the community of work. The binding ethical force of the basic situation of human life must be thematic in its own proper seriousness and not derived from something else, for example, from the church as the expression of religion. Thus the claim of religion to validity in the public realm cannot be extended to include the claim of the church to direct ethical authority over all other institutions. Any such claim would distort our vision of the basic obligations of the life that has been given us rather than furthering it. The express claims of religion should not be understood to imply a superiority to atheism in the sense that only when and where the church is explicitly present can we speak of the presence of God in the realities of life. On the contrary, the special task of the church is to make it known that the presence of God in the reality of the human world obligates us to take a specific, religious position in and through which is known the all-pervasive reality of God that reaches beyond all other specific contexts of life. That is the specific public task religion is to perform for society.

For recent discussion of the concept of religion, consult K. W. Dahm, N. Luhmann, and D. Stoodt, *Religion: System und Sozialisation*, 1972; D. Rössler, *Die Vernunft der Religion*, 1976; N. Luhmann, *Funktion der Religion*, 1977; T. Rendtorff, ed., *Religion als Problem der Aufklärung*, 1980; W. Trillhaas, *Religionsphilosophie*, 1972; H. Siemers, "Die Religion der Soziologie: Zur Problematik von Definitionen," in *Person*, ed. R. Pohlmann, Festschrift for H. Schelsky, 1980, pp. 93–114.

b. Taking Part in the Renewal of the Foundations: Personal Responsibility

Taking a stand toward the basic structures we encounter in the conduct of life means in this second aspect of our discussion that we are expected to make an independent commitment in the elementary situations of life. Responsibility makes us aware of the obligations the basic structures place upon our inner lives, and leading our own lives in a responsible

manner contributes to the renewed influence of the dominant presuppositions and keeps them open to new situations.

1) The Inner Obligations of Marriage

To lead a married life means to assume responsibility for a specific,
highly personal community and through the leading of one's own life to
contribute to the renewal of marriage and its validity.

Anyone who enters into a marriage desires that it endure. Marriages
are entered into not so that they might end in divorce but in order that
they might succeed. That a marriage succeed, and that its failure not be
permitted or tolerated, requires primary ethical concern, even though
the chief interest of public discussions is in marital crises and broken
marriages. Only when we know what unmet claim gave rise to the failure
of a marriage and what incompatibility led to it can we consider in a
meaningful way the ethical issues that are relevant to the consequences
of a crisis in marriage.

But we cannot take as our starting point the formulation of an abstract
ideal of what constitutes a perfect marriage. Rather, our theme must be
how marriage as a living community lays claim to each individual's way
of life. It is not the bonds of marriage, with all the overtones of force,
subordination, and external order, but a person's own free and productive contribution to the success of the marriage that will occupy the
foreground if marriage is to be discussed as a concrete aspect of an
individual's life.

Marriage derives its inner strength from the mutual commitment of
husband and wife to share their lives with each other. The answer to the
question of what is given here is not to be found in the mention of goods
and talents. The commitment expressed in the concept and the mental
image of love is a commitment of one's own life.

The ethical significance of the commitment of husband to wife and
wife to husband in marriage and for marriage can be given theoretical
form in the remark that this commitment is the exemplary case of
individual self-determination. This remark fixes the inner obligation that
marriage places on an individual's life at the point where a crisis can
begin. To bring oneself to the marriage, and not just goods and talents, is
the concrete demand of the task of giving life. It is necessary to give
oneself to marriage, holding nothing back, with no reservations and no
conditions. Subjective control over the possibilities of life must be sur-
rendered to the fellowship of marriage and be integrated into it. There-

fore an ethic of marriage cannot be reduced to a moralistic casuistry. No casuistry can comprehend the situation of a person in community. Marriage as a living community is based on love and harmony, which the marriage partners are to bring to the marriage and to cultivate throughout the marriage. This responsibility is of a specifically individual nature, just as much subject to contingencies as are the individuals who find themselves together in the relationship. Therefore the calling of marriage is different from the experience of feeling called to functions in the realms of politics or the economy. That is, in these realms life is always subject to a goal-directed limitation of one's involvement, and the objective functions are distinguishable from the person who is involved.

Commitment in marriage can be expressed in the concept of partnership. This modern understanding of marriage gives good expression to the inner responsibilities, in that one's self-commitment to marriage involves the community whose partners are the married couple and to which they bring themselves. The conduct of life is then oriented not to patriarchal or feminist structures but to the commitment of the partners to each other. The connotation of partnership derived from business partnerships or from the partners to a formal agreement could easily lead to the erroneous conclusion that the marriage partners were related to each other only for the purpose of attaining some goal the basis for which could cease to exist under certain circumstances so that the partnership could then be dissolved. In such a case, marriage as a partnership without the full participation of the persons involved would be accepted as only a partial community and would thus have an inadequate ethical basis. For the understanding of marriage "from within," see (in addition to the literature cited in section 1a above) Th. Bovet, *Ehekunde*, vols. 1 and 2, 1961–62; H. Ringeling, *Theologie und Sexualität: Das private Verhalten als Thema der Sozialethik*, 1968.

If the conduct of an individual's life within marriage falls under the category of self-determination, it is clear that faithfulness to the marriage is an intrinsic obligation. Marital fidelity is a part of faithfulness to oneself. Together, the two constitute an obligation we must fulfill in our lives.

The inner responsibilities of marriage become reality in the process of a shared life. Thus it is not something that is given at the beginning, when a marriage is entered into, but it is a responsibility that develops. Each individual's life is in this respect a contribution to the single biography of the couple. Marriage as a living process therefore means that the marriage is fulfilled not in basic principles but in the concrete living situations it involves. Any marriage in which the partners repeatedly asked each other whether they should continue to live together or even whether they wanted to do so would not have much chance of success. The same principle that is valid for one's personal life is valid also for life in marriage: the yes to life must be expressed as a concrete affirmation of the givenness of life.

Yet at the same time no marriage is without conflicts. The marriage partners, because of the shared nature of their life together, are not masters over all the conditions that affect their marriage. For the success of the marriage they must continuously assert and give productive form to their inner independence from all the things on which life makes them dependent. Marriage is a learning process that in the various stages of the marriage poses different tasks and demands. Thus nothing could be more erroneous than to demand of a marriage that all the intentions professed at the beginning be carried out consistently. Rather, the course of life must remain open to the changes and transformations that the marriage partners experience with each other and through each other, the things they must suffer and to which they must give structure. For this reason at all stages of life the marriage presents new tasks for individual growth. Even the conflicts that the partners go through in which they seek to dominate each other result in an increasingly unitive nature for the marriage, that is to say, an intensification of its binding mutuality.

Here the marriage lays claim to the duration of each individual's life. The challenge of marriage is not fully recognized or comprehended apart from its duration, which reaches even to old age and death. Crises arise in marriage because one's own life falls short of the reality of marriage. Crises assert the reservations of unconditional self-realization over against individual self-determination in marriage. The possibilities of life in a generalized and unspecific sense are then esteemed more highly than one's own married life. To this extent the crises arise wherever the marriage makes specific claims on the individual's life in contrast to the large number of possibilities that could or might exist. For this reason, when marriage crises lead to the dissolution of the marriage, they are a process in which contact is lost with reality—a rejection of one's own actual biography. They arise from the desire to begin one's life over again or to structure it differently. A marriage crisis is a life crisis because it reveals a contradiction to one, to one's own biography, in the shape of the dissolution of a community one had chosen to establish. Basically in every marriage crisis with the potential to lead to the end of the marriage, however it may be dealt with, there is someone who is reluctant to give life concretely, and thus someone who is in opposition to the basic meaning of marriage. Therefore there is no ethical right to divorce that has the same validity—that is, is based on the same level of reality—as the community constituted by marriage, nor could such a right be placed alongside it. Divorce cannot claim as its basis any reality of life comparable to marriage but is always in conflict with a committed life. The legal possibility of divorce is almost universally recognized and must be kept open because the realm of public law is not, and must not be, lord of the individual's life but is to serve the living of that life. The institution of divorce, however, exists to regulate the consequences of conflict, and not the conflict itself, and it cannot therefore be the source of a marital crisis or of the failure of a marriage.

It is a way of limiting the role of the legal system in divorce to the regulation of legal conflicts for the legislature to change the grounds of divorce from guilt to the fact that the marriage is already dead. The legislature thus recognizes that marriage law should not take a stand on the question of guilt. In support of this restraint of the law there is the consideration that the roots of the guilt behind a desire to divorce often lie in a shared life that has not reached a crisis and in which therefore the guilt cannot be clearly or fairly apportioned between the marriage partners. This legal situation, however, should not lead us to conclude that guilt has nothing at all to do with a divorce. The ethical significance of the legal principle can only be that the guilt involves an element of mutuality and is thus the joint responsibility of husband and wife. But we must also emphasize the other factor, that not every conflict is an indication that the marriage is dead, in the sense of no longer existing.

The legal principle that a marriage can be regarded as dead is in sharp contrast to the autonomy of the married couple and in its own way underlines the inner obligation, imposed by marriage, by virtue of which the mutual responsibility for a shared life cannot simply be abrogated by conflict. Thus it is necessary to consider ethical responsibility in the context of marriage conflict. The binding force of marriage for the duration of life, as an anticipation of the entirety of the shared life, is such that in marital strife it involves the future of the marriage and cannot be understood simply as a rigid maintenance of a responsibility that was once entered into. The productive force of this responsibility is the overcoming of conflicts in regard to the future of the marriage. But in time and content the success of a marriage cannot be separated from the success of the lives it involves. This is a concrete indication of the seriousness of our duty to the future in marriage. In every crisis leading to a dissolution of a marriage, one of the partners is the one who suffers and at whose expense the other seeks to realize an advantage for his or her own life. The self-determination that makes use of the other, abandoned partner is always a negation of the basic ethical responsibility that a person undertakes in entering into a marriage. It is therefore important to insist that the dissolution of a marriage implies guilt. But guilt does not bring about a complete separation but is another feature of the relationship of the couple to each other. Even where the dissolution, separation, or divorce comes about, the living human relationships of the marriage partners to each other do not simply cease. It is therefore always necessary to seek for ways in which the dissolution can come about in a humane manner that corresponds to the mutual acceptance the husband and wife accorded to each other—that is, for ways in which the divorce still involves the basic meaning of marriage as a living community with elementary responsibilities. Under these presuppositions, it is our ethical task to reflect on how to deal with the marriage crisis in a way appropriate to the nature of marriage even when it comes to a divorce. In the case of a separation or divorce the couple enter into a realm where their relationship to each other is unstructured, but they still do not really escape from the reality of the marriage context, with its claims on the whole of life.

For discussions in church circles of divorce and marriage law, see F. Böckle, "Ehe und Ehescheidung," in *Handbuch der christlichen Ethik*, vol. 2, 1978, pp. 117–35; E. Wilkens, ed., *Ehe und Ehescheidung*, 1963; Council of the German Evangelical Church, ed., *Zur Reform des Ehescheidungsrechts in der Bundesrepublik Deutschland: Eine Denkschrift der Familienrechtscommission*, 1969; J. K. Döpfner and H. Dietzfelbinger, eds., *Das Gesetz des Staates und die sittliche Ordnung: Zur öffentlichen Diskussion über die Reform des Eherechts und des Strafrechts*, 1970; Interkonfessioneller Arbeitskreis für Ehe- und Familienfragen, *Eheverständnis und Ehescheidung*, 1971. See also the comments of Th. Strohm et al. in *ZEE* 15 (1971) in a special issue, *Reform des Eherechts und des Ehescheidungsrechts*.

Marriage as a public institution poses a problem today for the understanding of the individual relationships between husband and wife. What is the ethical relevance of the public and thus legal status of marriage for the conduct of an individual's life? Every marriage ought to contribute to the renewed importance of marriage in general. To this extent at least marriage is not merely a private matter, however private and concealed the inner processes of a given marriage may and must be. It differs from the private relationship of two persons to each other in that it is entered into in public, that is, "before God and these witnesses." The public aspect, in being an expression of the obligation to contribute to the renewed validity of the institution, involves the ethical dimension of bringing the conduct of one's individual life into a context of duties that transcend the individual.

Thus today, when much is being said about "marriage without a wedding certificate"—in the sense of a marriagelike community of life— this usually arises from a general reserve toward institutions, and thus at heart from a reserve against all the social interdependence involved in institutions. Often marriage without a wedding certificate is promoted in order to express the individual and quite personal bonds of community between a husband and wife for themselves alone, free from external controls. Such a marriage is designed then not to avoid the mutual obligations of marriage but to stress its personal nature. To this extent it is to be understood as an alternative to civil marriage. If the desire and intention of the partners is to have a marriage in the full sense, as this is required by the nature of marriage, it is difficult to see why such an "alternative," personalized form of marriage could not be achieved within marriage itself. A publicly formalized marriage is also open to this possibility. It is experienced as a restriction of free relationships only when it is no longer fully affirmed or desired. But this can also take place under the formula marriage without a wedding certificate. Such expressions as "a marriage-like" arrangement, or "trial marriage" imply not only reservations about the public form of the marriage ceremony but also about the duration of the marriage. In defense of such reservations it is often argued that people are reluctant to submit to external restraints. The position of absolute autonomy thus implied anticipates, however, the break-up, or failure of a marriage relationship, or "marriage-like" arrangement. That is to say, they express the awareness that the relationship is not being entered into with the determination to have a true marriage. Thus these expressions are misleading in reference to the attitude that is required. The marriage, or the relationship that is substituted for marriage, is made dependent on goals controlled by each partner for him or herself, and thus independently of each other, goals which bring them together, but also pull them apart. The shared life in marriage then becomes a function of goals that unite the partners only partially and for only a limited time but do not form a basis for a distinctive, shared life together.

In sociological terms, this approach involves a privatistic and, in the pejorative sense, individualistic concept that usually goes hand in hand with the rejection of other responsibilities in politics and society. Even in this negative respect, therefore, marriage is seen to be an exemplary basic situation for dealing with the ethical realities of life. If there were a possibility of undertaking "citizenshiplike" relationships or "laborlike" activities, there are those who would avail themselves of the opportunity.

The problems involved in marriage without a wedding certificate generate a model for our understanding of the ethical relationship of individual life to the social life that transcends the individual. It is the institutional nature of marriage that provides an occasion for reflecting on a deepened understanding of human self-determination that is not exhausted in mere self-realization but always demands a transcending of self. A church wedding gives expression to this by placing the intentions of the couple to lead an ethical life together under the assurance of God's blessing through prayer and intercession.

For further discussions of "unmarried" communities of life, see G. Landwehr, ed., *Die nichteheliche Lebensgemeinschaft*, 1978, esp. the essays by H.-J. Becker ("Die nichteheliche Lebensgemeinschaft [Konkubinat] in der Rechtsgeschichte") and T. Koch ("Ehe und 'nichteheliche Lebensgemeinschaft' als Thema der Ethik"); George O'Neill and Nena O'Neill, *Open Marriage: A New Life Style for Couples*, 1972; H. Ringeling, "Sexuelle Beziehunger Unverheirateter," in *Handbuch der christlichen Ethik*, vol. 2, 1978, pp. 160–76; idem, "Freie Lebensgemeinschaften in der Sicht evangelischer Sozialethik," *ZEE* 24 (1980): 143–48; *Partnerschaft und Identität: Die nicht-eheliche Lebensgemeinschaft*, Loccumer Protokolle 3, 1980; W. Müller-Freienfels, "Tendenzen zur Verrechtlichung nichtehelicher Lebensgemeinschaften," *ZEE* 24 (1980): 55ff.

2) Citizenship and Accepting the Responsibilities for Political Community

Political responsibility means placing one's own freedom and personal commitment at the service of the community. Politics lays claim to the citizen's life for participation in the public life of the community, because the citizen's independence is dependent on the community.

Until the quite recent past the Christian understanding of politics was guided by the concept of a divine authority legitimizing the state, and as a consequence, making the citizen a subject of the state. The main support for that position is the classic passage Rom. 13:1: "Let every person be subject to the governing authorities. For there is no authority except from God, and those that exist have been instituted by God." Thus political ethics was largely based on authority, and by contrast, a citizen's own productive and constructive contribution to the life of the political order was not regarded as an independent ethical issue.

But that is precisely the theme of this second aspect of political ethics. In contrast to ethical tradition, we therefore begin here by exploring the citizen's political autonomy. Then as the argument proceeds, the inner theological connection with the concerns of Reformation ethics will become clear. A modern ethic must present clearly the way the fundamental insights of the tradition can be reformulated under the conditions of a modern constitutional state whose legitimacy rests on a rational basis. It is not possible here simply to break off the discussion. All those who want the help and protection of the government are under an obligation to contribute in their own ways to the existence and the life of the political community. The question of how citizens are to conduct their lives in the political realm involves not only the way citizens have opportunities open to them through their participation in the community but also how they must give themselves to that community. If life together under the political order were dependent solely on external force it would have no satisfactory basis. Our task here is to present the ethical qualifications of life in its political aspects as an order that human beings have established and for which they are responsible.

The task can be defined in terms of the theoretical notion of self-determination, the political autonomy that human beings enjoy as citizens. Autonomy in the living of our life consists in our individual self-determination as citizens, that is, our participation in the political community. This self-determination having to do with the ethics of politics must be distinguished from our direct self-determination, which involves our own personal development.

Self-determination as autonomy is a concept of political ethics. It indicates the aspect under which the political community lays claim to our individual lives. The discussion involves certain alternatives. If human autonomy involves primarily our own being and our abilities as humans in and for ourselves, then the compatibility of our freedom with the freedom of others will always be seen as a problem of secondary importance. In that case freedom and human worth belong to our essential nature as humans. The defense and preservation of this human worth will then be the highest requirement of political activity.

But this is an abstract argument, although—or perhaps because—it has the appearance of being simple and uncomplicated. It is abstract because realization of self-determination always involves claims on other individuals or on the community. For this reason the idea of a direct self-determination of human beings does not leave scope for the original social nature of every life and thus leads the ethical discussion in a false direction.

The entire matter is seen in a different light if the autonomy of human beings as citizens constitutes the starting point of the discussion. Autonomy then means that the political community, to achieve its own realization, requires the productive and constructive participation and cooperation of its citizens because only in that way can it attain inner cohesiveness and be distinguished from a political order based solely on external force. The necessity and the ethical form of autonomy must be developed by reference to the reality of the political community and must be related to it. Then autonomy will mean an individual's self-determination to be a citizen. The meaning of a citizen's autonomy in an ethical and political sense must thus be clearly distinguished from the abstract, general arbitrariness involved in being an autonomous subject. The determining factor in the significance of political autonomy is that it has as its content the concrete expression of the political community in the conduct of each individual's life. Thus it cannot be a question of individuals who, after balancing all the factors involved, decide for or against participation in the political community. The specific nature of political autonomy makes such an abstract decision impossible. And it would be aberrant to decide, in pursuit of absolute self-determination, against participating in the political life of the community in order to achieve politically relevant results. Political self-determination involves, rather, assuming the ethical responsibilities of the political community by living as a citizen, and thus it becomes relevant for one's personal life.

On the presupposition of a concrete application of political and ethical autonomy, it is apparent that the state is dependent on the free and independent participation of its citizens. This is the necessary condition for the realization of the inner cohesiveness of community life. No community can exist indefinitely without the participation and cooperation of its citizens. The political question is whether this fact is explicitly recognized and acknowledged and therefore plays a role in the formation of the political community's life. Consequently, a citizen's autonomy is itself dependent on the political life of the community and must be expressed in relation to that community. In this way the limits that are placed on a state by the political autonomy of its citizens can be given relevant form. The state cannot make use of its citizens in the same way that it would make use of something that was at its free and arbitrary disposal. It can make claims on men and women only as citizens, that is, in their required but freely given agreement to participate in the community. The ethical aspect of autonomy challenges individuals to be ready and willing to work for the development of the political life of the community beyond their own immediate self-interests. And the ethical definition of citizenship implies that the primary form of mastery required of each person is mastery of self. Only those who have learned self-control are able to play a productive and constructive role in the political life of the community. Those who, on the contrary, seek to impose their own immediate interests on others will experience the political community as oppressive and therefore will struggle against it. The life of a citizen finds concrete expression in a readiness to participate in the shared life of the community. Political freedom is the freedom to be the citizen of a shared community and to make that freedom real in relation to oneself.

Following this line of argument, it is important to consider the relationship of the traditional Protestant ethic of authority to the Reformation understanding of freedom. Thus we pick up the discussion as developed earlier.

The ethical point of the Reformation doctrine of freedom may be formulated as saying that Christians are free because, on the basis of their experience of the freedom bestowed by God in Christ, they are ready and willing to lead and to structure their lives for the benefit of others. The theological understanding of the meaning of being Christian is thus the ethical paradigm for the autonomous citizen, because the life led by the individual Christian has as its goal the service of the common good. That is the concrete application of Christian freedom.

There is therefore good support for the thesis that the relationship between the basis of Christian freedom and the conduct of a Christian life prefigures the modern problem of autonomy. This becomes clear when we reconstruct the discussion of the theological understanding of freedom. If the life of a Christian merely served to make it possible for him or her to be Christian or to demonstrate that this is the case, this direct self-determination would be primarily interested in demonstrating how religious a person was. The conduct of such a life would not be oriented to the concrete reality of the political community but would seek to prove the validity of the individual's own point of view toward the faith. Ethics would then be a function of the self-expression of faith. In this debate, Reformation ethics quite decisively agreed that Christians, because of their freedom, enter into the political community and commit themselves to participating in that community. But then the directness of their status as Christians is not the point of reference for their ethical duty. Rather, their Christianity is made manifest only by means of their participation in the concrete political community and the responsibilities of it that require the free participation of men and women for their realization. To that extent at least, the ethical understanding of Christian freedom can be reformulated in the context of modern, rational political activity.

This being granted, we can see clearly the political and ethical sense of the requirement that the state accept its limits with respect to the freedom of its citizens. If the state is dependent on the free and self-motivated activities of its citizens, it cannot at the same time make use of them as if they were at its unlimited disposal. This is, however, a limit established within the political realm and not one imposed on it from outside. That is to say, it is not based on a contrast between a human autonomy that existed in its own right and only secondarily took on political relevance, on the one hand, and on the other hand, an existing order of the state that only secondarily made use of human beings for its purposes. This limit, rather, is constitutive for the common political life as an ordinance of freedom. The tradition of Protestant ethics has endeavored to give expression to this viewpoint through the thesis that the authorities are instituted by God and thus do not have sovereign power over the conditions under which they function but that they function in relationship to God and therefore are called to account for their actions. The rational constitutional state must respect and preserve the autonomy of its citizens for the same reasons—that is, because it is not the absolute master of its power—in order to establish its inner authority on the basis of that autonomy, without which it cannot function. For the same reason, individuals as citizens are obligated to place their freedom at the service of the common good in order to work for its achievement: they must act politically. The freedom to conduct one's own individual life finds its concrete form in political responsibility.

On the historical background of the ethical concepts of citizenship presented here, see the summary given by M. Riedel in "Bürger," in *Geschichtliche Grundbegriffe*, vol. 1, 1972, pp. 672–725. See also R. Smend, *Bürger und Bourgeois im deutschen Staatsrecht* (1933), in *Staatsrechtliche Abhandlungen*, 2d ed., 1968, pp. 309–25. On the concept of self-determination, see F. Wagner, "Der Mensch zwischen Selbstbestimmung und Abhängigkeit," in *Anthropologie als Thema der Theologie*, ed. H. Fischer, 1978, pp. 145–64. On community service as a concrete expression of citizen initiative, see the writings by Th. Strohm and others in the issue of *ZEE* 19 (1975) dealing with this subject.

3) Work as Vocation

Work as vocation is the responsibility toward one's individual obligation to participate in the community of life that results from work. The necessity of working is thus incorporated into the independent participation in a vocation that is involved in the leading of one's own life.

Work as vocation sets the theme for the claims made on one by an active life for and in the community constituted by one's work. This does not mean on one as a source of energy for performing work, for example, in the sense in which one could be replaced by a machine, but on one as a person whose life must be structured to participate in work. The concept of vocation connotes human self-determination to take part in work. The ethical requirement that the individual work must therefore be defined in relationship to preparation for and participation in a vocation.

The history of the concept of an ethic of vocation can be traced to Martin Luther. The decisive step was the transference of the concept of spiritual vocation from the privilege of a special calling to life in a religious order to the activity of a secular calling, an active life in one's profession and social rank. The ethical obligation to perform secular work is based on the belief that each person is called to his or her work and in and through secular tasks is doing the will of God. The place to which the person is called and in which the vocation that is God's will is to be found is not the distinctive place of the individual's own choice of a spiritual rank but the daily round of work in the world. The inner obligation to lead one's life through an outward calling provides the real ethical significance of work in a vocation.

To be sure, the outlook involved in the Lutheran ethic of vocation fitted fully into the order of a society based on rank, so that vocation and rank could be understood as synonymous. The modern structure of labor in conjunction with the capitalist form of economy produced great modifications in this respect. The place that rank and vocation had occupied was taken by the free labor force that was offered on the labor market and employed in return for wages. The division of labor found in modern industrial production transferred the meaning of work from individual vocation to the greater satisfaction of needs through a process of exchange. Negotiations over wages came to replace discussions about the meaning of work. As a consequence, it was money as the means for self-determination and not work itself that was central to the concrete expressions of the self-determination of the workers.

The result was that work came to be regarded as a form of alienation, because reduced as it was to labor that could be replaced at any time, it was not possible to find any individual sense of obligation in the sense of vocation. Nevertheless, labor can be regarded as alienation only because it lays claim to and defines an individual's life without there being any possibility of an ethical self-determination in regard to it. Thus even in criticism of it the claims of the concept of vocation make themselves heard.

From the point of view of the purpose of work, the question of the ethics of work can be completely obscured by the search for improvement in one's life apart from one's vocation—the attempt to find equivalent satisfaction in the world of leisure.

Neither the thesis of human alienation through the work process nor the assumption that the loss of work as vocation will be compensated by leisure deals adequately with the task implied by the concept of vocation. It has its basis in the fact that even under changed and changing conditions of the organization of work and of economic forms, work lays claim to the way in which individual human beings live, and does so in a manner that cannot dispense with the responsible self-determination of men and women in relation to work.

Helmut Schelsky has formulated the sociological situation by saying that work as vocation "is the most important factor for the social structuring of human life in our culture" ("Die Bedeutung des Berufes in der modernen Gesellschaft," in *Auf der Suche nach Wirklichkeit*, 1965, pp. 238–49). The social aspect of work can function in an integrative or in a disintegrative manner. The meaning of vocation for an individual's life is made clear by the problem of unemployment, insofar as unemployment is the experience of loss and raises the question whether the individual has any place in society, that is, is being "used" or is superfluous. The unemployed person is thrown back on his or her self and is in danger of losing a sense of identity. The blow to one's way of life becomes clear in cases of a forced change of occupation, because one's personhood is intimately connected with the occupational qualifications one has acquired, and with the social position attained through work. A change of occupation or retraining for another job implies extensive changes in the social world of the worker. The connection between occupation and life style also becomes clear in our present society, where one's work and one's leisure develop in different directions. The separation between the work of one's occupation on the one hand and leisure time on the other raises for the individual's way of life the question of whether he or she is living in two different worlds or different times. The social significance of work as occupation is also an important factor in a person's way of life. The relation of adults to society or to their social environment is to a large extent determined by their occupation. Security in social life, the permanence of a specific life style, the place that one holds in society are largely determined by one's occupation. Vocation and work have specific meaning for social standing and individual worth, for social rank and the signs that one "belongs." In work and professional activities are where working men and women have most of their social contacts and therefore their social activities. An occupation provides the primary experience of society and of the social environment and, as a result, is of significance for the experience one has of social reality in contrast to mere opinions. This perception of reality is mediated and defined through the work experience. Thus work is a component in the formation of the individual's experience of reality.

These sociological factors underline the relevance work has for the way an individual's life is lived. But they do not answer the question of where the individual's position in relation to work as vocation is defined in concrete terms. Indeed, against the background of these historical and sociological factors that question arises anew. It is the question of where the binding influence of the community defined by one's work takes specific form for the living of one's life. In this aspect, an occupation means training, qualifications, and preparation for the occupation in the quite real sense of the practice of an occupation through being trained by others. Directly appealing to people to work industriously and inspiring them to joy in their work by influencing their attitudes are not adequate ethical factors here; the training of persons to perform work by providing the skills and qualifications necessary is the concrete means for attaining self-determination.

An ethic of vocation must allow men and women to bring their unique ways of life to the workplace by means of their objective self-determination. From this it follows that the world of labor must be so constituted that it furthers a specifically vocational training of those who work and enables them to practice their vocation. This establishes a first definition of the humanization of the world of work that is rich in ethical consequences. Its goal is always to enable men and women to be masters of their work, not its servants.

Freeing individuals from domination by their work, which by its nature could also be performed by a machine, is the point of the efforts to structure working conditions appropriately. This relationship of machine to man also involves a program the goal of which is to turn work over to the machine in every instance where it is technically practicable and possible to do so, and to liberate human beings from such work. What has been expressed as a hope and expectation ever since the first machine was used for industrial production can lead again and again in the context of a labor economy to the situation of the human's being replaced by the machine and thus becoming unemployed. This problem of the economic structures accompanies every program for the "humanizing of the workplace," but it is not sufficient reason for preserving inhumane conditions that that would preserve the workplace. The problem presents us with the demand for a transformation of working conditions that can provide workers with individualized training for their vocation.

For literature on the historical and systematic content of the concept of vocation, see M. Weber, *The Protestant Ethic and the Spirit of Capitalism*, 1977 (Germ., 1905); K. Holl, "Die Geschichte des Wortes Beruf," in *Gesammelte Aufsätze zur Kirchengeschichte*, vol. 3, 1928, pp. 189–219; G. Wingren, *Luthers Lehre vom Beruf*, 1952; W. Bienert, *Die Arbeit nach der Lehre der Bibel*, 1954; H. Gatzen, "Beruf bei Luther und in der industriellen Gesellschaft," doct. diss., 1964; T. Rendtorff, "Beruf," in *Historisches Wörterbuch der Philosophie*, ed. J. Ritter, vol. 1, 1971, pp. 833–35; W. Conze, "Beruf," in *Geschichtliche Grundbegriffe*, vol. 1, 1972, pp. 490–507; J. M. Lochmann, "Werk und Werkgerechtigkeit: Arbeit in christlicher und marxistischer Sicht," *ZEE* 22 (1978): 105–17.

4) Education:
Participation in Culture

The involvement of lives in the task of culture is the basis for providing nurture. The education of the individual has as its purpose making individuals responsible for the renewed vitality of the basic elements of the culture that is transmitted through education.

"Man is the only creature that needs upbringing" (Kant, *Über Pädagogik*, in his collected works, ed. W. Weischedel, vol. 6, p. 697). The necessity of bringing up children gives the individual the concrete task of participating specifically and independently in the community that is mediated to us by culture. This second aspect of the cultural task leads us to explore what it means to enable an individual to achieve self-determination with respect to culture through education so that the ethical responsibility of this participation takes on independent form.

Bringing up children is a concrete application of the giving of life, and it sets the theme and is the starting point for human dependence. Individuals can attain to their own independent position regarding the elements of culture that they encounter in their upbringing only through an encounter with the authority of those charged with their education. Therefore in the present-day discussions of education it is essential to emphasize the ethical points of view that stress the education of the individual as cultural formation rather than a merely functional view that sees it as a process of socialization. To be sure, the socialization theories of the social sciences rightly place emphasis on the insight that upbringing in a broad and comprehensive sense involves all the processes through which a child or a young person learns how to live as a member of society. Thus socialization theory presents a view of the educational process that goes far beyond upbringing in the strict sense. Even so it is important to maintain, or to give new vitality to, the distinction between socialization in the wider sense and the explicit upbringing of the individual, because otherwise the process of education would become more and more anonymous, with the result that there would be no way of establishing responsibility. The goal of the express upbringing of a child as the child's cultural formation is to enable the maturing person to adopt his or her own position toward culture and to make decisions within the bounds of the wider social world in which he or she lives. Upbringing should enable individuals to act autonomously within their society. If upbringing were equated with socialization, this task could no longer be clearly formulated.

The school gives the clearest example of a process of eduction that is determined by its content. The ethical task of the school starts with responsibility for enabling young persons, through their schooling, to move beyond their immediate participation in family and society, that is, their everyday life, and through the reflective thinking stimulated and formed by the content of their education, to attain a position of relative distance from the world in which they live. Only in this way can individuals come to a free and independent self-determination that leads to a true realization of culture and establishes its true inward authority. The school as the institution designated for the purpose of education has therefore a responsibility for the social relationships between teachers and pupils, and among the pupils themselves, only in that it is where they can learn how to act in their relationships in society.

The problem we encounter here can be stated in basic terms. Human beings can be brought up only by other human beings; they cannot be brought up by themselves. That is to say, the question of education, precisely where its goal is individual independence, encounters the problem of autonomy, a person's self-determination with respect to dependence on others. Thus if we say that the goal of education is to make individuals completely self-determining, in strict contrast to being determined by others, our contention inevitably leads to a criticism of educational institutions. School becomes an instrument of force, of the violation of human freedom. But it is easy to see that such a critique misses the mark, because it makes the result of the educational process— the relative independence of the person—into its presupposition and thus brings about the negation of the entire task. The relationship between authority and freedom, which is at issue in education, cannot be settled by rejecting authority in favor of freedom in the educational process or by sacrificing authority in the interest of the child's unrestricted self-determination. But neither can it be settled by devoting education solely to training and protecting the individual in order to spare him or her from experiences of alienation and debates about the nature of reality in the process of education. The relationship between authority and freedom must rather involve content that is distinguishable from the child's immediate world of experience. The content of education need not at every point have current applicability to the world in which the child is living but should challenge the child to move beyond what is immediate. Only in this way can there be self-development that frees the individual so that he or she does not remain dependent on the teacher but becomes capable of moving freely within the culture that is mediated by education.

Thus, it is in education as what enables the individual to become self-determining in relation to culture that ethical responsibility is concretely applied to participation in the community formed by one's culture, participation through living one's own life. The ethical task consequently involves a general cultural formation through education, not limited to specific activities in the society or to specific skills but free and relatively indeterminate in relation to such concrete goals and itself its own goal. That is, the ethical task involves the formation of persons who are able to function independently in their culture.

Only when there is clarity about the ethical significance of this basic aspect of education can we establish standards and criteria that permit us to identify the appropriate emphases in the complex relationship between education and socialization. By means of an education that aims to achieve self-determination for each individual, the cultural community achieves in and for itself not a state in which it simply has at its disposal the men and women who become a part of the community but rather one in which it enables each succeeding generation to accept the inner obligations of the culture for their individual lives. An education should achieve at each of its stages the goal of enabling the rising generation to adopt the culture independently, that is, to accept through its own insights the authority of the existing culture—which first comes to it from the outside—in order to be able to contribute to the transformation and renewal of that culture.

Upbringing anticipates the formation of an individual's independence. It derives its legitimation from the preparation of young persons for their own free participation in their culture. Therefore a successful education is one through which persons come to assume responsibility for renewing the vitality of the basic elements of the human culture that has been transmitted to them by their education. Hence it is essential to the concept of education that it can be terminated. This is, to be sure, always relative to the individual. But here is where its validity must be proved. However important the intention of a program of "lifelong learning" may be—that is, the thesis that in order to participate in culture, one must be willing to accept the challenge of a permanent process of education—it would be false if it negated the possibility of completing the process of education. For only a limited education is compatible with the goal of human maturity. The completion of the education is seen in the person's maturity, which is the individual's self-determination to participate in culture. Maturity then expresses the idea that the person in his or her own life can be called upon for the preservation and renewal of the cultural community and is involved responsibly in working for its realization.

For a discussion of education and socialization, see H. Ringeling, "Naturliches Recht: Sozialanthropologische Fragen einer Familienethik," *ZEE* 19 (1975): 261–77; idem, "Welches Menschenbild wollen wir? Sozialisationsziele in moralwissenschaftlicher Sicht," *ZEE* 23 (1979): 243–51 (other references are cited here). See also E. Lichtenstein, "Bildung," in *Historisches Wörterbuch der Philosophie*, ed. J. Ritter, vol. 1, 1971, pp. 921–37; W. Trillhaas, "Bildung und Sittlichkeit," in *Handbuch der christlichen Ethik*, vol. 2, 1978, pp. 492–505; *Evangelische Beiträge zur Bildungspolitik*, published by the Evangelical Church of Germany, 1976.

5) *Spirituality:*
The Subjective Side of Religion

As spirituality, religion is the individual application of human self-determination to the reality of life which forms the basis of the individual's freedom and independence from the existing world and so gives courage for the renewal of an independent perception of the ethical task.

By spirituality we mean here the specific nature of an individual life as shaped by attitudes toward life in general and specifically attitudes toward God. In relation to the church as the institutional form of religion, spirituality is the "subjective side of religion" (W. Trillhaas, "Frömmig-keit," in *RGG*[3], 1158) that finds concrete expression in an individual's life. This defines the place of spirituality in life. Ethical responsibility, as it finds expression in the formation and cultivation of spirituality, is not found first in the application of religion to an active life. Spirituality is more than and different from the practice of a church-centered life. It is a distinctive and independent contribution toward making religion real. As understood in Protestantism, spirituality always involves the expression of religion in the life of the church, but it is not identical with the activity of the church as an institution. For our understanding of spirituality, the difference between it and formal church life is signif-icant, because spirituality expresses the perception of religious relation-ships in each person's life and is thus individual in nature. The ethical task whose concrete form is to be explored here can be defined theoret-ically by saying that spirituality is the individual's personal commitment to religion.

Spirituality must be explored in distinction from the life of religious institutions, because a religious approach to life is demanded in each place where we find ourselves, even when it is not necessary or possible to give it specific expression. Because the church is not present in every state and condition of life, it needs spirituality as the free and unconfined way of making such an approach.

Spirituality expresses itself by inner composure and reflection on the basic relationships of life, by maintaining an active life in order to keep one's inner sense of obligation alive. Spirituality is the practice of reli-gious reflection in the context of one's private life. This can be understood as reflection on oneself, not as abstract reflection on the self's own existence or as self-centered introspection but as reflection on the specific situation in which one finds oneself in the context of a concrete, empirical life, with the claims, tasks, and demands that are placed upon it. Further, piety is personal reflection, because each person must give a meaning to his or her life, a meaning that is not invented but received from the whole community and context of life, that is to say, from community with God. In this sense, spirituality is the individual's own commitment to religion, the practice of bringing the sum total of life's experiences to bear on the whole of life. Thus spirituality has its *Sitz-im-Leben* not in a specific form of life, for example, in an external religious ordering of life, but in living one's life in a secular context.

One additional perspective must be brought to bear on this line of ethical argument: spirituality is not simply something that is immanent in life. In spirituality the relationship of each person to the self finds expression in such a way that each one confronts his or her self, becomes aware of his or her own life's conduct. Thus it is possible to speak of forms of spirituality, of forms of expression in which this relation to the self becomes distinguishable in the context of and in contrast to the daily practice of life. Spirituality lays claim to one's own time and practices for composure and reflection. Spirituality means taking time for orientation toward the inner responsibilities of life and for letting them play a role in one's own life. In such forms as prayer—beginning with grace at meals—in Bible reading, etc., spirituality makes use of the forms of expression of the institutional church or is present in the religious institutions themselves. At the same time it differs from them in many and varied nuances and forms for each individual. The ethical responsibilities of spirituality cannot be reduced to a fixed catalogue of spiritual practices.

Therefore it is possible for spirituality to enter into rivalry with the church, for example, in the pietistic model of the *ecclesiola in ecclesia.* This rivalry, in which individual spirituality makes the claim that it is the "true" church in contrast to the "mainline" churches, is possible because the life of the institutional church, for the sake of its inner authority in each human life, requires individual spirituality. Spirituality has something to contribute to the institution and is not merely a recipient of the church's guidelines and instructions. The rivalry can be expressed in the claim that it is not necessary to go to church in order to be a good Christian, that Christianity and churchliness are not identical. Something important is contained in this rivalry between spirituality and institution; the empirical church and the community with God that is mediated by religion are not coterminous.

But there is also a danger in this rivalry. It appears when spirituality seeks, through the distinctive way it structures the inner authority of religion for the individual, to frame its rivalry with the church as a negation of religious institutions as a whole. In that case spirituality is distorted as an immediate religious self-realization; it becomes a sect and falls into making religion an instrument for its own purposes. In doing so it loses its own ethical significance for ethics.

In the face of this threat, the content and theological meaning of

spirituality for ethics must be given new emphasis. As spirituality, therefore, the knowledge that human beings are not solely comprehended in
what is at hand, that is, that they are not merely the product of natural
and social relationships, takes on specific relevance for each individual.
Spirituality is the individual expression of the fact that humans can be
distinguished from their world in the context of their experience of
empirical reality. As spirituality, human independence in the midst of
the dependences of life takes shape as productive resistance against
absorption into the functions of society through too much activity.
Spirituality provides the inner meaning of human worth. The human
ability to distinguish between the self and the self's relationships, and
humanity's gentle resistance to being absorbed by society, derive their
vitality from the religious knowledge that freedom has no other basis
than that provided by our relationship to God. That is the productive and
constructive contribution of spirituality to life in society, its specific
application of the ethical obligation placed upon us by life. Human
independence and freedom and the dignity they confer should not be
thought of first of all as demands we must make on others or on society.
These would be abstract demands if their only content were concern for
an end to dependence. The specific contribution of spirituality to our
shared life is that it enables us to assure ourselves of an independence that
in the precise sense of the word is *original*. But that can be the case only if
our awareness comes from the ground of the independence, that is, from
our relationship to God. Spirituality thus provides the meaning of the
"inner" independence and freedom of human beings, which is the presupposition of all imaginable, empirically attainable human freedoms,
because spirituality flourishes in individual lives and in the struggle with
those dependences that we experience as real.

Inwardness has fallen into disrepute not only in theology and ethics but
almost everywhere. But this is totally unjustified, because without a well-
developed inwardness there can be no clearly defined outwardness.
Without a living inwardness, otherwise well established demands for
freedom lose contact with the life that men and women must be
responsible for and that they must strive to realize—tasks in which no one
else can substitute for us.

The importance of the concept of spirituality for historical and systematic
ethics is set forth by D. Rössler, in "Frömmigkeit als Thema der Ethik," in
Handbuch der christlichen Ethik, vol. 2, 1978, pp. 506ff. See also W. Trillhaas,
*Protestantisches Christentum: Perspektiven und Gestalten des neuzeitlichen
Christentums*, 1975, pp. 9–24.

c. Evaluating Our Goals:
Justifying Our Actions

Taking a stand toward the basic structures we encounter in the conduct of life means, in this second aspect of our discussion, that we must be prepared to justify our actions. Our goals and expectations should correspond to those actions which in the basic structures of life demand responsibility. This requires explicit evaluation if we are to be free in our actions from bondage to false expectations.

1) The Goal of Marriage,
or the Expectation of Happiness

The expectations one has of marriage are, to begin with, simply the expectations the husband and wife bring to the marriage.

Anyone who enters into a marriage chooses a specific possibility among the many that life presents. The mutual choice made by the marriage partners is, as a choice among the conceivable multiplicity of possible encounters between men and women, a concrete action amid the fullness of life. It is not necessary here to enter into the question of how this choice is made in the course of life, or whether it is really a choice among various possibilities or, instead, something freely given by another. It remains true that the choice among many possibilities is part of the awareness of the marriage partners as they relate to each other. The choice of the partners involves expectations that before the marriage are vague and general. Dealing with these expectations in marriage involves turning the general expectations into reality, that is, transforming them into mutual acceptance between husband and wife. Each becomes for the other the concrete replacement for the general expectations brought to the marriage. Those expectations must not be allowed to come between the marriage partners and distort the achievement of their oneness in marriage.

General expectations of happiness threaten the reality of the marriage if the couple take their orientation from the expectations and allow them to create a separation between expectation and reality. Such a difference can have fatal consequences. It can be expressed in the temptation of the husband or wife to think that he or she could have married someone else, that is, to let the various possibilities come to dominate the reality. In many divorces this is what leads to the final break. In a broken marriage a general expectation of happiness triumphs over the concrete expectation of mutual faithfulness. The couple must work together to free themselves from the clichés about happiness and fulfillment and must set the concrete reality of their shared life against the potential chaos of general expectations. If the external norms of society are adopted by the couple and used against each other as conflicting goals, the results are destructive. Each then feels compelled to evaluate the other in terms of the general norms and to decide if the partner is adequate for attaining the ideal of happiness. But when the partners see each other in the light of general expectations of happiness, they see each other in a foreign light, and not in that of their own living relationship to each other. Marriage is thus always a process of striving to free oneself from general, abstract ideals.

This applies particularly to the sexual expectations one brings to the marriage or to the marriage partner, because general norms of sexual happiness and fulfillment are formulated in terms of the uninhibited expression of sexual relationships through exploration of all the possibilities. As the reverse side of emancipation, such exploration can lead couples into a new bondage, because they think they must live up to the sexual norms. This bondage is expressed in the search for as yet undiscovered pleasures. The assumption that such expectations can be fulfilled better by a trial marriage is following the false path of believing that marriage is defined solely or primarily in terms of sexual fulfillment. The measure of a good marriage is not the satisfaction of a general need for happiness; the transformation of one's expectation of happiness into mutual acceptance is the way to discover the concrete fullness of life. The inner measure of a marriage is not what one partner demands from the other in order that he or she may have a good marriage but what the one gives to the other, because one can honestly expect from a marriage only what one is able and willing to contribute to it.

The religious metaphor in Eph. 5:23–33, which depicts the relationship of married love in terms of the love of Christ for the church, expresses the thought that the fulfillment of unity in marriage depends on an expectation that is presented in a picture of total commitment free from any reservations. The significance of this metaphor for the history of marriage in Christian culture has been clearly set forth by H. Schelsky.

If we take into account the high value ascribed to social independence, as expressed in the acceptance of general concepts of what constitutes happiness, then marital fidelity, even in conflict with such expectations, is a measure of how free marriage is from being dominated by society.

Thus among our ethical presuppositions a knowledge of sexuality is relevant for our understanding of marriage. For as a result of the attention that has been paid to sexuality since Sigmund Freud, the multidimensional social and cultural nature of sexuality is an important object of discussion.

An ethical discussion of sexuality can begin with the observation that human sexuality is experienced as a power that is active within a person, manifesting itself as an independent force with which the person must come to terms. Speaking of an independent "sexual drive," however imprecise the concept may be, expresses in a significant way this state of affairs. Human sexuality constitutes a task that must be dealt with in the course of life and that occupies a prominent place in the biographical account of an individual's process of maturation.

The power of sexuality consists in its ability to draw a person out of a narcissistic relation to self and to open the person to the reality of social relationships. Sigmund Freud's observations point toward the importance of seeing the working of an elementary drive in the process of human maturation. The goal of this process is to give expression to love through sexuality. This goal is, however, always in conflict with the opposite possibility of turning love, as a personal relationship to another person, into nothing but sexuality and thereby reducing it to a function of self-gratification.

It is this element of self-gratification that led the Christian tradition to define sexuality as concupiscence, meaning that it leads to an absolute self-centeredness. Thus it is sin, because it makes the other person into an object for one's own use and thus reduces fellowship with God and other persons to a means for achieving one's own ends. This argument is basic to the theological-ethical position that has carried much weight in traditional Christian thought. The consequence is not a negation of human sexuality but the recognition of the task of integrating it into our understanding of the ethical reality of life. Herein lies the task that sexuality poses for the living of our lives.

The conflict arising in the maturation process must be dealt with in the actual living out of our lives. According to Freud, the contradictory possibilities in human sexual development can be observed in two phases occurring at different times. Autoeroticism arises as the first phase in consequence of the symbiotic relationship between mother and child, and it constitutes the first stage of human independence. In it the individual develops a self-understanding in which independence is realized as pleasurable concentration on the organs of his or her own body. This is polymorphous in nature and is not restricted to the genitals. From the observation of early childhood sexuality, Freud worked out for the developing individual an explanation of sexual "perversions." These can be regarded as regression into the sexuality of early childhood and arise in the conflict with the further development of sexuality, which is the means for achieving social relationships that accord with reality. Perversions constitute an attempt to reject reality.

The second phase involves growth beyond the narcissistic stage, the transfer of libido to objects other than one's own body. According to Freud this maturation signifies an intensive transition from the "pleasure principle" to the "reality principle." The maturation process is not simply identical with human psychological maturation. It alters the individual's relationship to the surrounding world in that it involves movement toward an affirmation of reality. This maturation process can succeed or fail, and thus constitutes a crisis.

A child lives by the pleasure principle in that it acts according to the concept that the world around it is there essentially in order to satisfy its own needs. Maturing, then, means learning to live in harmony with reality. It means learning to deny oneself immediate gratification at times, to accept reality as something objective and resistant to us in that it is not simply there in order to provide us with immediate pleasure. The task of bringing our life into accord with reality is accomplished with respect to sexuality by the incorporation of our sexuality into heterosexual relationships. In addition, the function of sexuality for life becomes productive in the renunciation of permanent, immediate gratification, that is, by sublimation of our sexuality through the use of the power of its drives in the cultural relationships of human society.

On Freud, see vol. 5, *Sexualleben*, of the series of studies edited by A. Mitscherlich et al., 1972. For the historical background, see D. S. Bailey, *Mann und Frau im christlichen Denken*, 1963; W. G. Cole, *Sexualität in Christentum und Psychoanalyse*, 1969. A concise summary is found in J. Scharfenberg's "Die Frage nach der Geschlechtlichkeit in tiefenpsychologischer Sicht," in *Religion zwischen Wahn und Wirklichkeit*, 1972, pp. 229–42; S. Keil, *Sexualität*, 1966; W. Trillhaas, *Sexualethik*, 1969; *Denkschrift zu Fragen der Sexualethik*, ed. EKD, 2d ed., 1971; H. Ringeling, "Die Grundlagen geschlechtlicher Freiheit," *Wissenschaft und Praxis in Kirche und Gesellschaft* 65 (1976): 404–18; idem, "Kriterien einer christlichen Sexualethik," *Diakonia* 8 (1977): 292–302.

For the ethical line of argument it is decisive that human sexuality cannot play the leading role in the development of the task that it poses for us. It would be a mistake to think that the way we live is a function of our sexual drives, because sexuality in and of itself presupposes and demands integration into the conduct of life. Responsibility for the way we live cannot be delegated to our sexuality. Every attempt, every program along that line is in strict contradiction to the task posed by sexuality and in the final analysis is a negation of that task. From the point of view of studies of human sexuality such attempts constitute regression. But on the other hand there is also no validity to the traditional argument which maintains that the relationship of sexuality and culture or of sexuality and ethics can be subsumed under the function of heterosexual drives in the service of reproduction, and which seeks to support an argument from "nature" on this basis. Ability to reproduce, however elementary its relation to sexuality, is in and of itself ethically neutral. That is, it can be achieved within the marriage bond, and just as easily in open promiscuity.

Sex, as an elementary drive in human self-realization can play a productive role in the way we live only if it is affirmed and its power is acknowledged. The conflict that results from the tendency of sex to dominate human beings should not be suppressed or denied. In that conflict we see a relationship to reality, a dependence on something other than the rational and moral ego, which can be experienced in sexual commitment as both a strengthening and a fulfillment, and which one can have neither individually nor alone but only through sexuality.

The success of sexuality always implies not only the receiving of love but also the expressing and giving of it. We are speaking here of the requirement that we deal with our sexuality in a responsible and reflective manner. Such ethical, reflective thought finds concrete expression in the formation and preservation of limits within which sexuality is protected and developed and in which it can develop in integration with the totality of individual relationships between human beings concerning the opposite sex and not simply be realized for itself in unrestricted independence. The fundamental solution to this task is marriage. Thus, ethically, all other sexual relationships are to be defined and modified in reference to marriage. The affirmation of life in the concrete expression of sexuality does permit the inclusion of premarital sexual relations. But the responsible distinction between sexual relations that lead to marriage and thus according to their intention at least are governed by marriage and such relations that tend toward promiscuity cannot be defined merely in terms of sexual activity. To this extent it is valid here to say that sexuality cannot assume the dominant role in the way we structure our lives.

In many and varied aspects homosexuality constitutes a conflict in the way we live our lives. The recent attention to homosexuality has been made possible by the decrease in the absolute religious and moral rejection of homosexuality in the Christian world and the new awareness of the individual conflicts resulting from homosexual tendencies in people's self-understanding and in their relationship to persons of the same sex. It is also influenced by the attempt to portray homosexuality as an alternative of equal value to heterosexuality and to promote marriage-like homosexual partnerships. The attempt to reduce the conflict to the level of purely social prejudices would make the acceptance of homosexuality a part of a program for the transformation of society.

An individual acceptance of homosexual conflict is possible in the field of pastoral concern only if homosexuality is not regarded as an alternative life style and in principle a general form of sexual expression and if ethics does not gloss over this conflict but limits it to being regarded as an individual conflict. That is to say, the general acceptance of homosexuality as a valid form of sexual expression is not in the best interests of the homosexual. It would impede the recognition of the individual problems in the life of the homosexual and impose general expectations that cannot be resolved.

On the other hand, the clear ethical distinction that marks homosexuality as a form of sexual life that can never become universal can lead to a definite affirmation of the differences between the sexes as something to be accepted, and by analogy a recognition of orientation to one's own sex, so that homosexual tendencies can be integrated into the conduct of one's life rather than one's life integrated into those tendencies. Certainly society needs to support homosexuals in their dealing with this conflict.

On homosexuality, see M. Dannecker and R. Reiche, *Der gewöhnliche Homosexuelle*, 1974; R. Lautmann, ed., *Seminar: Gesellschaft und Homosexualität*, 1977; G. Looser, *Homosexualität—menschlich—christlich—moralisch*, 1980.

The discussion of sexuality in the present century has involved so many different promises and expectations that new conflicts and hypotheses have resulted, the insolubility of which has come to be a burden for individual and institutional attempts to deal with sexuality. This is the contemporary counterpart of the dominance of the ascetic tradition in an earlier phase of Christianity.

All the problems that can be identified in the field of sexuality lie between two extremes. The first is an attitude toward human sexuality that is on principle negative and that tends to a mastery of it as a hostile force threatening our humanity. The other would accord to sexuality the dominant role in the structuring of the way people live, with the goal of eliminating all hindrances to immediate sexual satisfaction. Sexuality is a constituent of life, but it is to be regarded as a task of the giving of life and thus as the basis and occasion for specific reflection on life, because sexuality in relationship to the way people live can be a source of fulfillment as well as conflict.

2) The Secular Nature of the State and the Evaluation of Political Life

The political task includes accountability for the goals that can and do serve the political order. The secular nature of the state demands specific political accountability. The expectations citizens have of the state and the exercise of power by it must take into account the state's secular nature.

The demand for accountability in political life can be addressed to the politicians. It is expressed in the expectation that those who are politically responsible must also formulate the guidelines, goals, and ideals of politics and fulfill their responsibility to present to the public purposeful political perspectives, thus exercising political leadership that has significant and meaningful content. The expectation can be personalized in the challenge to political leaders to be more than pragmatic, one-day-at-a-time politicians. More is expected of them—that they give meaning to politics in order that through what they say and do the basic obligations of politics may be renewed.

Such an expectation makes it clear that individual politicians, unless they are laying claim to absolute authority, can play only a representative role in establishing the meaning of political action. That is, they must be accountable for the basis of their politics in such a way that their policies and actions are not tied to their own person or their own views but can be understood and adopted by others.

Political accountability can be defined as a hallmark of political activity itself. It includes the expression of political legitimation that results above all from free and secret elections. Elections that express acceptance of a specific political program are examples of political accountability in that through them agreement can also be withheld. Accountability can be demonstrated by the setting of significant goals, but it is put into practice and determined through actions that can be distinguished from the contents of a political policy. Thus the task can be formalized and the necessity of accountability can be seen in the connection between political actions and specific procedures that establish legitimacy. In this way overdramatization of questions involving political accountability is avoided and openness is maintained for various options and alternatives. In any case, political actions are decided not solely and directly through the power of words and ideas but through the "legitimacy of the actions taken" (N. Luhmann).

This means then that accountability for the content of political policy is a matter not of the presence or absence of politics but of the place it holds within the structure of the body politic, of whose activity it is a part.

In a more basic sense, political accountability can involve accountability for political life itself, for the sources of its normative nature, and for its relationship to other basic facets of human life in marriage and family, economics, culture, and religion. It gives rise to a critical investigation of the nature of political life—to the question of what boundaries can be placed on political life and of what the circumstances are under which political activity itself can be called to accountability. Thus it can be raised to the status of a dispute over the political fundamentals in which everyone is involved, in which the definition of basic values is sought, and in which the temptation of politics to want to be the custodian of ultimate dogmas of well-being or to claim for itself a higher historical mission can be brought before the judgment bar of political reason. We are dealing here with the fact that there has been in modern times a permanent political crisis, expressed above all in the form and by the claims of totalitarian regimes. As a result, politics must confront a mistrust in principle precisely at the point where it must lay claim to the basic trust of the individual as citizen.

Each of these aspects of political accountability involves all the others. All derive their ethical relevance through their relationship to the ethical concept of the public good. This concept covers all the expectations that are brought from every side to political life at the level of the common life of the community. If politics is more than and different from the balancing of differing interests and their regulation so that they are compatible, it is also challenged to accountability on the question of the relationship of the public good to human salvation as Christian salvation. It is in the context of Christianity that the awareness was formed of the necessity that the state be secular, that is, the necessity that the state and politics be independent and be aware of their limits in contrast to and in express distinction from religion. The question arises of how this accountability of political life within its proper boundaries can be carried out if political life is confronted by expectations that are no longer adequate for dealing clearly and rationally with this distinction. The pressure on political life from those who expect happiness and fulfillment in life is the crisis of politics. It raises the question of whether, under the pressure of specific expectations, public life can still be regulated.

The ethical concept of the public good is limited by the possibilities of what politics can accomplish. The secular nature of the state means that the political task must be defined in terms of its difference from and its relation to the Christian religion. That is the meaning and the systematic intention of the Reformation doctrine of the two realms. As a result of the Enlightenment, religion found itself in a precarious situation in this respect, because the Enlightenment's political agenda included the negation of religion. Thus politics tended to expand to compass the realization of hopes for ultimate salvation which had been the theme of religion.

The eschatological promise that was imminent in the Enlightenment understanding of the process of history pointed toward a totally transparent world in which human beings would exercise rational mastery over all the conditions of human social, historical, and individual existence. The goal of history, the collective happiness, the sovereign sway of rationality, would coincide with a world that was free of all contingent events. The human will was directed toward a new creation of the world, which derived its determination from the conviction that the Christian world was a failure, that the disappointment arising from the fact that the expectation of the end had not been fulfilled demanded a new and productive response. In this sense, the Enlightenment as the historical process of the modern age was itself a religion. It was nourished by the incentive of finding a substitute for the old religion. (G. Rohrmoser, "Politik und Religion am Ende der Aufklärung," in T. Rendtorff, ed., *Religion als Problem der Aufklärung*, 1980, p. 203).

The totalitarianism of the twentieth century is the point at which the Enlightenment was taken seriously beyond its application to Christianity.

The dechristianizing of the Enlightenment loosed the force that led to political totalitarianism, which must be termed religious according to the concept of religion that expresses the ultimate intention of the Enlightenment. (Ibid.)

Political practice is then conceivable only in totalitarian terms, that is, as something that needs to be accountable to nothing higher than its own will. The phenomenon of "totalitarianism as a kind of secularized theocracy" (Rohrmoser, "Politik und Religion") can be understood only in the context of the history of Christianity.

The meaning of the doctrine of the two realms is to be viewed against the background of the political experiences of the twentieth century. This is not the place to reconstruct the history of the discussion of the doctrine since the 1920s. But it is the appropriate place for a systematic revival of this significant bit of Protestant and Lutheran political theology. At the beginning of the present century, Ernst Troeltsch raised the question of the meaning of Protestantism for the rise of the modern world. He was convinced that the historic relationship of politics and religion could be elucidated only on the premise that the independence of the modern world from its Christian origins was brought about by the Enlightenment. In his interpretation he also advanced the thesis that Luther and the Reformation belonged not to the modern age but to the premodern period, and this led him to distinguish between early Protestantism and neo-Protestantism. If the distinction between the two realms in which God rules had its political relevance in the concept of Christendom, it follows that religion, in the theological form of neo-Protestantism, had to be defined anew in terms of the emancipated modern world.

Theologically, the revival of the doctrine of the two realms in the 1920s, and then especially in the period of the Third Reich and the years after it, meant the attempt to take the independence of a political world that regarded itself as wholly secular and to contrast that with the independence of religion in such a way that the contrast did not become a mutually exclusive rivalry between religion and politics as, in the opposite direction, it had as a result of the radical conceptions of the Enlightenment. Rather, it established the secular independence of politics as the heir of the Reformation in its own boundaries. Thus, a theme was revived indirectly that had been formulated in the political philosophy of German Idealism.

> The emancipation of the state from the control of the Christian religion is not only a part of the completion of the Reformation, not only the permanent condition of freedom, but also the indispensable presupposition for the rationality of politics. Politics can remain rational only in a society in which Christianity is a living force, just as the experiment of democracy can succeed only as long as a Christian ethos is acknowledged as its intellectual and religious basis. (Rohrmoser, "Politik und Religion," 207).

In fact, however, under the assaults of the totalitarian ideology of National Socialism, the revival of the doctrine of the two realms initially developed only in terms of the independence of the church and its political responsibilities in relationship to the state. But the doctrine was not adequate in that situation, because it made the church's understanding of its relation to politics dependent on the concept of the totalitarian state. Not only had the National Socialist regime denounced the church's political activity, but in its totalitarian understanding of politics it was not open to accepting the limits which the church had placed on activity in the political realm. In this context it would have seemed plausible to emphasize, not so much the doctrine of the two realms, as the church's claims on politics contained in the concept of the lordship of Christ. One of the misunderstandings that resulted is that, in the decisively altered political conditions after 1945, the question of the Christian understanding of politics was discussed as the particular political task of the church. At the same time the admittedly more complex question of the relationship between church and state in terms of the distinction drawn by the political situation received little attention, precisely because it lay outside the immediate realm of the church's practical competence. The church cannot and should not take the political realm as its own proper responsibility, unless it is willing to forget the meaning of the heritage of the Reformation in this area. Therefore its responsibility is to transfer to the political arena the discussion of the distinction between the two realms. This is the fundamental problem in coming to terms with politics as we confront it in contemporary Christian political ethics.

In our day the distinction between God's activity in political tasks and God's acts for human salvation must be asserted in opposition to the world's claims to political domination, just as in the time of the Reformation it was asserted in opposition to the claims of the church to world domination. For political domination of the world has in the process of modern history taken the place of the total control of reality which the medieval church once claimed for itself.

In order to clarify and substantiate this thesis, I will attempt in the following to reformulate the theological justification of the doctrine of the two realms by an analysis of politics and the task of justifying political activity.

Political activity as the control and exercise of power is subject to the limits imposed by time and by finite conditions. For its legitimation it depends on being able to justify itself in terms of the political will of the people. But the special function, the specific task of political activity does not follow directly from the sum total of the will of individuals. It is subject to the common will, upon which all individual wills and individual interests are dependent. Human political will, to which politicians owe their access to power and the exercise of that power, must take shape in distinction from the direct desire for meaning and happiness on the part of individuals and thus must constitute the will to life in community. Thus it is clear that the political will has its own proper authority.

But then it is not only totally unrealistic but also inappropriate to expect a true and ultimately valid self-realization of humankind solely through the political shaping of the world. A politically based life in society cannot establish the humanity of men and women. It can only lay claim to the service of humanity in a politically relevant society. To this extent politics is dealing with the world in which humans live and is a function and a component of that world. Only by means of far-reaching and long-range formulations can political activity help preserve the human world. No demand for political activity has meaning if it is expressed in promises that life in general will always be successful.

The significance of this state of affairs becomes clearer when competence in political activity is contrasted with an open and public presentation of God's truth as superior to all humanity. Here we see the political meaning of religious freedom. The proclamation of the gospel is not the proclamation of a rival political system. It is the proclamation and the affirmation of a freedom the meaning of which goes beyond any possibility of realization through politics. Today we prefer to focus on the question of the political consequences that flow from such an affirmation of freedom of belief. The answer is found in rationality—that is to say, where the establishment of limits, the ability to form a consensus, and a factual basis for political action in the service of the community take on objective, institutionalized form and become the criteria for determining the direct political will of the people. Such an understanding has developed in post-Enlightenment times out of an interest in a humane understanding of political life.

In the context of the doctrine of the two realms this distinction means that political activity—even in the form of providing structure for the world—is a function of God's preservation of the world. But not even in connection with this function, is it capable of bringing salvation. Any intention of doing so would only involve political reason in unresolvable contradictions. This is not to say that political reason is less competent than theological reason and that even in its own field it thus needs to be permanently informed by the latter. For such ecclesiastical arrogance, theological reason would need to provide proof of its alleged superiority.

In contrast to the situation under totalitarian political systems, which follow of themselves from a religious exaggeration of politics and thus provoke the liberal demand for limits on the power of the state, liberal democracies are threatened by a totalitarianism from within. This is involved in the "revolution of rising expectations," which places political life in a dangerous situation if the justification of politics in the sense of its acceptance by the citizens is made dependent on the fulfillment of the sum of all their expectations. That gives rise to a situation in which the state and its institutions face a rejection in principle, or one in which the acceptance of political responsibility depends on the precondition, revocable at any time, of one's own personal interests and expectations. In the concept of a "popular democracy" leading to violent attempts to seize political power for private alternative concepts of politics, the common good and the constitution that provides for it are destroyed in the interest of the private expectations that one brings to politics. A pious religious consciousness inclines a person to support such rejection and aloofness, although not with the use of force but rather in intention, and this fact shows how necessary it is that the doctrine of the two realms be applied to religion and that its relation to religion be made clear. It is precisely where churches or religious groups join in political protest or in rejection of politics in the name of a concern for humanity and a commitment to human values that the unavoidable question arises, What concept of humanity is their guide? The Christian understanding of humanity includes an acceptance of political tasks that have content other than the immediate fulfillment of human goals. This problem is a challenge to the church. If we take into account the political function or the political consequences of religious involvement, then every religion has a political dimension. It depends only on the context in which responsibility is accepted. The Christian religion has a strongly political dimension the Christian nature of which consists in the willingness to apply the Christian understanding of freedom to oneself. In this respect, Martin Luther's definition is still normative today: "The Christian is the free lord over all things and subject to no none." And therefore it is also true that "the Christian is the servant of all and subject to everyone" (*On the Freedom of the Christian*, 1520). Only when we see that the distinction made by the doctrine of the two realms places duties on both state and church, politics and religion, does the question of the justification of political life take on its appropriate form.

The early discussion of the doctrine of the two realms is documented in *Reich Gottes und Welt: Die Lehre von den zwei Reichen*, ed. H. H. Schrey, 1969. Cf. also the comprehensive study made by U. von Duchrow: *Christenheit und Weltverantwortung: Traditionsgeschichte und systematische Struktur der Zweireichelehre*, 1970. See too E. Troeltsch, *Politische Ethik und Christentum*, 1904. On the more recent discussions, see esp. M. Honecker, *Sozialethik zwischen Tradition und Vernunft*, 1977, and also his "Thesen zur Aporie der Zweireichelehre," *Zeitschrift für Theologie und Kirche* 78 (1981); U. Duchrow, ed., *Die Vorstellung von zwei Reichen und Regimenten bis Luther*, 2d rev. ed., 1978; N. Hasselmann, ed., *Gottes Wirken in seiner Welt: Zur Diskussion um die Zweireichelehre*, 2 vols., 1980; K. Nowak, "Zweireichelehre: Anmerkungen zum Entstehungsprozess einer umstrittenen Begriffsprägung und kontroversen Lehre," *Zeitschrift für Theologie und Kirche* 78 (1981); W. Huber, *Kirche und Öffentlichkeit*, 1973. Important for the whole discussion is E. W. Böckenförde's "Die Entstehung des Staates als Vorgang der Säkularisation," in *Säkularisation und Utopie*, 1967.

3) Economic Activity between Self-Interest and Investment

Economic activity is subject to a particular demand for accountability, because it involves interest in material gain. The ethical accountability of economics must take concrete form in its dealings with profit and with various interests. The goals toward which decisions about investments are oriented provide us with significant examples for our consideration.

A dominant motif in Christian ethical tradition is the criticism of wealth. The rich are depicted as the opposite of the pious. In the preaching of Jesus this motif is unmistakable. Therefore we must first of all clarify the meaning of this criticism of wealth and its relationship to the goals of economic activity. Wealth, as well as both the striving for wealth and the living in wealth, can be regarded in the Christian tradition as an orientation to life that is in direct competition with faith and with trust in God.

For example, this is seen very clearly in Jesus' words, "For what will it profit a man, if he gains the whole world and forfeits his life?" (Matt. 16:26a). The parable of the rich young ruler (Matt. 19:16–26), who asks what it is that he should do beyond the fulfillment of the Ten Commandments in order to inherit eternal life, culminates in the demand that he should sell everything he possesses and give it to the poor—that is, he should renounce his wealth. Why is it that economic wealth is regarded as a rival to a life of faith? It is only because and insofar as economic wealth produces a distribution of the means of life such that human interests seem to be satisfied in a manner that, in empirical terms, means extensive independence from others. The criticism of wealth is thus directed primarily at exposing the delusive character of such independence, because it does not bring true life but remains subject to the limits of earthly life and thus of death. All those who have their hearts set on riches are relying on what is perishable, and not on life. The opposite pole of wealth is thus poverty, which when freely chosen, places one's life in a realistic position with reference to the goal of obtaining life. Poverty is the religious and ethical program for attaining independence from material goods, a life commitment to the goal of life itself, a goal that extends beyond this earthly world. Does this contrast provide an answer for the ethics of economics?

It cannot be used to try to derive from the proclamation of Jesus guidelines for economic activity. Those who would transpose the choice of asceticism and poverty into a general commandment are turning the whole matter upside down. At the heart of the matter is our involvement with life, but the search for a religious and ethical orientation toward the goal of our actions cannot be brought to a successful conclusion by a total negation of economic activity.

For a discussion of the problems and perspectives of the ethics of economics, consult the early work of G. Wünsch, *Evangelische Wirtschaftsethik*, 1927, and the discussion of that book by A. Hakamies, *Georg Wünschs evangelische Sozialethik im Lichte seiner werttheoretischen Auffassung*, 1975. See also G. W. Locher, *Der Eigentumsbegriff als Problem evangelischer Theologie*, 1954; A. Rich, *Christliche Existenz in der industriellen Welt*, 1957; W. Trillhaas, *Das Evangelium und der Zwang der Wohlstandskultur*, 1966; G. Hartfiel, *Wirtschaftliche und soziale Rationalität*, 1968; A. Muller-Armack, *Religion und Wirtschaft*, 2d ed., 1969; H. D. Wendland, ed., *Sozialethik im Umbruch der Gesellschaft*, 1969; M. Hengel, *Eigentum und Reichtum in der frühen Kirche*, 1973; R. Kramer, *Die christliche Verantwortung in der sozialen Marktwirtschaft*, 1973; H. Schulze, *Theologische Sozialethik*, 1977.

One cause of the difficulty of discussing the ethics of economics is that theologians and ethicists do not find it easy to come to grips with economic issues and that, in their primary experiences, they find themselves at considerable distance from that field of activity. But the difficulty also rests on the specific and close relationship between economics and religion, which brings into play the rivalry between the practice of religious ascetic life and any orientation toward economics. In an enigmatic way this affects their respective understandings of reality, because in both possibilities we can see an intensification of what is to be gained in life. But that is something more than and different from a rivalry between moral positions.

This rivalry and this relationship are the systematic concepts that form the basis of Max Weber's ingenious historical and sociological reconstruction of the relationship between Protestant ethics and the forms of modern capitalism: *Die protestantische Ethik und der Geist des Kapitalismus*, 1905, republished 1968. This was the stimulus for Ernst Troeltsch's extensive investigation of the social history of Christianity, *Die Soziallehren der christlichen Kirchen und Grupen*, 1912, 1965. It is still disputed whether Weber's thesis provides a historical explanation for at least the beginnings of the release of economic forces in the modern period of Western industrial society or whether, on another plane, it serves as a paradigm for the systematic relationship between the ethics of religion and economics and thus is to be regarded as a bit of theory in the sociology of religion, an indirect debate with the Marxist theory of history. In any case, for our discussion it would be inadequate and not even relevant to develop an ethic of economics as a pure appeal to the religion or morality of workers and management. The question must be explored in a different direction.

What is it that lets economics be regarded as a rival equivalent to religion, that is, as the object of absolute commitment in life?

Economic activity opens a specific access to the fullness of life through the exchange of the products of labor, especially through the convertibility of the economic value of specific goods. This access to an indefinite range of possibilities for life is achieved through money. Money functions in the exchange of goods and is thereby the means to the participation in the fullness of life insofar as that can be realized through material possessions.

In speaking of the rivalry to an orientation to life in religious or ethical terms we can say that a person's heart is set on money, that is, on the functions that wealth can perform. This is based on the experience that thereby the way is opened for participation in the fullness of life and for more possibilities than any individual can have unaided. This leads us to the search for an ethically binding concrete expression for involvement in the fullness of life that can be defined and tested in economic terms and that can determine for us what we should spend our money for.

The traditional answer is that wealth, money, and possessions find ethical justification only if they are used for a good purpose. Thus the giving of alms is the best-known justification for wealth. The good purpose is the alleviation of the needs of others, of the poor. However helpful that demand is, it is still subject to economic forces. This is because the ethics of economics, its orientation to a goal, is seen as a secondary good purpose, which is added on to economic activity. Indeed, in order to be able to give charity you first have to earn the means to do so. Only those who have can give. The rich as benefactors occupy a respectable position but one that presupposes economic activity, the surplus from which can be used for the needy.

The Christian diaconate has always been aware of the differences and the similarities between economics and a religious orientation. This can be seen in two aspects: first, in that the investing of wealth in meeting the needs of the poor is a religiously based realization of the fullness of life, because in the poor we encounter Christ himself (Matt. 25:31–46; 2 Corinthians 8), and second, in that wealth cannot be justified in itself but takes on value only when put to a good use, the rich being under ethical obligation not because they are rich but because they are called upon to be good stewards of their means. In the present day there is a corresponding connection between the church's organized ministry of compassion and the loss to the economy of the goods and money used in this way.

With this understanding it is possible to frame a specific requirement for justifying economic activity; that the goals toward which it is oriented not be merely self-serving. Gain can be understood as the increase of possibilities for exchange and thereby the potential creation of a fullness of life that can be expressed in terms of possessions. But gain is in itself an abstract category.

As far as economic interests are concerned, the ethical demand for accountability is seen largely in terms of self-interest. It involves one's own personal interests, and makes use of the economy in relation to others for strictly economic purpose. But it is not at all certain that the critique in terms of economic self-interest is adequate. The responsibility inherent in economics and proper to it in dealings with the enrichment of life that it produces is to be discovered in another quarter. Money as gain must, in order to be economically relevant, be reinvested in the economic process in order for it to be productive. That is more than and different from one's self-interests as a consumer. A concrete expression of the orientation that economic interests have toward goals can be seen in the investments that are made. Money must be invested; it is nothing in itself.

In this strictly economic context we encounter again the old problem that wealth is perishable. The usefulness of money for an individual's life is limited by and disappears with the end of that life. By contrast, through investment the gains that one has made become involved in the concrete economic expression of the fullness of life. In contrast to the common view that money has value in and of itself, because anything can be bought with it, in economic terms money is seen as the equivalent of the fullness of life in the decision how it will be invested. In our decisions how to invest what we possess our reflective thought about life becomes relevant in economic concepts. This involves not only the problem of justice as distributive justice, the distribution of the means of life, but also and especially the problem of investment, which gives prominence to the question of how we are to deal with the fullness of life.

Here we should look at the objection that investments are made solely in economic terms—on the basis of which investment promises the best changes for the greatest earnings. That is certainly relevant, but it is not decisive. The chances for maximum gain are dependent on the success of the investments. And the chance for gain is not a fixed entity nor an independent goal of our activity. The success we expect is dependent on the renewed activity of the investment.

Ethical responsibility for economic activity confronts us with the task of transforming the general, and in itself abstract, orientation to economic gain by using the perspective of specific decisions about investment as is required by economic activity itself, and also of measuring our decisions in the light of our responsibility for that which is being invested.

Thus by inquiring into the goals of economic activity we can define an ethical principle that does not negate economic factors but defines the interests involved as having, through the concrete expression of these interests in making investments—that is, in the context of the economic process—a content vaster and more adequate than mere self-interest.

The discussion of the ethical and theological dimensions of our concept of money has been revived in recent years by W. Kasch, as seen in the volume he edited, *Geld und Glaube*, 1979. See also E. Küng, *Wirtschaft und Gerechtigkeit*, 1967; H. C. Lüling, *Freiheit und wirtschaftlicher Liberalismus*, 1979.

4) Technical Culture and the Use of Its Tools

Explicit justification is demanded of cultural activity wherever its accomplishments have impact beyond its traditional range of influence. A clear example of this is found in the interrelationships of the modern natural sciences and technology. Ethical justification here involves primarily responsibility for control of the tools of scientific and technological activity.

Is it permissible for human beings to do everything they are capable of doing? With this question we take up a line of discussion that can serve as a pattern for dealing with an extremely complex set of problems. The goal is to formulate a concrete example of ethical reflection. The application of this issue is found in the question of whether it is possible to control the tools of our scientific and technological culture.

It is necessary to state the initial question in more precise terms. The question of whether humans should and may do everything that is possible is to be clearly distinguished from the erroneous assumption that they can actually do anything they want to do. In the light of our highly developed natural sciences and the technologies they have produced, that assumption bears no relationship to reality. It is impossible to do everything we want to do (even though it might seem possible), because science and technology are able to guide and concentrate human expectations concerning the control of nature in such a way that generally it is only what can be done that is desired.

In general, however, even with the means of science and technology at their disposal, humans will to pursue (in the sense of defining goals) only the traditional goal of their culture, that is, to obtain through a control of nature the optimum quantity of the necessities of life. This same goal is seen also, for example, in the development of self-control through education, as expressed in the philosophical ideal of the control of nature through the intellect. But this intention is not free of ambiguity. At every stage of cultural development it is necessary to determine anew what the desired optimum actually is.

That is the significance of the current debate initiated by the Club of Rome (D. L. Meadows et al., *The Limits of Growth,* 1972), which has gone far beyond that study in creating a new awareness of the environment. For science and technology cannot of themselves determine for human culture what the optimum is. We may well expect that the hostility to technology and the criticism of science evident in this discussion will in the long run prove to be ephemeral.

Science and technology do not discover and develop the desired goal, however it may be presented in detail, but rather they develop the means for exercising control. The debate concerns such means, and it is here that the specific demand for justification must be made. The means are the concrete expression of what is possible, of what human beings can do. They also pose a distinct ethical problem, because control of the means for taking action is what distinguishes scientists and technologists from all others who live in the same cultural community.

The same holds true for other areas of a culture. For example, the control of the necessary means for expression distinguishes the artist from an ordinary person in art.

The ethical discussion should not be defined by general hopes for progress and expectations of happiness nor, on the contrary, by fears of progress and expectations of disaster. The concrete discussion of the ethical issues must deal with the problem of how to control the tools that have been made possible by science and technology. Science and technology are not justified by virtue of serving the general human goals of improving the conditions of life, in the sense that every means for doing so is right. Their specific need for justification results from the question of control, which always involves the ability to place limits on the means that are employed. This is the way to approach the concrete problem of how we must deal with the possibilities inherent in specific scientific and technical activities. This covers a large range of individual problems. Among them one problem occurs again and again: the distinction between scientific experiments with life and the technological application of the results of those experiments in the context of the way human life is lived. Is it responsible to use the whole realm of human culture, including the total environment, for conducting scientific and technical experiments? Can a general abolition of the distinction between experiment and reality be justified? The distinction between the totality of human culture and the scientific and technological activities conducted within it must be maintained. The ability to control and limit the use of the tools of human activity is a clear criterion in this area.

A contemporary example can make this clear. Investigation of the accident at the nuclear reactor at Three Mile Island in the United States disclosed that the accident would not have occurred if the employees had permitted the automatic technical devices to function instead of intervening in the process. In the last analysis it was not technical failure but human error that was responsible for the accident. Not the inadequacy of technology but human inadequacy is to be identified as the troublemaker. As a result, the demand might be made for improving humans rather than improving technology, in order to allow technology to continue its course unhindered. Clearly the results of the investigation are highly ambiguous. It is disturbing to feel that Three Mile Island proves that such accidents cannot be avoided through technology but are contingent on human nature itself. It is also highly disturbing to feel that as a consequence control over the tools of human activity must also involve control over the men and women involved, who are then in effect placed on the same level as the scientific and technological apparatus. A further cause of discomfort is that clearly the experimental nature of science and technology is extended to investigate the conduct of human life.

This example also makes clear the ethical impact on the debate about nuclear energy, which includes many other problems—social, political, economic, and aesthetic—that cannot be explored here. Neither the problem of safety in atomic power plants nor the long-term problem of atomic waste disposal seems amenable to clear scientific and technological solutions. In this situation the construction and operation of nuclear power plants is often justified on the grounds that further progress in science and technology will probably continue the progress made earlier and result in the discovery of the necessary solutions to the problems. This means, however, that the human world involved in the nuclear energy industry must expect that in addition to the promised benefits, it will become a sort of grandiose laboratory or an arena for technological experiments. The opposition that has arisen to this state of affairs must not be blamed on those who express their opposition. An unconditional yes to nuclear energy would mean that the distinction between experiment and reality were no longer maintained. A responsible yes can be given only on the condition that the instruments of atomic power can be controlled.

There are many comparable though less conspicuous examples of this sort of problem to be found in other areas—in medicine, for example. Friedrich H. Tenbruck (*Kritik der planenden Vernunft,* 1972) has pointed out that sociology faces an analogous problem that goes beyond the broad sociologizing of consciousness and extends deep into the practices that turn social culture into a kind of experimental field. In this area it is much less clear what kind of control is necessary.

The task of ethics is not merely to place external limits on science and technology but to show that those limits are a concrete application of scientific and technological responsibility itself. Such a demand means that the relation of science and technology to the totality of culture must be defined in such a way as to make it clear that the goals of human culture cannot be perfectly attained anywhere. Every activity of human culture produces something approximating the fullness of life. No such instance is in itself the achievement of ultimate goals, but each one is merely a specific instrument for some activity or for expressing goals, and it must therefore be called to accountability.

The discussion about controlling the means of human activities has become heated in connection with the problems of using nuclear energy and involves the whole of society. Only a few of the writings that serve as examples of the discussion can be cited here: G. Altner, *Zwischen Natur- und Menschengeschichte*, 1975; idem, *Das Kreuz dieser Zeit: Von den Aufgaben des Christen im Streit um die Kernenergie*, 1977; idem, *Atomenergie—Herausforderung an die Kirchen: Texte, Commentare, Analysen*, 1977; W. Dreier and R. Kümmel, eds., *Zukunft durch kontrolliertes Wachstum—Naturwissenschaftliche Fakten, sozialwissenschaftliche Probleme, theologische Perspektiven: Ein interdisziplinärer Dialog*, 1977; W. Ch. Zimmerli, ed., *Kernenergie—Wozu? Dedürfnis oder Bedrohung*, 1978; W. Korff, *Kernenergie und Moraltheologie: Der Beitrag der theologischen Ethik zur Frage allgemeiner Kriterien ethischer Entscheidungsprozesse*, 1979; H. Nowotny, *Kernenergie—Gefahr oder Notwendigkeit: Anatomie eines Konflikts*, 1979; F. H. Tenbruck, *Kritik der planenden Vernunft*, 1972. Tenbruck's argument is stated more sharply in the lecture "Der alte und der neue Fortschritt: Mythos und Realität," in G. Rohrmoser, ed., *Fortschritt und Sicherheit*, 1980, pp. 147–62.

5) The Fullness of Life and the Means of Salvation

The church is called to ethical accountability over the way it perceives the relationship of faith to the kingdom of God and the way it lives up to it in practice. This task of justifying its faith is expressed concretely in its use of the means entrusted to it.

Religion represents "that perspective of all human reality which perceives the possibility of renewing and transcending this reality" (D. Rossler, *Die Vernunft der Religion*, 1976, p. 123). Christianity, the Christian religion, understands itself as the expectation of fulfillment and the hope for salvation, which makes the fullness of life real for men and women, undistorted and unfragmented. Every statement related to that hope, every attitude that is oriented toward it, is one of faith and not of sight. There is no misunderstanding what Paul says here: "While we are at home in the body we are away from the Lord, for we walk by faith, not by sight" (2 Cor. 5:6b–7). Concretely understood, faith is a relationship to the fullness of life, not that fullness itself. The church is the place where this relationship takes explicit form.

"The church is to be understood in terms of a purpose that is different from itself. . . . The kingdom of God is historically and actually the purpose for which something like the church exists" (W. Pannenberg, *Thesen zur Theologie der Kirche,* 1970, p. 9). The way in which the church fulfills this "purpose" is the ethical problem of ecclesiology in the sense to be presented here, the concrete ethical reflection on the church in its relationship to the kingdom of God. (On this question, cf. vol. 1, pp. 182–88.)

The definition of Ernst Troeltsch that "religion is the power of the beyond in this world" (*Collected Writings* 1:979) does not mean that the church by virtue of its eschatological orientation should be regarded as an alternative to the responsibilities encountered in the reality of human life. The relationship of the church to the kingdom of God is not such that the church through its life and work is to take direct responsibility for the realization of the coming kingdom of God, so that from a position of superiority to the world it can subject all reality to itself.

The church is the concrete expression of the religious relationship of human beings to God only through the means that are entrusted to it for that purpose, and not independently of them or through other means.

This is indeed said of Christ himself. The eschaton is here when Christ "delivers the kingdom to God the Father after destroying every rule and every authority and power. For he must reign until he has put all his enemies under his feet. The last enemy to be destroyed is death" (1 Cor. 15:24–26). But the resurrection of Christ is the content of the faith the believer affirms, not a metaphor of religious or ecclesiastical self-realization.

Religion as "church" is the concrete expression of the communion of the saints. The doctrine the church holds concerning itself is not that it possesses salvation but that in the future relationship oriented to the fullness of human life it will take the form of a community. The concept of the church is constituted not by the strength and power of religious self-consciousness but by the "means of salvation," the means by and through which the relationship to salvation is to be apprehended. The Reformation tradition sums up these means as "Word and sacraments" (Augsburg Confession VII), and that is the key to the way this relationship is structured. This does not provide a comprehensive description of the essence of the church as the unfolding of the fullness of what the church waits for in hope. Any attempt by the church to construct a picture of itself as something like a counterworld to the ethical reality of human life invariably ends in the complaint that it is impossible for the empirical reality of the church to convey such a picture. Between the religious expectations and hopes to which men and women are called as they look toward the fullness of life, on the one hand, and toward participation in the reality of life as ordained by God, on the other, it is only the means committed to the church that are effective, as they are explicitly distinguished from all other means of acting and of giving shape to life. In theological terms that is the correlate to God's activity in reaching out and embracing humanity, as expressed in the symbol of the kingdom of God, the doctrine of God's justifying grace, and the doctrine of the justification of men and women through the fullness of God's grace. The ethical task of the church is to give to the correlation of justification and eschatology a concrete expression in which the possibility of the renewal of life is present to liberate us here where the ethical reality of life is found in the way human life is lived.

The church has the responsibility to use the means entrusted to it so as to express fully their relationship to the fullness of life present in the symbol of the kingdom of God. Not drawing boundaries against outsiders but being present in the reality of human life everywhere, not elementary cultivation of special sanctity but openness to all without distinction, not the demand for satisfying the commandments of the church but the invitation to participate in the religious life—these are the things that must mark the church as the institution where religious orientation is to be found.

If these aspects are combined, the church is the institution of freedom in religious relationships only as the open church, the church of the people, in whose midst the relationship of God to God's world is manifest and made accessible through human activity.

The church is thus itself accountable for the faith it serves, in that it places its trust in these means and therefore believes in itself. In every age the specific temptation of the church has been to regard itself as lord of the means of grace, to want to be more than and different from what God has called it to be. Viewed historically, the specific temptation in Roman Catholicism is juridical clericalism. Its goal has been to control the success of the proclamation of the gospel and the reality of the sacraments, and to subject them to an ecclesiastical hierarchy in order to have at its own disposal the public nature of the relationship to the divine fullness of life, at least with respect to the members of the church. Here the ethical demand summarized strikingly in the Reformation slogan "without force, only through the Word *[sine vi, sed verbo]*" (CA 28.21) serves to call the church to limit itself to those spiritual means proper to it.

The specific temptation in Protestantism is a moral clericalism. It always appears when the church or individual church leaders desire more than that to which they are called and, for example, try to exert direct influence on human concerns in politics and daily conduct in order to control the success they desire so greatly for their proclamation. This clericalism encounters its boundaries in the Reformation concept of the priesthood of all believers, which places a limit even on moralistic clericalism.

The ethic of the church is a necessary corrective for such ecclesiastical claims, which are by no means the result of incorrect intentions but arise out of the fullness of the content of faith and the desire that once and for all the expectations it arouses be fully realized. The correction is necessary in order to define the role of the church in relationship to the other basic situations of life. In this connection it is essential to note that the means of grace entrusted to the church are for the benefit of women and men in all the areas where they lead their lives. Word and sacrament are to be heard and received in the community—not by institutions such as marriage, state, economy, or culture—but by women and men in the world who are subject to the basic responsibilities of life. In this way the church bears witness that people, as those created by God and called to the Christian faith, are not fully defined by their relationships in the world but that in those relationships they are challenged to independent responsibility. In this sense, as it involves women and men, the church is to be an institution of freedom.

For this section, see W. Lohff and L. Mohaupt, eds., *Folkskirche—Kirche der Zukunft? Leitlinien der Augsburgischen Konfession für das Kirchenverständnis heute,* 1977; Council of the Evangelical Church of Germany, *Aufgaben und Grenzen kirchlicher Äusserungen zu gesellschaftlichen Fragen,* 4th ed., 1971. For comments on this document, see M. Honekker, "die Denkschriften der EKD als Paradigma ethischer Argumentation," in *Kirche im Spannungsfeld der Politik,* Festschrift for H. Kunst, 1977, pp. 131–42.

The task of the church in relationship to the other basic institutions of life is to be prepared to strengthen and promote the acceptance of the elementary relationships of life, to enter into the always necessary renewal of their validity, and in affirmation of the religious relationship to the ultimate validity of the fullness of life, to clarify and critically to define the goals of human action. The church will be faithful to this task if it finds its own independence by holding to the means given to it for the concrete fulfillment of its task and does not for the sake of influence or success or under the pressure of specific expectations ascribe greater value to other means—such as power or moral pressure—and thus obscure that freedom in whose service it must stand.

For the definition of the content of the "fullness of life," see also the section "The Good and Salvation: On Success in Living."

2. Responsibilities of the Active Life: Applications of the Giving of Life

Responsibility in the active life requires that we take a position with respect to the consequences of our actions, and that we consider the effects that our actions will have on others. This is an application of the commandment to give life. In this sense an active life always involves the formation of tradition, passing on to others the possibilities of life. The question of the capability and worthiness of our actions to contribute to the tradition is not directed to the past; it is oriented to the future, but not to a future that is totally open and undetermined. It affects the future in that it anticipates it and prepares the way for it. That is the productive significance of the formation of tradition as the handing on of specific possibilities for life.

Responsibility in the active life is thus the theme of the second exploration of the concrete application of ethics. Continuing the applications developed in the first section, examples are considered in the following areas:

1. The responsibility of parents for their children
2. The form of political activity
3. The criteria for economic activity
4. The forms of cultural tradition
5. The structure of the relationships of religious life

Responsibility for an active life as a commandment in the formation of tradition finds its continuity in our efforts to be independent and responsible individuals. The tasks involved in being capable of and worthy of establishing traditions are closely connected with the forms in which our activity for others is expressed. This line of argument thus leads us to an active consideration of the limits that are imposed by our goal of enabling others to be independent. In this respect we must be able to establish the credibility of our actions.

The three aspects of the problem that must be dealt with concretely and in detail in the five areas of activity can be brought together in the following maxim for guiding our conduct: Act in such a way that the results of your life contribute to the formation of tradition, aid in the renewal of independent and responsible conduct, and can stand the scrutiny of their credibility in the process by which traditions are formed.

a. Making Life Possible for Others: The Formation of Traditions

Taking a responsible stand in our active life means, in the first place, orienting our actions in terms of their consequences. Any formation of tradition that is productive and is oriented toward the future must anticipate the participation of others and promote increased independence. This involves the concrete consideration of the future consequences of the specific ways in which we live our lives.

1) Parenthood and Family Planning

Parenthood involves parents in the task of forming traditions for the world in which their children will live. Thus the actions of the parents must be guided by the duty to act in behalf of their children's future. This task includes the goals and the means of family planning.

Parenthood confronts a couple with the task of contributing to the formation of traditions that will be viable in the future. Thus parenthood requires a plan that involves the durability and stability of the marriage and a distinctive formation of tradition. Children require a world in which to live, a world that must in every respect be provided for them by their parents. Thus parenthood confronts parents with questions about the world into which the children will be born and in which they will live. Questions about the issues that define their plans for life demand concrete answers. Parents must be aware of the active role they play in the formation of tradition.

In forming a life plan, parents must make themselves aware of the preconditions that will be a part of what they hand on to their children. Parents do not have control over the means necessary to shape the world according to their plans for their children. They do not have at their command those activities that are involved in the totality of political, social, economic, and cultural factors that will shape the world in which their children will live. Rather, parenthood makes concrete the interdependence of the way parents lead their lives and the historical reality in which they lead them, so that parenthood is the area in which our attitude toward the context of our tradition becomes a major theme.

The importance of this interdependence for ethics takes concrete form primarily in the personal responsibility of parents for their children. It cannot be transferred to impersonal social forces. Thus it is appropriate for the legal system to protect the primary responsibility of parents and to strengthen their independent position in society rather than favor the delegation of this responsibility to society.

"Family planning" is the contemporary catchword for the formation of tradition through parenthood. The ethical line of argumentation can be made concrete by the use of specific examples. While in earlier times entering into a marriage implied without question a readiness to have a family, today it is a question of whether and at what point in the marriage a couple want to have children. This question now constitutes a new and decisive stage in many marriages, and the possibilities of family planning raise new problems and many tensions. The planning of the family has come between the marriage partnership and the family, since the married couple have at their disposal the means of avoiding and regulating conception, means that make possible, and therefore today demand, a highly reflective awareness of the need for planning.

Any ethical approach that defines the questions involved in family planning too quickly and exclusively as questions of the "permissibility" of using the means of avoiding and regulating conception fails to deal with the issues. The question of whether a couple want to become parents at all and what that means for them leads to the much more important question of whether they are ready and able to enter into the process of the formation of an individual tradition and to let their own plans for their lives be shaped by that decision. The question of the means to be used in family planning is therefore of secondary importance to the question of the points of view which guide that planning. The regulating of conception is an element in the consciousness of those who contemplate parenthood. It involves above all the question of what should and can be planned in an ethically responsible manner.

Within certain limits it is possible today to plan when and whether parents will have children. But by contrast, what kind of children they will have cannot be planned. Family planning by no means makes it possible to plan for the type of children one would really like to have. Instead, family planning is the concrete expression of a readiness to accept the children who are born and to accept the task of constructing for them a world that is capable of handing on a tradition. From this point of view it is an easy but dangerous mistake to hold that family planning is a method that the parents can use for their own self-realization and for determining what they would want their children to be like. Family planning can only represent the anticipation of the task that the parents undertake for those children who are born to them and grow up under their care. Family planning is not a means for controlling the life plans of children but is an expression of the parents' readiness to submit their way of life to an ongoing process in which tradition is handed on. The ethical dimension involved in conscious planning is more important for the relationship of the parents to the family and to their children than is the question of the means used to prevent or regulate conception. It is only through the ethical awareness of what parenthood means that the question of the means employed can be seen in the proper light. Any ethical argument that makes the means used to avoid or regulate conception the major or even sole criterion can easily lose its path. For example, the extensive rejection of family planning by official Roman Catholic moral theology tends toward a negation of consciously accepted parenthood in favor of a "natural" reproductive function of sexuality. In this way the ethical evaluation of conception becomes isolated from the context in which the life and traditions of parenthood and family function. The decision to become parents must always imply the anticipation of assuming responsibility for children, and therefore it demands the intention to plan carefully. An isolated, naturalistic way of approaching the question that is exhausted in a casuistic rejection of the means of contraception overlooks, for example, the fact that between a "natural" regulation of conception on the one hand and the "pill" on the other there is no perceivable difference in relation to the overarching responsibility for careful planning.

Such distinctions cannot be accorded any ethically valid significance. They could be ethically significant only if the choice of means also included a definable differentiation of motives and intentions as, for example, if in the former case nature were allowed free course, while in the second the human agent intervened in an autonomous and impermissible manner. But that is an abstract contrast, because in both cases parenthood is not a purely "natural" process; in the concrete reality of life of any marriage, parenthood always demands a conscious structure of relationships and is dependent on them. It is hard to see why in the prevention or regulation of conception the use, for example, of seemingly "natural" methods is any less "manipulative" than is the use of chemical agents. We cannot recognize here any ethical distinction in principle.

The ethical obligation to engage in family planning finds its concrete expression in the readiness of the parents to incorporate their own life style into the formation of a family and to let their plans for their lives be placed in the service of a tradition that lays claim to the time and space necessary for the well-being of the children.

These considerations lead us to the conclusion that abortion is not a means appropriate to family planning. On the contrary, the termination of a pregnancy is the rejection of parenthood and in principle is also the negation of the specific responsibilities that children bring. If abortion, the killing of the fetus, is accepted as a method of family planning, then the negation of specific unwanted children would also have to be regarded as a part of family planning. But that is totally contrary to the ethical responsibility of family planning. Thus the problem of abortion belongs to the discussion of life situations of conflict and how to deal with them.

The official position of the Roman Catholic Church is formulated in *Humanae vitae, On the Proper Order of the Transmission of Human Life.* Encyclical of Pope Paul VI, July 25, 1968. For the discussion of the encyclical, see the book edited by Aktionskreis Humanae vitae, *Humanae vitae oder die Freiheit des Gewissens,* 1968; F. W. Menne, *Kirchliche Sozialethik gegen gesellschaftliche Realität. Zu einer soziologischen Anthropologie menschlicher Fruchtbarkeit,* 1971; *Denkschrift zu Fragen der Sexualethik,* prepared by a commission of the Evangelical Church in Germany, 1971. See also the interdisciplinary discussion in R. Blobel, A. Flitner, and R. Tölle, eds., *Familie und Geburtenregelung,* 1969; J. Grundel, "Empfängnisregelung und Bevölkerungspolitik," in *Handbuch der christlichen Ethik,* vol. 2, 1978, pp. 148–60.

2) *The State and Public Order under Law*

Planned political action, as a part of the formation of tradition, is subject to the duty of acting justly. The obligation imposed by this duty finds concrete form in that the actions of the state are subject to the authority of law.

"The LORD loves justice" (Ps. 37:28). Political action is oriented to the future as long as it has as its content the forming of a plan for the life of the community. In relation to this principle we will now consider examples that illustrate the criteria for the formation of tradition. Seen in historical and sociological terms, the modern state as the organized form of the political will is the locus of the authority for the framing and codifying of law. But the concept of a state governed by law involves the principle that the state itself is subject to the law and cannot use arbitrary actions as a substitute for obeying the law. The state is a community under law. This concept brings together a wealth of very complex historical and systematic aspects that bear on the question of the relation of laws established by the state to laws existing prior to or outside the state. We will explore here only the question of the significance that the authority of the law over the state has for our understanding of state actions as planned political activity. The ethical relevance of this question is that law gives a binding form to the mutual acceptance of those involved in the actions of a community and those affected by the community. With the help of law, mutual acceptance can play a role for the shared life in community that goes beyond personal relationships.

See also W. Pannenberg, "Christliche Rechtsbegründung," in *Handbuch der christlichen Ethik*, vol. 2, 1978, pp. 323ff.; and "Aufnahme und Auswertung," in *Recht und Institution*, ed. H. Dombois, vol. 2, 1969.

Insofar as the state is responsible for the political life of the community, it must recognize the binding force that this "acceptance," this mutual recognition, has for the state itself in its plans and actions. This finds expression in the understanding that the state governed by law is subject to the legal order in all its actions. The legal order is the express form of such a plan of the political community through which the current political will is incorporated in a clearly defined tradition and is subject to the continuity of the life of the political community. Thus the activity of the state confirms its responsibility for the tradition in its binding force through the specific forms of legal order. This holds true for both the protective and the productive tasks of the state. The protective task is expressed as the protection of life against violation through force. The productive task of the law finds expression as the positive form of the political community in terms of the public good. In both instances the activity of the state is to be measured by its capability for honoring tradition and being worthy of the tradition. That is to say, the activity of the state is subject to specific forms defined in law that are valid independent of the current political will and thus make the actions of the state dependent on them. The basic element in the continuity of state and politics is that they are both subject to law. This holds not only in terms of limitations and obligations; current state actions and political plans must also always see themselves as strengthening and continuing the elements of the continuity of law in the midst of change.

As regards the formation of tradition, the task of the state to protect its citizens takes concrete form above all in the state's monopoly on the use of force. This monopoly excludes the possibility that citizens or groups in society could use force against each other. Moreover, this monopoly is the negation of force as a device that could be used in the course of political life. The state's monopoly on the use of force establishes on a permanent basis the ethical responsibility of each citizen to take part in the life of the community. The way is opened for the inner life of the community to be realized freely, that is, without the threat of force or the possibility of its use. The law places binding restraints on everyone and draws an ethically and politically significant distinction between the will of the individual and the realization of that will in the political realm. The only roads open for community action are those that acknowledge a common order that is binding on all, the order of law.

For the same reason, however, the state's monopoly on the use of force is also subject to law. It is not that the state has a de facto monopoly, but that its monopoly on the use of force is governed by law which requires that the state not use force to carry out its own specific plans and that it therefore cannot place itself above the rule of law, which it must protect and to which it is answerable. The only basis for this monopoly is the state's duty to protect its citizens from violence. Therefore even the official means for upholding this order are under the obligation that they be used only in accordance with the law, just as the state is under obligation to preserve justice. The goal of the monopoly of force is not to enable the state to use force but to avoid its use entirely. And it follows that political activity is obligated by the state's monopoly on the use of force to promote the formation of political traditions such that reasons for using force may be decreased or eliminated, but in any case not increased.

Therefore wherever violent protests break out in a society they are as a rule an indication of some degree of dissatisfaction with the politics of the state. In such situations it is inadequate to appeal to the protective function of the law; rather, the state is challenged to provide a qualitative answer in terms of productive law.

To be sure, on the same grounds the state is obligated to preserve its ability to enforce the law and the constitution through actions in which it uses criteria in the choice and employment of its officials that are consonant with this obligation. The means used in the application of these criteria, such as the installation of officials in public office, must correspond to the spirit and the basic principles of constitutional law. See L. Kaiser, "Der 'Radikalen-Erlass'—Prufstein eines demokratischen Rechtsstaates?" ZEE 23 (1979): 106–17.

This provides us with guidelines for carrying out the productive tasks of forming tradition, that is, through the application of the same basic principle to the active maintenance of the power of the state. The exercise of power and authority, for whatever goals and purposes, must be combined in a form such that power and authority can maintain continuity with each other in their development, with the result that the political will expressed from time to time can be distinguished from the traditions of the common life on which it is based and the legal system in which it is manifested. This task is made possible through the division of powers, as it has developed in its basic outlines in the classic form of the liberal state, that is, the state under law which protects the rights of the individual. The separation of the powers of the state is the express political form of the inner freedom of the community's life in the relationships within the political power that exists at any given time. It makes it possible for freedom to contribute to the tradition within the political order, and it stands opposed to every totalitarian expression of will. Therefore the division of powers and the subordination of the then current political authority to that division is a sure sign that the authority of the state is in the service of forming the tradition expressed in political activity. The division of power among the executive, legislative, and judicial does not complete the political task. It is the form in which the openness of the state for the life of the community is expressed. The interaction of the three powers presupposes the distinctions among them. The separation of powers is the formal manifestation of the task of relating political power and authority to the traditions of the political community, traditions over which the political authority does not have control but to whose preservation and renewal it is committed.

The three powers of the state do not exhaust all the effective public political powers that affect the productive task of political activity. Political parties, organized public opinion, churches, labor unions, and a host of social groups also share in this task. All of them are subject to the express form of order under law as it is defined in the broadest sense by the constitution. But more than that, they must allow their own actions and their political intentions to be measured by the degree to which they promote and strengthen, or negate, the basic structural forms of community life. Even though the arguments and discussions around this task are in reality endless and complex, there is still no well-founded exception to these guidelines that could claim general validity. Only under this condition can the various groups work productively for justice and win respect as the representatives of real legal claims within the life of the community. In the case of such real claims it still holds that groups are not justified in the use of force within the community but must contribute to the life of the community through their adherence to the law. Even the churches in their public claims, however these may be expressed, are not exempt from the legal authority of the state but are bound by it, and it is their duty to uphold it.

For the historic and systematic understanding of the constitutional state, see E. Wolf, ed., *Der Rechtsstaat. Angebot und Aufgabe,* 1964, reprinted in Th. Strohm and H. D. Wendland, eds., *Kirche und Demokratie,* 1971; H. Zillessen, *Protestantismus und politische Form. Eine Untersuchung zum protestantischen Verfassungsverständnis,* 1971; E. W. Böckenförde, *Entstehung und Wandel des Rechtsstaatsbegriffs, Staat, Gesellschaft, Freiheit. Studien zur Staatstheorie und zum Verfassungsrecht,* 1976; M. Kriele, *Recht und praktische Vernunft,* 1979; H. Hattenhauer, *Die geistesgeschlichtlichen Grundlagen des Rechts,* 2d ed., 1980.

On the position of the church in the constitutional state in relation to law, see W. Huber, *Kirche und Öffentlichkeit,* 1973; M. Honecker, *Recht und Moral, Der Wirklichkeitsanspruch von Theologie und Religion,* Festschrift for Ernst Steinbach, 1976, pp. 109–28.

3) Economic Systems and Economic Accomplishments

Economic activity that seeks to provide the means to sustain material existence must develop an economic system that is able to achieve that goal. It is in the light of this goal that we are to give concrete expression to the task of tradition building in economic activity.

"To every one who has will more be given" (Luke 19:26). A number of examples from the preaching of Jesus show that economic procedures can serve as analogies for our activities in respect to the coming kingdom of God. Parables such as those in Matt. 25:14–30 and Luke 16:1–15 do not give us instruction about how to conduct ourselves in economic activities but use economic illustrations for religious instruction. In this present approach to an aspect of economic activity, when we seek to identify an appropriate place for ethical argument within the realm of economics we will follow the point of view of Wisdom literature, which is influential in the New Testament as well as in the Old, and will attempt to formulate out of the elementary issues of life a point of contact for the question of how to live our lives.

The criterion of the formation of tradition is relevant for economic activity in all its forms that involve the task of making possible both on the national and the international scene adequate material provision for a growing population. In this respect our sole concern should be to develop a line of approach for ethical argumentation on the basis of which or in reference to which a thorough discussion can take place about the contribution of economic activity to the process of the development of tradition. It is not, however, our concern here to consider all the aspects of the economic order that might be relevant. Therefore the factors currently involved in this question will be touched on only briefly.

The far-reaching changes that the organization of modern capitalism has produced can perhaps be summarized as follows: Economic activity is no longer oriented toward the qualitatively or quantitatively clearly defined and agreed-upon needs of an individual or of the majority of the population, but toward a particular undertaking as an activity for the increase of capital. It is an economy that seeks to increase gain.

> The relatively unspecific older expression of a "profit economy" is being used here as it was used by Werner Sombart in his book *Die deutsche Volkswirtschaft im 19. Jahrhundert*, 2d ed., 1909. I am doing so because I did not want to plow through the complex area of economic theories and discussions of capitalism in detail. See, however, the recent study of J. Kromphardt, *Kapitalismus*, 1980.

The ongoing, unending task of providing the means for sustaining life involves an organization of economic activity that determines the debate about the satisfaction of everyday needs and is therefore to be evaluated in terms of how efficient it is. An economic system oriented to profit does not derive its form from the concrete issues of satisfying the needs of the individual.

Such a system is characterized by the overcoming of the limits imposed by specific goals. The emancipation of the profit-oriented economy from existing concrete needs is, to be sure, not an emancipation from the need for the means of life in general. Such an economy determines the needs for the satisfaction of which its efforts are expended, and even creates new needs. In the transition from an economy for satisfying needs to one that creates new needs, this emancipation from the concrete form of our existing needs for sustaining life becomes obvious.

As a result we encounter problems at a level for which ethical tradition and moral teachings provide no direct equivalents and which are much more abstract than the problems we have previously found in the tradition. Ethical interest has focused first of all on questions that arose as consequences of the emphasis on the profit motive in economics and that in the nineteenth century were summed up in the "social question," that is, primarily in the problems of the industrial proletariat. Or it has given its attention to the question of whether this economic form in its totality is acceptable, because the service function of the economy for the satisfying of recognized needs has been replaced by the interest in accumulating capital.

Capitalism as a system of "egoism" has, under the influence of the socialist critique of capitalism developed by Karl Marx, been condemned as contrary to the social nature of economic activity, and because of this anomaly is doomed to perish. In particular, Marx's critique of capitalism in *Das Kapital* was expressed as a theory of the inevitable crises of the capitalistic economy, which must result in a revolutionary transition to a socialist economy.

The great debate in this century about the form of political order has been shaped by the debate between the politics oriented toward the views of Marx on the one hand and liberal political economy on the other. On this subject, see J. A. Schumpeter, *Kapitalismus, Sozialismus und Demokratie*, 3d ed., 1975 (English original, 1942); W. Eucken, *Grundsätze der Wirtschaftspolitik*, 1959, 4th ed., 1968; J. Tinbergen, *Wirtschaftspolitik*, 2d ed., 1972; H. Albert, *Ökonomische Ideologie und politische Theorie*, 2d ed., 1972; J. Kocka, "Organisierter Kapitalismus oder Staatsmonopolitischer Kapitalismus?" in *Organisierter Kapitalismus*, ed. H. A. Winkler, 1974, pp. 19ff.; B. Frey, *Moderne politische Ökonomie*, 1977; J. P. Wogaman, *The Great Economic Debate: An Ethical Analysis*, 1977; J. Sharpf, *Die Rolle des Staates im westlichen Wirtschaftssystem*, 1978; S. Katterle and A. Rich, eds., *Religiöser Sozialismus und Wirtschaftsordnung*, 1980.

The debate about the form of a profit-oriented economy (if we set aside all other expectations and hopes, fears such as alienation, or condemnations such as egoism) is to be decided by the concrete question of its ability to produce the desired results. The reaction to specific crises is itself an essential element in giving concrete form to the task of forming economic traditions within a capitalist economy.

If we bring together all aspects of the problem that can and must be identified, then the ethical argument can be summarized in a few points.

The capitalistic organization of a profit economy is relatively different from a planned or centralized economy in that it seeks to realize its "plan" in a sum of individual undertakings, but its achievement does not depend on an individual accomplishment. It derives its life from the commercial whole. As a system it consists of the organization of individual interests into a common interest mediated by the economy. Thus it is capable of and worthy of establishing tradition only from the point of view of the community economy. The debate must be concentrated on not permitting the economic organization to become separated from its specific social context, in relation to which it is possible to exist. In reference to the way in which the form of the profit economy is organized, the formation of tradition means in concrete terms the ability of the economy to contribute to the political and social realms, that is, to participate in a more comprehensive formation of the context that satisfies the material needs of society. To this extent the form of the economy always exists in relation to a plan for the shared life of the community. Both the formation of strong labor unions and the economic policies of the state are ways of bringing to realization such a plan in an organized economic order. They are not alternative ways of organizing the economy but serve in specific ways to bring the economic activity into relation with the common interests, or, to put it differently, they communicate the common interest of society to the economic processes. We can determine whether the way an economy is organized enables it to achieve the goals set for it by seeing whether it is able to serve the common interest.

The development of a profit economy is in principle egalitarian, that is, there is no basic reason why only certain persons or groups should be involved in it. Instead, it is the form by which persons and groups work together in the economy for the good of all. This form, however, is filled out and brought to completion by individual economic activities. Thus the key to its success is that in some way or other everyone must actually be included in these activities.

The explicit development of this egalitarian factor in the economy is therefore a necessary and unavoidable task. This task finds concrete expression in the market orientation of a profit economy insofar as the world of commerce is characterized by activity in an open market. The criterion of an open market is that in the relationship of supply and demand there is no specific and normative catalog of what should be supplied or demanded. The distinctive achievement of a profit economy is that needs are no longer specified, and thereby the market is made subject to economic forces. The distinctive responsibility of the market structure is not defined in terms of specific goods but solely in that everyone should have access to the market and no one should be excluded. The ability of this form of economic activity to contribute to the ongoing tradition is determined by the degree to which the individual interests of a profit economy to control the market can be successfully opposed by the common interest in having the market open for everyone, for example, through increased demand for goods and services. In economic and political terms, the order by which such a system contributes to the tradition finds its concrete expression in expanding access to the market and keeping it open to everyone without nullifying the accomplishments of the economic system itself. The form of the economy makes necessary a division of property which, beyond the individual interests of those directly involved in the processes of a profit economy, makes it possible for everyone to participate in the market. Among other factors, the economic significance of the policies of the state lies in the forming of an economic order capable of contributing to the ongoing tradition. In this way economic political policy participates in the task of keeping the economic system, for the sake of the accomplishments it can make, capable of participating in the tradition.

This line of argument assumes that we cannot expect any economic system to solve all the problems of life. For this reason it is misleading to stereotype all societies in which a profit economy exists as "capitalistic" societies, as if the solution to the problem of how we should lead our lives could be solved by the way the economy functions.

Though it is correct that all areas of life have an economic dimension and thus are affected by the type of economy under which they function, it is also true that the form of economic life does not provide the answer to all the problems of how we should lead our lives and therefore should not be looked to for those answers. That would lead to affirming the correspondence of ethical standards with the economic system. For example, this happens when the affirmation of a market economy is equated with the affirmation of personal freedom and human rights. Criticism of capitalism motivated by the fact that many of life's problems are in part caused by the organization of the economy and in part not alleviated by the economy ought to be directed to the right address.

If the question of ethical responsibility raised by the role of economic activity for the process of tradition building is posed in connection with the capabilities of the economy, that does not mean that a particular form of economic organization is singled out for ethical scrutiny. Rather, it is in this way that the criterion is set up by which responsibility is made concrete for each economic system. In addition, this approach also holds that each economic system does not fulfill its task only for itself but does so only in its interdependence with the state and society and in its openness to receiving correction.

4) The School as a Form of Culture

Our actions in relation to culture require that we construct a form of education that makes possible the future of culture. The school is the model for the concrete expression of the form given to cultural activities for our own formation of tradition.

Culture is the development of a context of tradition that transcends the individual in all dimensions of the way we lead our lives. Thus the concept of culture finds its theme expressed everywhere—in the family, the system of justice, the economy. The common traits and the distinguishing criteria are provided by the forms in which culture is manifest in all its differentiations. Under the presupposition of the ethical obligation laid on us by our cultural duty, the task of contributing to the tradition takes concrete form wherever our relation to culture itself assumes a form that lays claim to the way we lead our lives and to the way in which the formation of tradition is explicitly accomplished. This is the task that confronts us in our schools and, in more general terms, in the entire system of education and formation.

Thus under this present theme we are taking up once again the earlier discussions and developing them further.

The establishing of schools and the requirement of compulsory education are forms by which our cultural traditions are shaped. The task of the school may be distinguished from that of parents in that by a process of learning and training the school establishes a relationship between the student and the student's culture but is not itself a directly experienced expression of that culture. The school as a form of our relation to culture enunciates the theme that culture develops out of an active process of education for which specific persons are responsible. In a certain manner the school reconstructs the development of culture for each new generation. To be sure, it does not do so in the entire breadth and fullness of the living culture but in a form that builds up a relationship with and a relevance to culture by means of specific examples.

The critique of the schools is then essentially a critique of the way the schools disrupt the direct living experience of participation in the culture. This critique in the name of an immediate unity of individual life and the cultural context deals directly with the point that we are concerned with in our ethical investigation. The reason for this is that the school is the place where the difference between culture and nature is clear, and the formation of culture through education becomes the concern of each new generation so that cultural traditions are not only adopted and adapted but can be further developed in each individual's own way. Through the schools the process by which tradition is developed, the process to which we are indebted for the currently dominant culture, takes on its explicit form. The schools mediate the process by which we who shape the culture participate in its formation.

For the schools the formation of tradition means concretely that they must concern themselves with the substance of what gives meaning to culture. The schools and indeed the entire educational system are always involved in the whole cultural context and in its relevance to the tradition and its suitability for being incorporated into it. The debate about the content of the school curriculum is always a debate about the normative content of culture itself. Therefore the debate about curriculum, which is also in part a debate about teaching methods, is of great relevance for the way in which ethical responsibility is perceived in the process of shaping the tradition. In the schools and in the entire educational system there is transmitted an outline of the culture by which through content and methods a decisive orientation toward the culture is built up. Control of the educational system is thus always a highly explosive question that tempts political and social forces to try to bend the schools to their will and shape them to their own specific purposes.

It is all-important, therefore, to stress that the schools represent an independent form of instruction in relation to culture and have as their task the responsibility to contribute in their own way to the continuity of the culture. The emancipation of the schools from church control in the eighteenth and nineteenth centuries is a significant example of this. The schools must not be centers of indoctrination by which a specific contemporary pedagogy is allowed to assert itself. Rather, they must be able to maintain a continuity of content and to preserve a distinct distance from changing political and social interests. Because the schools are to contribute to the entire cultural tradition they should not be tied to a specific point of view or for the same reason exclude important aspects of the reality of the cultural life of the community. This latter remark is primarily directed to the role of religious instruction in the schools. Since religion is one of the essential dimensions of human life, by definition it cannot be excluded from the responsibility of the schools. Schools are not instruments for converting students or for developing them in spirituality. Religious instruction has the same responsibility as instruction in other areas—to enable students to understand the content of religion so that they can relate to cultural reality in such a way as to be able to participate in its traditions. Religious instruction should equip the student to deal constructively with religion as it is lived out in that culture.

This discussion of the school's responsibility to contribute to the continuing development of the tradition should not be taken as reducing the schools to the function of helping the members of each new generation discover themselves, not that helping students deal with the problems of finding their own identity could or should be excluded from the concerns of the school. But the special task of the schools is to help young people bring their relation to themselves into relation with the context of the whole culture and so equip them for contributing to the development of their culture.

For a discussion of the problems of the schools, see Ivan Illich, *Entschulung der Gesellschaft*, 1970, 2d ed., 1972, and the pertinent passages in H. von Hentig, *Cuernavaca oder Alternativen zur Schule?* 1971, 3d ed., 1973, pp. 70ff.

5) The Ecclesiastical Formation
of Religious Tradition

The church has been entrusted with the transmission of the faith. The communication, propagation, and renewal of the faith is the task of the religious tradition which finds its concrete expression in the form, task, and structure of public worship.

In the history of the propagation of Christianity the church has had a special responsibility for the continuity and the renewal of the way in which the Christian tradition is handed on. Concern for the future of the church, its existence, and its influence cannot be the ethical and theological motive for the task we are considering here. Concern for the future of the church is made unnecessary by faith, as stated in the Augsburg Confession VII: *Item docent, quod una sancta ecclesia perpetua mansura sit.* Concern for the future of the church cannot itself be a direct theme of ethics, but ethics does have a responsibility for the process by which the Christian faith is transmitted. It is, therefore, a theme of ethics that the faith is to be communicated and handed on. This structural responsibility for transmitting our religious relationships defines the practical task of the church. A part of our faith is its communication to others, because faith as our relation to God draws its vitality from a relationship to reality that is valid for all people everywhere. Faith is not limited to the special inwardness of individual experience. Its communication requires a form that is able to give expression to the relationship between making the faith your own and handing it on, between inwardness and outwardness, between the source and the future of the faith. In the fulfillment of this task our relation to God takes concrete form as public worship.

From this specific point of view we must now examine some examples of the ethical factor in ecclesiology. In the background of our discussion stands the important Reformation thesis that ethics is not an external task of faith but that it has itself a theological structure. One result of this is a concrete expression of our relation to God in the formation of religious tradition, which must make certain that it agrees with the basic structure of that relationship.

Public worship is the explicit form of religious communication and also the basic element in the process of forming religious tradition. Therefore the ethics of the church must take concrete form in public worship and in relationship to it. The development of specific forms of faith, of our religious relation to God, is subordinate to and dependent on the ability to communicate this faith. It is capable of being part of the tradition because it is public. The public nature of worship, however it has developed historically, is essential to the organization of worship. It is derived from our relationship to God and gives that relationship its social form. The empirical public nature of worship in all its aspects is the concrete expression of this relationship to God and distinguishes it from all secret gatherings. This public aspect imposes on the interest in intimacy and individuality the necessity of serving the universality of the faith, as is demanded by our relationship to God. For in worshiping God we worship the Lord of all of life, not our "own" particular God. This universality is not automatically present. Attaining to it is the task that faith must undertake in relationship to itself in its responsibility to the church. The specific task of the church in forming its traditions is expressed in the effort to move the forms of worship as far away as possible from individual piety and subjectivity and to achieve a certain objective nature for the religious forms. This objectivity, in the liturgy for example, assists the formation of tradition in that it can be repeated in every place and at every time, which means that it is relatively independent of the individuals who participate in it. So church offices, in their special relationship to the piety of the community at any specific time, have developed out of the contribution that worship makes to the formation of tradition. The leaders of public worship represent in their activity the responsible observation of the forms in which the transmission process is carried out.

The limits of objectivity are found wherever worship is freed from the participation of the believers and becomes so independent that the perception of the form of the tradition also becomes independent of the presence or absence of faith. Religious forms in their independence become rigid when in contrast to the participation of the believers they become legalistic and too objectified.

If the competence of church authorities to repress religious forms becomes independent of the structure of worship for communicating the gospel, then the priesthood as the bearer of the legal authority forms its own tradition within the larger tradition of the church until it reaches the point where worship appears to be possible even without the participation of the congregation, as long as a priest performs it. It is here that the Protestant critique raises is objections to the Roman Catholic private mass and the concept of sacramental acts as complete in themselves. For here the ethical content of the religious form is neglected in the interests of the form as defined by church law.

Thus the formation of tradition ceases to be an open process and becomes the preservation of a body of traditions that is closed in upon itself and to which the laity owe only their obedience. This independent legal control of the tradition process is in sharp contrast to the task of transmitting the faith. Instead of a living transmission we have conflict over the authority of the church.

The leaders of the Reformation recognized this clearly and therefore stressed the other element in worship that contributes to the formation of tradition, that is, the preaching of the Word. They demanded that all religious activities that took on a specific form be in accordance with the preached Word. This demand brings into play that element of the formation of tradition that requires the involvement of the congregation as a part of the communication of the faith. The preacher is the public representative of the faith in the act of proclamation, that is, the function of the faith as proclamation, in which there are no distinctions among believers. Called by the community and serving as its representative, the preacher represents in the sermon the present religious relationship. Moreover, the sermon can be repeated. On the one hand the preacher is not required to be absolutely original, as if the sermon were the first time the foundation were being laid for the transmission of the faith, but neither can the preacher undertake to present anything that is not the content of the ongoing tradition. The sermon is concerned anew with being capable of and worthy of representing the tradition, and thus with the individual structuring of our religious relationships. The sermon is the form of an individual religious relationship and is as such always something "new" and not something repeated in an identical form, as is the liturgy.

The limits of the individual form of preaching are evident wherever the sermon becomes so much a self-portrayal of the preacher's individuality in religion that he or she seeks to take a stand outside the community tradition or explicitly negates this context. The special responsibility of the office does not assure the preacher, as the one who holds the office, absolute control over it; that is, it does not authorize a subjective approach without preestablished obligations. The office of preacher is a representative office for the congregation. The preacher's goal must be to arouse the congregation to a renewed and ongoing formation of the tradition, and that must be measured by the compatibility of the sermon with the tradition.

The ethic involved in the formation of religious tradition is directed toward letting worship be clearly seen as an example of the result of religious tradition formation which shows the difference between the religious practice itself and that on which it is based. The knowledge that faith lives through a reality that it does not control must be clearly portrayed by the church. This situation, which is an issue in fundamental theology, confronts the church with the challenge of keeping the form of religious presentation open to a variety of adaptations, and thus of making it possible to renew the vitality of the faith. Freedom of belief is the inner standard by which the authority of church forms is judged. Therefore the form of the church's tradition must exclude the use of force in two manifestations: that of legal force in the threat of punishment (church discipline), and that of inner force in the form of a demand for absolute conformity with a specific religious point of view held by a preacher, or a group, or a congregation within the church. In this sense freedom of belief is always basic to the church's ethic, which in the form it takes has a responsibility to serve the formation of tradition, which includes religious practice but is never entirely subject to it.

For the unity of liturgy and ethics, see the works of H.-D. Wendland in *Botschaft an die soziale Welt*, 1958. On the problem of ethics and preaching, see D. Rossler, "Das Problem der Homiletik," in *Theologia Practica* 1 (1966): 14–28; H. M. Müller, Die Authorität des Predigers in pastoralethischer Sicht, *Predigtstudien*, 1974, pp. 11–24.

b. The Structure of Independence:
Responsibility for Tradition

Assuming the responsibilities of an active life means, in the second place, awakening a sense of responsibility and structuring independence in such a way that the individual is able to make a commitment to the tradition. Responsible involvement in the process of forming future traditions involves commitment to an active life for the renewal of this duty.

1) Upbringing as the Path to Independence

Parents owe their children a good upbringing because only through good training are children able to assume responsibility for living independently. The ethical authority of training and education lies in anticipating that children will be independent in the future and in enabling them to be so.

"The moral commitment involved in entering into a marriage is fulfilled in the second birth—the intellectual—of children, through which they are brought up to be independent persons" (G. W. F. Hegel, *Enzyklopädie*, p. 521). It is not independence but dependence that has the first word in the process of education. Parents owe their children an education because only through education can children become capable of leading their own lives in a responsible manner. Although in the process of growing up dependence has the first word, it does not have the last. The process of education has its obligatory structure because it must lead to independence. The individual problems of those involved in the process—parents and children—are to be oriented toward this goal. Education is the result of a multiplicity of individual acts and is the sum total of these acts. That sum then constitutes the tradition context in which independence grows out of dependence. As teachers, parents are concerned to see to it through many individual steps that their children will be able to lead their own lives. This begins with everyday instruction in walking, eating, and speaking, and culminates in the children's being able to stand on their own feet and move ahead, that is, in being able to lead their own lives. At each step in the educational process an element in the tradition is given to the child and determines the child's accomplishments and activities. Thus education provides an orientation by which the child is enabled to participate in the tradition.

For parents, education always means the anticipation that their children will become independent. The educational task requires that we acknowledge its obligatory nature. As the authorities in bringing up their children, parents must come to terms with the fact that their authority does not include total control but is always guided by the purpose of helping the child to become independent. It would be a negation of the authority of education to direct it toward maintaining permanent dependence, making it obedience training instead of education. Such authority is closely related to the process of tradition and must lead each child in his or her own way to become capable of affirming the tradition. Between authority and freedom there is no contradiction but only a difference of degree along a continuum. The authority of education fulfills itself in the independence of the child.

It would also be a negation of authority in education to withdraw in favor of allowing children a seemingly natural independence and to let the guiding rule be that children ought to know best about what they want to do. Educators would then not be accepting the task that is implicit in the dependence of children—that of transmitting to them the content and orientation of the tradition in which they are to lead their lives. For teachers to give up their responsibility in the interest of the child's freedom would be to negate the child's independence and fail to build it up. They would be failing their responsibility to the concrete formation of tradition by which they should provide the content of that independence. Education as the anticipation of independence therefore means building up the context of tradition for children in such a way that they will be able to find their own individual places in life.

For children, education always means the transition from what is to what ought to be. The formation of autonomy is the way to achieve a position in relation to the reality of life and to acknowledge the normative obligations for leading one's own life. On their way to maturity children must come to accept that life constitutes a task to be performed. Independence means dealing adequately with this task in one's own way. Independence is attained by many small steps through which what parents and others do for the infant and for the child becomes increasingly what is expected of the growing child. Independence is the capability of assuming responsibility.

Anyone who thinks that independence means complete freedom to do or not do anything one wants will never attain true independence. Independence is not freedom to act arbitrarily. The independence of a person growing toward maturity stands in relationship to the context and traditions of life and must culminate in the individual's own contribution to tradition. The demand for absolute freedom can take the radical form of wanting to get rid of one's parents, that is, by the negation of the authority through which independence is shaped and formed. That, however, is always a pathological example of a freedom that does not understand its own distinctive nature.

The ability to give and accept criticism is also a necessary element of the process by which we reach independence. Because the criticism voiced by adolescents is directed toward those who have made the world the way it is or made children into what they are, it is always a sign of continuing dependence. To persist in such criticism is to insist on this dependence as one of the conditions for independence. As regards such dependence, criticism does not liberate the individual but extends his or her dependence because it expresses the need to impose duties on others but not on oneself.

Independence therefore means the acceptance of duties in one's own life, and this marks the transition from dependence to responsibility. Responsibility is the form in which freedom is expressed in our lives in that it does not negate dependence but accepts it and turns it into something creative. Because only those can be free who are capable of accepting responsibility, freedom is that form of independence which is ready to and capable of taking on the task of working within the context of tradition for the living of life. Criticism finds concrete expression in the assumption of responsibility. Criticism succeeds when it is addressed not to others but to one's own life style. Only those can be considered mature who in framing their criticisms also accept the question of who is responsible for solving problems and meeting challenges, and then address the question to themselves.

These ethical premises summarize the aspects of the educational process that can be identified in the progression from authority to freedom. At the end of a successful upbringing, the parent-child relationship is dissolved. The departure of a child from the parental home is often a painful process, especially for the parents, but it is necessary and desirable. For the children, it often brings a dramatic feeling of emancipation. Parents and children can now enter into a new relationship on the basis of a new independent life that has moved beyond direct dependence. The art of bringing up children lies in anticipating and desiring this freedom from each other and in bringing it into being as the child matures.

Neither authority nor freedom can guarantee that children or those bringing them up will have at their disposal all the means that could be desired for the process of forming tradition. For all who are involved, it is equally the case that the process of handing on a tradition involves communicating the way life is to be lived in a context in which the binding ethical force of the realities of life becomes concrete. Thus through upbringing the individual comes to learn what is involved in the total reality of human life. In the fullest sense maturity means that the individual can be a source of authority for others on their way to their own independence.

2) Democracy and Political Toleration

Political toleration is the concrete expression of responsibility for the political independence of citizens in the relationship of a majority to minorities in a democracy. Thus toleration is the ethical criterion for the capability of contributing to the tradition in political activity.

Throughout the world today almost without exception democracy is the concept that gives legitimation to political authority, as expressed in the slogan "All power proceeds from the people." By virtue of this general acceptance, the concept of democracy has taken the place held historically by the concept and practice of monarchy and its traditional legitimation. By the same token, however, democracy as the form of the state assumes ethical responsibility for the political task. Therefore it must make possible the exercise of authority, the use of force, and the establishment of law and order. A democracy must also respect the independence of its citizens, who as a body provide the state with its legitimation, and it must recognize the freedom and the authority of the people. In the relation of these two demands to each other and in their binding force we see the ethical problem that toleration poses for politics, and it is the structure and content of this problem that we must now consider. Toleration is the concrete form that this task takes and that we shall now explore in the example of the relationship of majority to minority in a democracy.

As regards this relationship, toleration in political matters is not some supplementary moral requirement which would demand that in the heat of political debates the participants should maintain tolerant and friendly relations. It is that also, but as an ethical claim it is not merely a matter of intentions but is a specific part of the democratic process by which decisions are to be reached. Mutual toleration is a requirement that is binding on a democracy.

Majorities are the makers of political decisions. In the reality of the political scene they play a role in the formation of a capacity for making decisions and taking actions so that decisions can be reached in the presence of dissent. Situations that make a majority decision necessary are not unambiguous but are characterized by the complexity of the issue or the task that demands a political decision.

When confronted with a variety of possible actions for which groups with differing or even entirely opposed interests contend, a binding decision must be reached. Thus under the principle and in the process of reaching a majority decision, the social nature of political action becomes manifest. That is to say, every decision reached by a majority is in its content and in the manner by which it is reached related to alternatives favored by a minority. Majority decisions are by definition not absolute decisions. Even when they must be accepted by everyone, by the whole body politic, it is the majority that must bear responsibility for them.

This responsibility has two aspects: It is responsibility to the whole and responsibility toward those who are currently in the political minority. By no means may an unconditional identity be asserted between the majority decision and the whole political realm, but only a conditional representation of the whole by the majority decision. This is the boundary beyond which lies political totalitarianism. Toleration means that majority decisions are not closed to public criticism, but indeed permit it. The attempt to turn decisions of a political majority into absolute decisions leads to a negation of their own conditional nature. Toleration is a determinative criterion for the way in which majority decisions are reached.

The demand for toleration means that the majority also has a responsibility to the defeated minority. It therefore can and should require agreement with its decisions only within a framework of legal and political authority that does not eliminate the independence of minorities. This means that the content and form of decisions that are reached under these preconditions must not be so constructed that they seek to force the full agreement of the minority. Respect for and legal compliance with majority decisions can be demanded of the minority, but not total agreement with their content. Consequently, the decisions must be such that they can be tolerated, but that no one is forced to agree with them.

For this breadth of toleration, the acceptance of freedom of religion is the most important example, both historically and in terms of its nature. In questions of faith there can be no majority decisions. Therefore in a democracy the legal separation of church and state is essential. But separation does not mean a lack of relationships between them. The existence of an independent church keeps alive the demand that the state respect differences of belief, a demand basic to the concrete relationships of church and state in a democracy. Majority decisions that require uniformity of belief are in political terms not simply inappropriate; they are incompatible with the relationship between majority and minority.

The majority can require acceptance by the minority only if this does not imply unlimited submission to the intentions and goals of the majority. The social nature of the body politic in which a majority can be constituted and which needs a majority that is capable of making decisions is not completely and unconditionally subject to the majority and can be made totally subject to it only through the use of unjustifiable force. A political majority that practices toleration of dissent must be content with being accepted by the minority only within limits. When minorities are forced to go underground politically, that is an indication that the majority is extending its power into all areas of life in such a manner as to leave the minority with no alternative except to surrender. The requirement that the majority grant toleration to the minority is more than just a formal principle.

If this be granted, it is also the case that the minority must abide by the decisions of the majority. Minorities must acknowledge the existence of the majority and its competence to make decisions; that is, minorities must be tolerant of the majority if they are to be democratic minorities. If a minority does not accept its own political situation but feels that it is the real, the only true majority, it will conclude from the hindrances placed in its way that it has the right to fight against the actual political majority with all the means at its disposal. As a rule it is not at all interested in whether the majority is capable of showing toleration. Whenever it can, it will use that toleration only as a means for preparing to overthrow the majority and will not accept the demand placed upon it that it be tolerant of others. In such a case the minority negates its own political limitations, as seen, for example, in its inability to win majority support for its goals. The claim to be exclusively right and the inability to form a majority then coincide. Therefore the minority too is confronted by the demand to show toleration, not only in its relationship to those on the "outside," but also in its understanding of the role it is to play as a minority if it is to prove itself capable of participating in a democracy.

The requirement for political toleration also involves the possibility that a new majority will come to power, and this places one more limit on the claim to exclusive authority made on behalf of majority decisions and relativizes any such claim. The constitutional possibility of forming a new majority underlines the time limits under which any majority must function. In terms of structure, toleration means that even though the ruling majority does not desire a loss of power, it cannot use every means at its disposal to avoid such a loss but must accept the possibility in principle. The clearest indication of the spirit of tolerance in the exercise of power is whether the structure remains open to the possibility of a new majority being formed, or whether this is seen as a marginal case to be avoided by all means, in extreme cases even by the use of force.

The requirement to be tolerant of others is not limited to organized majorities or minorities but also extends to the manner in which individual citizens conduct their political activities. Democracy is not an instrument for exercising one's own freedom or ambitions without reference to others. Those who regard as democratic only those things that are in agreement with their own will and that lead to the expression of that will confuse political democracy with immediate self-fulfillment. The acceptance of democracy always includes acceptance of toleration in allowing others to determine how they will lead their own lives. The demand that we be tolerant also includes democracy itself. If democracy as a political form presupposes autonomy in the way one lives in the sense that it does not lay claim to the total person, then there must also be freedom beyond the political realm. This means acknowledging and respecting the limits of political democratization instead of demanding in an intolerant manner that it be practiced everywhere. Democracy is the form in which our political life is conducted, but it is not the necessary form for all of life. This would lead to an overextension of the political side of life that would ultimately destroy the condition of freedom on which it is based.

The constitutional and structural problems of democracy have been discussed above. The questions discussed here are the sensitive points that distinguish between the political practices in a liberal democracy and those in a totalitarian democracy.

On the question of the relationship between minority and majority, see V. Scheuner, *Das Mehrheitsprinzip in der Demokratie*, 1973, and his *Der Mehrheitsentscheid im Rahmen der demokratischen Grundordnung*, found in the Festschrift for W. Kaegi, 1978. On the problems of democracy, see R. Niebuhr, *The Children of Light and the Children of Darkness*, 1947; H. Arendt, *Elemente und Ursprünge totaler Herrschaft*, 1975; J. L. Tolman, *Die Ursprünge der totalitären Demokratie*, 1961; G. Leibholz, *Strukturprobleme der modernen Demokratie*, 3d ed., 1967; Th. Strohm and H.-D. Wendland, eds., *Kirche und moderne Demokratie*, 1973; U. Matz, ed., *Grundprobleme der*

Demokratie, 1973; O. Barbarino, *Staatsform und politische Willensbildung,* 1949; H. Steinberger, *Konzeption und Grenzen freiheitlicher Demokratie,* 1974; M. Greiffenhagen, ed., *Demokratisierung in Staat und Gesellschaft,* 1973.

3) Material Security for Independent Living as the Responsibility of the Sociopolitical System

A society that depends on the labor of men and women is responsible for guaranteeing them the freedom to lead their own lives apart from their work. This responsibility is the concrete expression of the ethical task of social policy.

Criteria for the effectiveness of economic systems have been discussed earlier. Now in reference to the labor force, we must examine the ethical basis for a social policy that would ensure that the workers have the material requirements for independent living beyond their function as laborers. One's work does not constitute the whole of one's life. Wherever the two are identical, where men and women are regarded only as part of the labor force and are so used, they are being exploited. Social policy is an answer to the separation between dependency in one's work and one's individual life, a distinction that has become normative for the modern workplace. It strengthens and protects the freedom of working men and women over against their economic dependency. The ethical basis for an appropriate social policy cannot be established by moralistic appeals. It grows out of the structure of the workplace itself. This context must be taken into account in developing an ethical line of argument.

The organization of economic activity needs, indeed is dependent on, human labor. In theory it is assumed that workers freely make their labor available. This assumption is valid only if it be granted that a person's labor is a part of that person's freedom and independence, and is not, as in traditional societies, limited to a specific occupation by virtue of one's birth or social origin. That one's labor is a part of personal freedom does not mean that an individual is free in the sense of being able to live without working. It means only that one's ability to work belongs to that person. This assumption implies the responsibility for seeing to it that workers are able to lead a relatively independent life in reference to their work. The discussion here will be limited to this question. Social policy involves responsibility for this freedom.

The organization of economic activity and the workforce are dependent on each other, but the nature of this dependence is not symmetrical. The employer needs available workers but is not dependent on any specific individual workers; that is, respect for the personal lives of individual workers is not involved in this relationship of dependence.

Conversely, individual workers are dependent on the organization that provides employment as their means of livelihood. But respect for the specific interests and goals of a specific enterprise is not yet determinative for them. This enables us to explore the problems of the context in which responsibility for the private lives of individual workers can and must become an issue.

What can be the starting point here for moral discourse? It is possible to speak of the independence of work in the individual lives of workers only under the condition that none are fully dependent on their ability to work. Only when persons are not identified with the work that they are capable of doing can its performance be demanded of them as an independent service. If, however, exclusive claims are placed on a person's ability to work, without taking into account individual circumstances, this is clearly exploitation in that the person can be "let go" when no longer able to work. This is the point of the metaphor of a "safety net" in the formation of social policy.

If, therefore, the economic organization must rely on a free and independent labor supply (in contrast to forced work, to the exploitation of emergency situations, and to slavery), then it is necessary for the possibility to exist of achieving independence through one's work. It is a binding obligation of the economic system and a criterion of its ability to participate in the ongoing tradition that working men and women be free to determine their individual, independent lives, however little that may serve the immediate interests of the individual enterprise for which they work.

In this way social policy becomes a binding obligation for both society and the state. This obligation takes on concrete form in health insurance, provision for pensions, unemployment insurance, and many other provisions that constitute a system of social security that provides long-term, continuing material provision for individuals to lead their lives beyond their current ability to work.

In relation to the basic obligation to provide such security, the question of whether it is based on voluntary participation or on legal requirements is secondary. The decisive matter is to recognize that this responsibility is an urgent requirement growing out of the general concept of freedom for economic activity. The mutual dependence of organized economic enterprises and the labor force provides adequate arguments for distinguishing clearly between a system for the social security of individuals that makes it possible for them to lead individual and independent lives and any system based on the giving of "alms" or "charity." It is a matter of just claims and requirements that follow directly from the independence of individual workers who, because they bring their work as a contribution to the economy, are not simply identical with their contribution, as is a machine. Therefore this contribution can reasonably be expected from them only if at the same time their independence is explicitly acknowledged in relationship to the work they are accomplishing.

This line of argument should not and cannot prescribe in detail implementation of social policy. It only serves to identify concretely the area in which the individual lives of working men and women form the basis of binding economic responsibility. This ethical orientation is not something tacked on to economic practices for humanitarian or moral reasons that are essentially foreign to those practices. On the contrary, it sets the theme for an ethical task that is integral to the economy. It follows from such an ethical argument that the system of providing social security for working men and women is oriented to the needs of their individual ways of life.

Social policy is the expression of the economic order in the service of the way of life of working men and women and is the economic condition for the permanence of freedom in relation to work.

So formulated, this task stands in critical relationship to a theory that defines human beings exclusively as belonging to an economic class and regards them only as those who contribute their labor as a commodity. To be sure, here too, as in the case of Marxist theory, we are dealing with the independence of the labor force, not in relation to the way of life of individual workers but in a relative and abstract way in relation to capital. The formation of a differentiated system of social security is thus the formation of a system that encourages and ensures individual independence, and in terms of its basic nature is incompatible with an economic theory of class struggle in the strict sense. Theories of class struggle, by contrast, depend on the force of impersonal laws of economic development in which they rely on the total identity of workers with their labor and thus negate individual ways of life in favor of a determinism based on the class to which the individual subject belongs.

On the revisionism debate in relation to class struggle and social policy, see R. Luxemburg, "Sozialreform oder Revolution," in *Politische Schriften*, ed. O. K. Flechtheim, vol. 1, 1975; L. Basso, *Rosa Luxemburgs Dialektik der Revolution*,

1969; S. Miller, *Das Problem der Freiheit im Sozialismus. Freiheit, Staat und Revolution in der Programmatik der Sozialdemokratie von Lassalle bis zum Revisionismusstreit*, 3d ed., 1974; S. Papcke, *Der Revisionismusstreit und die politische Theorie der Reform*, 1979.

Social security as a concept of social policy for the protection of the individual has been current since about 1920 and was recognized as one of the basic freedoms in the Declaration of Human Rights of 1948. On the discussion of social policy in the Federal Republic of Germany, see H. Achinger, *Soziale Sicherheit*, 1953; G. Weisser, in *Handwörterbuch der Sozialwissenschaften*, vol. 9, 1954; E. Boettcher, ed., *Sozialpolitik und Sozialreform*, 1957; and the study produced by the Kammer für soziale Ordnung of the Evangelical Church of Germany, *Die Soziale Sicherung im Industriezeitalter. Eine Denkschrift*, 1973, republished in *Die Denkschriften der EKD*, ed. Kirchenkanzlei der EKD, vol. 2, *Soziale Ordnung*, 1978.

4) Forms of Etiquette
as the Culture of Everyday Life

In their conduct of daily life, human beings have a responsibility for seeing that culture can be capable of being handed on; that is, in relation to other persons they must observe certain forms of etiquette. Good manners are the expression of virtue in daily life.

The way the conduct of individual life contributes to the durability and permanence of the process in which tradition is formed can be illustrated in good manners as the concrete expression of the way culture is shaped and renewed.

In terms of its concrete expressions, ethics must not ignore seemingly trivial areas. Anyone who knows the history of ethics in detail, particularly in the areas of duty and virtue, knows that this tendency to ignore some issues has repeatedly been overcome, and with good reason. The forms of etiquette have their ethical relevance because they make it possible for individuals to act in a consistent and reliable manner. They place limits on a person's spontaneity or lack of spontaneity on the one hand and on encounters with situations and other persons on the other hand. They keep us from overdramatizing everyday life. For the individual they are the loose and easy bond of ethical orientation in daily life. They provide a viable form for what remains constant in interpersonal relationships, and thus they serve as a sort of cultural map for daily life. Those who have good manners can move everywhere and are independent in that they are not limited to a specific, familiar environment. Good manners make individual independence possible—and require it.

They are the medium by which persons in their relationships with one another do not negate their differences and distinctive characteristics, but mutually respect them. In this way they are the expression in daily life of the possibility of transmitting culture.

The most common complaint against manners is that they are mere externalities. To be sure, not every courteous gesture is an expression of true friendship, not every "Thank-you" is an expression of gratitude, not every "Please" a polite request. Manners are ordinary, everyday expressions of virtue and fill in the area in which the full commitment of personal concern is neither possible nor appropriate but which still requires an ethically acceptable expression.

There are two respects in which manners are significant for the way individual lives contribute to the transmission of human culture. The first involves dealings with strangers. It is obvious that formality is especially evident in our dealings with those we do not know well. Manners overcome the strangeness but also recognize and affirm it. To negate by false familiarity the strangeness of those with whom life throws us into contact can tend to be a form of violence, just as can the refusal to overcome the strangeness, expressed in brusque and hostile behavior. Politeness enables us to cope with the strangeness and establish mutual recognition, thus making proximity bearable without getting too close to each other. In an elementary sense, good manners are the forms of respect in the presence of that which is different. In their own way they enable us to restrain violence and thus help us deal with issues not only between individuals but also between groups, societies, and nations (international deportment!). The inward ethical significance of outward forms involves the need to respect and acknowledge that other persons are independent and autonomous beings, to respect the inalienable individuality of each person which must be preserved even in the closest and most intimate relationships, for example, between close friends and marriage partners. Thus the range of good manners extends from the external relationships of the world in which we live to the most intimate relationships and has in both realms the same significance.

The second respect involves the individual's own attitude toward the forms of polite behavior. Protest movements and youth movements criticize polite behavior above all because they regard it as a deception in which people pretend to be what they are not and show themselves in a false light. In such criticism direct self-expression is contrasted with the formality of mannerly conduct. Quite apart from the fact that every youth or protest movement develops its own codes of behavior in which participants express their immediacy over the long term (beginning with their clothing and extending to many elements of tone and form in their conduct) and thus pay their own tribute to the problem we are considering here, the real problem must be sought in another direction. It is true that manners express a kind of alienation, but no more so than the whole of culture does. For the individual in relation to the self, the acknowledgment of codes and forms of behavior means the acknowledgment of the limits of one's own standpoint, one's own will, one's own worth, one's own self-assurance. Those who brush aside all social forms in their relationships with others must be absolutely certain of the validity of their actions and their beliefs on which they are based. They must be completely convinced that their own point of view has universal validity. Otherwise it is merely a matter of being inconsiderate of others. Total directness toward others verges on violence against them. The ethical significance of polite conduct must be seen in relation to one's own conduct toward others, and this inner task that is the issue here is expressed in the concept "virtue." Virtues are the expression of the application to one's own life of the inward significance of good manners, and their goal is a consistency that comes from within. The alien nature of forms of good behavior can and must be overcome through the inward formation of a way of life. A "virtuous" life is one that finds in the inward significance of good conduct the equivalent of the outward forms. A criticism of good manners as such is the refusal to recognize the importance of this task.

In a certain sense good manners also play a role in the religious dimension of life in that men and women approach God through forms by which they acknowledge the otherness of God and the limits on the immediacy of their religious experience. Thus it gives an impression of arrogance when someone seeks to prove his or her piety by showing in pious expressions evidence of a direct relationship with God.

Beyond the acknowledgment and appropriate use of forms of conduct, the individual life participates independently in developing in daily life the worthiness of the traditional culture to be handed on. Good manners are elements in the living reality of a culture and mark the difference between culture and nature in a manner that has been entrusted to human beings and for which they are responsible. This task provides the inner standards and guidelines for even the changes in the rules of good conduct. It would be irresponsible to take arms against standards of conduct just because they are there, just as it makes little sense to negate them just because they have been handed down to us.

5) *Christian Independence and Religious Doubt*

The independence of Christians is the goal of the church's activity. A maturity that accepts religion with personal responsibility finds concrete expression in the ability to deal with religious doubt.

Although the ideal of the church institution may be the good church member, in practice the goal of the church is communication and transmission of the faith in order to equip Christians for independent lives. Being loyal to the church and being a Christian are not identical, either theologically or empirically. The attempt to make them equal leads the church into the temptation, in contradiction to its real task, to set up a false classification of "bad" and "good" Christians and to depict the criteria of acceptability in the church in the framework of the final judgment. False perspectives can lead here to false judgments and even to a churchly contempt for humanity. It is not this misuse of church practice that is the subject here, but its correct use when we speak of the conduct of the individual's life in relation to religion as a constructive task. From the standpoint of the Christian, this task is seen differently from the way it is seen from the standpoint of the church as an institution.

This is true in an elementary sense in reference to specific services of worship, which must always be open both to a theological interpretation and an interpretation in terms of the experiences of human life, because in terms of their theological significance they have to be related to human life. That is the theme of Christian morality and the morality of the church. For example, some religious observations are also family festivals and in this connection have proven worthy of being part of the tradition. Even the so-called official rites of the church, such as baptism, confirmation, marriage, and the funeral, are as church rites also concrete religious expressions in the context of individual life. It would therefore be a mistake to oppose manifestations of the relevance of these rites to the life situations of the people for the sake of making these activities unambiguously the concern of the church. On the contrary, the ability of religion to participate in the tradition is realized here in the living of daily life. The one, distinctive meaning of worship must here be differentiated and must move beyond the distinctive nature of its liturgical form.

Yet behind these forms of religious expression in the varying contexts of life there stands the quite different question of how independence in relation to religion can be attained. Responsibility for one's own Christian life cannot be delegated to the church but must find concrete expression for each individual. Religious maturity, through which each must take personal responsibility for his or her relation to religion, is a process in which this responsibility is achieved through one's personal struggle with the content of religion, one's relationship to God. In this life context, religious doubt can be a necessary element on the way to independence. Therefore when we speak of Christian autonomy in respect to ethics the emphasis is not on how the Christian is the representative openly and before others of what the church teaches and proclaims in general, being then, so to speak, an individual example of what the church is. Instead, we shall consider the significance of doubt in the formation of religious autonomy.

Here we continue from another perspective the issue raised above. The critical point in the relation of autonomy and faith can be seen with especial clarity when we consider the biographical context of the tension between self-awareness and faith. In childhood the concept of God is formed amid experiences that can be characterized by the concepts of authority and trust. The child does not first encounter God through religious instruction. The child learns this word in the everyday language of home through songs, prayers, and stories. In these and other language contexts, God appears as the ultimate and decisive authority. On the one side is God, the authority for our knowledge of good and evil, in the sense that God is the one who knows what is good and what is evil as well as the one who knows who is good and who is evil. On the other side, God is presented to the child with equal urgency and intensity as our ultimate refuge and trust, as the loving God to whom we can and must turn when no one else can help us.

In relation to these beliefs, doubt appears in the life of the child at a certain age. This comes about because the concept of God is always shaped by the world in which one lives; it is a reflection of the world in which the child lives with parents and peers. In this world the transition from childhood to maturity involves a process in which values are reassessed. Children must be freed from the conditions to which they have previously been subject. They must come to self-awareness. This process of detachment from others is necessary because human independence becomes concrete in the distinction between self and others. People become themselves when they distinguish themselves from others. This always means distinguishing oneself from the ideas and conceptions that were previously unquestioned. Children therefore begin to experience doubt as criticism of concepts and norms that have been passed on to them, and especially as a critique of the concept of God. As people mature they naturally distance themselves from this concept. In this maturation process, the God concept offers the first and also the most radical opportunity for a critique.

But this by no means signifies the end of faith in God. Criticism of one's parents does not make them disappear. To be sure, there are pathological cases in the relationship to one's parents in which the parents are totally excluded from one's consciousness. But it is indisputable that criticism of authority and of objects of trust (and thus also criticism of the concept of God) is one way we can attain to independence in our dealing with the meaning of the word *God*. This independence helps us move forward in our interpretation of the world in which we live. The experience of authority and dependence cannot be fully swallowed up by the experience of freedom and independence, because freedom and independence also need interpretation so that our independence as human beings can be truly perceived. Thus doubt has its place in this process of liberation, a process that leads to a new understanding of the constituent elements of life.

If we deal successfully with doubt, we gain confidence in our ability to cope with life. Thus religious doubt that grows out of the conditions of our human life culminates in the search for a maturity that can gain its comprehensive meaning in the question of faith.

Independence in our religious relationships does not mean a return to a childlike faith. Doubt does not lose its significance. Rather, in our relationship to ourselves as human beings it can play a significant and productive role in our awareness that we are involved in reality in a variety of ways. Thus we can say that the difference lies in whether "it is something that involves our knowledge, or involves our conscience, something that increases our possessions or something that strengthens our being, something that makes us better able to produce or to reproduce or something that makes us more sensitive and grateful" (Gerhard Ebeling, *Dogmatik Christlichen Glaubens*, vol. 1, 1979, p. 152). The "true" conflict would then be found in the self-contradiction that afflicts us as humans, compelling us in various ways to take a position in relation to reality.

Paul Tillich described this situation with profound insight. When he says, "Faith involves the ontological question" ("Der Mensch im Lichte des biblischen Personalismus," *Gesammelte Werke*, vol. 5, p. 170), he means that faith not only seeks to attain to subjective certainty and assurance, but has as its proper theme the question of ultimate reality. Doubt is thus not something that attacks faith from without, but it belongs to the essence of faith itself. "Faith and doubt are not in essential conflict" (p. 170). Faith has to do with the awareness of the tension that exists between persons and their ultimate concern. But then this tension is always a tension between oneself and doubt of oneself. "Faith includes itself and doubt of itself. Therefore it contains both itself and the ontological question, whose presupposition is radical doubt" (p. 171). Doubt that is to be taken seriously in the sense of a question about reality appears only where the question of God has a decisive significance, even if only in a negative sense. It would be an illusion to think that faith has to confront only "external" or so-called scientific doubts. "Doubt of God becomes doubt of the truth itself, and thus in its final dimension, doubt of the meaning of life itself," in as much as the question of God, while it can be suppressed, cannot be eliminated (Tillich, "Rechtfertigung und Zweifel," *Ges. Werke*, vol. 8, p. 89). Therefore we should not deny the seriousness of doubt. "In the theoretical sphere doubt is just as serious a matter as assurance of salvation is in the practical. Doubt is the struggle for participation in the ultimate meaning of life, in ultimate truth." Therefore Tillich can speak of the "justification of the doubter." That is the "break-through of the certainty that the truth which the doubter seeks, the meaning of life toward which the despairer struggles, is not the goal but the presupposition of all doubt, even doubt unto despair" (p. 91).

Those who doubt are engaged in a particularly intensive manner in the search for truth, for God. Each of them experiences individually the unresolved ambiguity of the world. Each is a representative of a life situation that is characterized, not by the clarity and simplicity of the truth, but by the contradictions in life's realities for which they are responsible. If we follow Tillich's interpretation, then doubt is the way the experience of the unconditioned in the relative becomes present reality. Therefore the church cannot be concerned with attempts to eliminate doubt but must accompany and encourage those who doubt.

On this whole discussion, see also H. Ringeling, "Begriff und Bedeutung einer kritischen Religiosität," in *Ethik vor der Sinnfrage*, 1980, pp. 31–46.

c. Responsibility for the Limits of the Active Life: Being Worthy of the Traditions

Taking a responsible stand in our active life means respecting the limits placed on our actions by the life that has been entrusted to us. That does not mean giving up activity but rather being authentic and worthy of trust in what we do. We must justify the way we live out the life that has been entrusted to us by making it worthy of participating in the tradition.

1) Responsibility for Lives Entrusted to Us: The Ethical Meaning of Infant Baptism

The criterion for the authenticity of what we do as parents in the upbringing of our children is the unconditional acceptance of life that is entrusted to us.

Responsible parenthood finds its criterion in the duty to create for the children a life context that is capable of participating in the tradition. The goal of our work in bringing up children is to be ready and able to accept, each in our own way, responsibility in and for the process of forming tradition. In both these respects we are accountable for what we do. The criterion for the truth and authenticity of our actions lies in the recognition and affirmation of the independence of the lives that are entrusted to us. This criterion must be explicitly perceived and explicitly set forth. We must become aware of the difference between the empirical, historical, and biographical process of parenthood on the one hand and on the other hand bringing up of children, with all its efforts and demands, its stumbling blocks and conflicts. This life, on whose behalf these efforts are made, is entrusted to us.

An example of how this may be done may be found in the following discussion of the ethical significance of infant baptism and the subsequent rite of confirmation.

The history of baptism in the Christian church may also be taken as an example of the development of Christian ethics. Beginning with John the Baptist's call to repentance, the interpretation of baptism has in various ways set forth the theme of entrance into the Christian life and the way that life is lived, while the time at which baptism is given and the manner in which it is performed have undergone many changes. (For the history of baptism, see the comprehensive study by C. H. Ratschow, *Die eine christliche Taufe*, 1972.) It is only in modern times that baptism as infant baptism, which for its interpretation draws on the words of Jesus in Matt. 19:14, has come to have such a close relationship to the family. The exegetical and historical disputes about infant baptism will not be explored in detail here, because the theological and ethical themes of these debates are not drawn from historical data but involve issues in systematic theology and ecclesiology. Nor is our theme here the theological doctrine of baptism, with its dogmatic implications. The discipline of ethics itself must take up a position on the ethical significance of baptism for the practice of infant baptism.

The Christian practice of infant baptism is, as a rite of the church, a symbol and a visible expression of the doctrine of justification as the core of the basic convictions that are essential to Christianity. As a rite performed by the church for human beings, it is the sign that God accepts humans, as this acceptance is mediated through Christ; that is, it is without preconditions of human accomplishments. Grace is bestowed to free us from sin. In this context, the church's rite of baptism is, as infant baptism, a symbol of the truth about life, a truth that is not under human control but is to guide and direct what we do in life. This is true in several respects. When parents bring their children to baptism, they recognize the child's right to lead an independent life that is not dependent on the actual, empirical future success or failure of that life. Infant baptism is the Christian symbol for a basic right to life, both in relationship to other persons and especially to the parents and all those who constitute the "world" in which the child lives.

Infant baptism makes it explicit that the parents do not control the child like a possession but are obligated to recognize the child's independence in an absolute sense, which is not conditioned, for example, on the expectations that the parents have for the child. The meaning of Christian baptism as a symbol that the person is accepted by God prior to any accomplishments, and is not conditioned on any accomplishments that the child might make in life, is to be expressed also in the unconditioned acceptance of the child by the parents and by all those who bear responsibility for the child. The role of godparents underscores and clarifies the representative nature of the activities for the child beyond the natural bounds, the responsibility of the concrete "world" of the child for a life which, in order to be able to be independent, must experience itself as accepted and supported as a life received from others. The responsibility of the godparents is an example through the life of the congregation of the social nature of life. Thus it is precisely the ethical meaning of infant baptism that gives concrete expression to the theological content of baptism as the commitment of life to God.

By contrast, the present-day criticism of infant baptism is based on a religious, individualistic understanding of our humanity in that it places the individual's decision to be baptized ahead of the baptism. These critics should reflect on what it means to give the individual the right to decide whether or not to live in a manner that accords with reality, that is, as something that has been received and therefore must be lived in a responsible manner in relationship to God. In any case, baptism based on a conscious decision can hardly negate the life context in which the affirmation of one's God-given life has its place in terms of theology and of one's own biography. Correctly understood, adult baptism can hardly be an alternative to infant baptism, because an adolescent or adult cannot be baptized in any other way than as a child, that is, in the recognition that God accepts us unconditionally, without any accomplishments on our part. An alternative to infant baptism could have a theological basis only if baptism had as its basis, theologically as well as ethically, specific human accomplishments. But then it would be a sort of self-baptism and meaningless as a religious rite.

On the debate over infant baptism, see the "Baptism fragment" from Karl Barth's *Church Dogmatics,* where baptism is discussed in the context of ethics. See *Church Dogmatics* IV, 4: *The Christian Life* (fragment), *Baptism as the Basis of the Christian Life,* 1967 (ET 1969). See also E. Jüngel, *Karl Barths Lehre von der Taufe. Ein Hinweis auf ihre Probleme,* 1968; and "Der ethische Sinn der Dogmatik," in *Realisierung der Freiheit,* ed. T. Rendtorff, 1975, pp. 119–34, esp. pp. 128ff.

The concrete role of baptism as infant baptism in the individual's life implies the subsequent rite of confirmation. Confirmation is a twofold validation of baptism. Through it both the ethical meaning and the theological meaning of baptism for the individual's independent life find expression, and in addition it takes place at the threshold of the person's independence. Confirmation is not an occasion for a general, abstract decision, but an occasion in which the individual now accepts God's yes to his or her life and the yes which the parents and godparents have spoken as the representatives in affirming the child's independence. At issue in confirmation is the authenticity of the person's own life in the context of the ethical reality of life. As a rite of the church, therefore, confirmation is bound to a process of Christian instruction in which the basis for the independence and responsibility of the life of the one accepted by God—as that life has been formed by the congregation and its representatives, the parents and godparents—is communicated to the young person in such a way as to bring conscious acceptance and affirmation. Confirmation is thus not a situation in which an isolated individual decision is made. Neither is it a substitute for baptism. Instead it expresses the meaning of baptism as the concrete social milieu in which the child has grown up. Isolating the confirmand's decision from this context could easily obscure the religious meaning of confirmation for the person's life. In it we see anew the recognition and the acceptance of responsibility for an independent life, but now we see it in a concrete rite in which responsibility for one's own actions is accepted and placed in the service of the formation of tradition. The "success" of confirmation is therefore to be seen in the totality of the person's own life, for the authenticity of which he or she is now responsible, supported by the truth of life to which baptism bears witness.

2) Human Rights:
The Limits and the Tasks of the State

The defense of human freedom finds concrete political expression in the affirmation of human rights. As basic rights they set the limits of the state's control over its people. Responsibility for their enforcement is committed to the state, both national and international, in the interests of faithfulness to tradition.

Political responsibility depends on the forms of law, and in a democracy it involves political tolerance. Both of these aspects involve reflective thought on politics, which must result in concrete policies in current political activities. This concrete expression is the content of human rights. That is the theme of this third investigation of the active life in politics.

The ethical significance of infant baptism in the context of the Christian church finds its counterpart in the state's formal acknowledgment of human independence. This is especially clear in the recognition of human rights as basic rights in the constitution and places the state under obligation to acknowledge these rights.

Human rights, as they are formulated in the General Declaration of Human Rights by the United Nations in 1948, claim today a universal validity similar to that of democracy. But their actual political acceptance and enforcement continues in many nations to fall far short of their claims. This is primarily because human rights must be made relevant not simply as such, but as politically relevant limits on a state's sovereignty and control over its citizens. The defense of freedom demands always both the recognition of these limits and the renunciation of specific forms of the exercise of the state's power. Because this concrete political demand involves and must involve human rights, these rights are again and again ignored in many nations or are given only verbal assent.

In recent years the discussion of human rights in ethical and theological terms has been quite lively. It is possible to get the impression "that the catchword 'human rights' has come to be regarded as a broad concept under which the prior social and ethical discussion can be subsumed" (H. Vogt, *Kirche und Menschenrechte,* epd-Dokumentation Nr. 5/75). The discussion of the basis for human rights and how to realize them is equally complicated and involved.

The current interest in human rights in theology and in the church must be seen against the background of a tradition that viewed human rights with skepticism and reservation, and in part rejected them entirely. That is especially the case with the Lutheran church and its theology in the nineteenth century. (See, e.g., H. Zillessen, *Protestantismus und politische Form,* 1971; T. Rendtorff, "Freiheit und Recht des Menschen," *Lutherische Rundschau* 18 (1968): 215–27.) It would be false to speak as if human rights had always been a constituent part of Christian ethics and thus to overlook or deny the serious conflicts that this issue created for theology and the church in earlier epochs. A constructive understanding of human rights is thus a marked advance beyond that tradition.

In dealing with the ethical questions to be considered now, it is essential to concentrate on the basic structure of human rights, which primarily involves two issues: the basis of human rights and the relationship between so-called individual and social human rights. For the state, recognizing human rights means recognizing the independence of individual lives within the political community. If this recognition is not to be mere rhetoric, it must involve the state itself. Its content is the explicit acknowledgment of the limits of the sovereignty of the state. It must be put into practice in formal and binding action by establishing and protecting human rights as basic rights under the constitution, so that in their content and in the way they are carried out they establish that the individual is not at the disposal of the state. This freedom from state control finds concrete expression in the right to live, in freedom of conscience, in religious freedom, and in freedom of opinion. Through human rights a human dignity is established that constitutes the criterion for the inner integrity of the political activity of the state and in relationship to which the capability and worthiness of political activity for contributing to the ongoing tradition is called to account. For the state, the ethical significance of human rights is that their express authority under the constitution and ongoing political acknowledgment means not a passive toleration but direct advocacy in a specific legal program. More precisely, this means that the validity of this human dignity cannot be dependent on whether the individual is demonstrably worthy of these human rights or that one can secure them for oneself or by one's efforts alone. That would have the ruinous consequence that human dignity would pertain only to those who could achieve it for themselves.

Here we touch on the central point of the basis for human rights. The history of human rights in modern times, especially in the Anglo-Saxon tradition, presupposes an original human freedom in the sense of a natural independence of each individual. This assumption stresses that the individual is not human by the grace of the state, but that on the contrary the humanity of each individual is the presupposition and precondition for the state. Here the word *natural* can only mean that freedom and dignity belong to the individual as a human being and must therefore be respected. But in fact this assumption led to the false conclusion that if the "natural" freedom and dignity of the individual is also empirical and political, the individual possesses a freedom that is real prior to and outside one's belonging to a political community. This assumption could give rise to the result that the actual validity of human rights is dependent on the way the individual is powerful enough actually to lay hold on this freedom. Seen from the point of view of the state and society, the acknowledgment of human rights is a given and has unconditional validity for both. It imposes duties on them and is to guide their actions. This understanding of human rights as something that must be accepted as given is comparable to the previously mentioned relationship between the ethical meaning of infant baptism and the significance of human rights. In this respect a theological ethic can and must speak of an inner connection between the Christian doctrine of justification and human rights.

See T. Rendtorff, "Menschenrechte und Rechtfertigung," in *Der Wirklichkeitsanspruch von Theologie und Religion*, eds. D. Henke et al., Festschrift for E. Steinbach, 1976, pp. 161–74.
Theological ethics represents here the position that human rights as rights to freedom are not the privilege of strong, independent individuals. The establishment of human rights is the task of the political community. Human rights must not be thought of as unmediated, natural human independence. Otherwise they would be merely a function of the natural life force and its economic consequences.

The political and ethical significance of human rights must be developed in terms of their political function. The legal significance of human rights is also its original social significance. It is in these terms that the relationship between human rights as freedom on the one hand and as social rights on the other is to be defined. It is only on the basis of the recognition of the right to freedom as the acknowledgment of the independence of an individual's life from specific political demands that we have clear guidelines for social rights. It is only by assuming that human life is not at the disposal of the state and of society that the individual's duty to accept responsibility to the state can be clearly seen. But in the process of achieving human rights there follows from this presupposition the task of structuring our social rights in a productive manner. Social rights are the necessary affirmation and confirmation of the right to freedom, and are also the criterion for authenticity in the perception of basic rights. Social rights explicate the ethical significance of the right to freedom for political and social activity. A merely formal acknowledgment of the right to freedom without there being any consequences for the structure of political and social reality would fall short of the claim to universal validity made for the acknowledgment of human rights in their basic significance. It would make them dependent on the ability of the individual to achieve. Social rights, in the sense of basic needs, confront political and social action with the productive task of enabling individuals to lead independent lives in their social context. But the task in the area of social rights, however they may be conceived in detail, is not to construct a specific form of social and political order compatible with human dignity and leading to its achievement. On the contrary, the task is to make the social and political order aware of the responsibility of making it possible for persons to lead independent lives in community.

In this respect the development of social rights lies open before us. To be sure, it is not therefore right simply to equate all political tasks, that is, the totality of economic, social, and legal policy, with the task of bringing social rights to realization. This would mean that the achievement of human rights was identical with the whole task of political and social activity. In this way the critical function of human rights as criteria for the truth of life in political community would be obscured. Human rights, even social rights, do not constitute the total task of political and social activity, but they are the inner critical standard by which such activity is judged. Therefore, especially in the currently expanding discussion of social rights, the inherent range of importance of human rights, from the right to individual freedom to social rights, must be kept clearly in mind. This specific ethical gradation in rank cannot be inverted, or else human rights would lose their evaluative function, which becomes evident in the perception and demonstration of the difference between specific political activities of the state and the claims of human dignity. At no point is it permissible for a specific social order to identify itself with the realization of human rights in such a way that it could say of itself that it is exempt from the criticism brought by human rights. Even social rights as the conscious and responsible perception of the basic meaning of human rights must remain subject to the criterion that no human beings can have other humans at their disposal, and in this sense social rights must be recognized as goals to be achieved.

As examples of the historic and systematic discussion of human rights, the following works may be cited: R. Schnur, ed., *Zur Geschichte der Erklärung der Menschenrechte,* 1964; G. Östreich, *Geschichte der Menschenrechte und Grundfreiheiten im Umriss,* 2d ed., 1978; M. Walker, *The Revolution of the Saints,* 1968; F. Hartung, *Die Entwicklung der Menschen- und Bürgerrechte von 1776 bis zur Gegenwart,* 4th enlarged ed., 1972; A. v. Campenhausen, *Religionsfreiheit,* 1971; E. Jüngel, *Freiheitsrechte und Gerechtigkeit,* 1968, in the collection of his writings, *Unterwegs zur Sache,* 1972, pp. 246–56; J. Lochman and J. Moltmann, eds., *Gottes Recht und Menschenrechte,* 1976; W. Huber and H. E. Tödt, *Menschenrechte,* 1977; J. Baur et al., *Zum Thema Menschenrechte,* 1977; M. Honecker, *Das Recht des Menschen. Einführung in die evangelische Sozialethik,* 1978; Kirchenkanzlei der EKD, ed., *Die Menschenrechte im ökumenischen Gesprach. Beiträge der Kammer der EKD für Öffentliche Verantwortung,* 1979; J. Moltmann, *Menschenwürde, Recht und Freiheit,* 1979. For special discussion of social rights, see H. Zacher, "Freiheits- und Socialrechte im modernen Verfassungsstaat," in *Christliches Gesellschaftsdenken im Umbruch,* ed. St.-E. Szydzik, 1977, pp. 75–105.

3) *Justice as the Criterion for Economic Activity*

Economic activity establishes and determines the nature of worldwide relationships of interdependence that challenge us with the critical question of the worthiness of these relationships for participation in tradition. Justice is the criterion for the concrete ethical evaluation of economic activity.

Economic activity, which in reference to the form of the economy is subject to the demand for productivity and is responsible for the material security and the independence of the workers, cannot be permanently abandoned to a seemingly self-sufficient autonomy. In the activities of the economy, reflective ethical thought must be explicitly brought into play. In this third aspect, therefore, we are to explore in what way the task posed here for ethics can find concrete application in the concept of justice.

The most important discussion of the theme in Protestant theology is still Emil Brunner's *Justice and the Social Order* (ET 1945), where the various concepts of justice and their contents are discussed. The question is repeatedly examined as to what orientation can be derived from the biblical, especially the New Testament, concept of justice and primarily the concept of the justice of God. Even though we take it fully into account that the theme we are exploring does not as such lie within the field of view of the New Testament authors, in considering the structure of the concept of justice, New Testament emphases point out the direction we should go. In the exegetical discussion, E. Lohse opposed the thesis of E. Käsemann and P. Stuhlmacher that God's justice is the apocalyptic demonstration of the power of God to which humans must submit; instead he held that the justice of God is God's compassion, God's helping and guiding relationship to human beings in contrast to the law which judges us. In christology this compassion is proclaimed as freedom from the burden of sin by Christ's taking the place of the sinner (2 Cor. 5:21). See E. Lohse, *Grundriss der neutestamentlichen Theologie*, 1974, pp. 83–87; E. Käsemann, "Gottesgerechtigkeit bei Paulus," *ZThK* 58 (1961): 367–78; P. Stuhlmacher, *Gerechtigkeit Gottes bei Paulus*, 1965. We may draw from this exegesis the conclusion that justice in the theological sense is the establishment of a relationship between God and the human person, and that this relationship is defined by God in Christ having assumed the dependence of humanity on the law. This understanding of the concept of justice in terms of a relationship and the way that it points to the assumption of our dependence on God must lead us to the ethical understanding of justice.

John Rawls, author of the most recent classical theory of justice, says, "Justice is the primary virtue in social institutions, just as truth is in systems of thought" (*A Theory of Justice*, 1971, p. 3). Rich in tradition, justice is one of the fundamental categories of orientation in ethics. The task of ethical argumentation is to attempt to define the place of the critical function of the concept of justice in reference to the discipline of ethics. In this the worldwide interdependence of economic activities must be kept in view. The universal extent, historical and systematic, of the concept of justice makes it particularly suitable as a criterion of truth in the investigation of the problems of economic activity, which today transcend national contexts and national economic processes. At the same time, the concept of justice is well suited for dealing with differing ideological positions and moral demands. How then can justice be valid as a criterion of truth in economic activity? And how can it be translated into truthful dealings? Is the economic realm at all open to the idea of justice, or is justice a demand that can only be raised in opposition to the economic system? Is the widespread view correct that sees injustice at work in economic activity as such and finds justice only where express political action stands in the way of the course of economic activity? Or is it the case that the problem of justice first and foremost appears as an economic problem because there is where it has its life setting?

Regarding justice as a criterion for economic activity thus requires that the concept of justice be formulated in reference to a range of problems that are themselves identifiable in economic activity. The traditional teachings about justice (as distributive justice; as the doctrine of "to each his own"; as the distinction between a proportional and an arithmetic concept of justice and its relation to the idea of equality; justice as the provision for freedom and equality) all have an economic aspect in that they are oriented to material goods, to inequality in their distribution, to property and its use. And they are related to the basic concepts of just treatment and just acknowledgment as the concrete expression of just treatment.

The critical function of justice in the process of forming economic tradition must be seen in terms of the inescapable necessity of economic activity and as a criterion in the context of economic activity. We are dealing here with the problem-oriented meaning of justice, and this provides a specific direction for our questions. Its goal is not a general, abstract concept of justice that would impose from the outside a plan for the solution of problems. Neither can it involve an absolute, moral, or philosophical demand for justice that would pose as an alternative to the problems in economic activity. The concept of justice is oriented to the solving of problems only if it can be relevant to the realm of economic relationships.

To define the place and role of the concept of justice we must deal with "absolute" concepts of justice. In the case of classic Marxism, there is no explicit theory of justice oriented to actions, nor can one be constructed. Under the premises of Marxist socioeconomic theory of justice, problems of justice or of injustice arise only as the consequences of a society consisting of mutually antagonistic classes. There the call for justice in the sense of a balance of justice between capital and labor would be rejected as "repressive" because a demand for justice would only hold up the course of the class struggle. Under these circumstances, justice would itself be shaped by the conflicts and could not be complete justice.

It is possible to enter the realm of freedom, not by concepts of justice and activity to achieve it, but only by a revolutionary abolition of the antagonisms of the class society itself. Thus absolute justice does not define a goal that is oriented to the solution of problems, but one that is seen as the alternative to the existing state of affairs. Under prevailing conditions the demand for justice must appear to be obsolete. Either the orientation to justice only contributes to the lessening of the conflicts of the class society and thus to the hindrance of the revolutionary process, or in a communistic society there is no longer any problem of justice because there is no inequality, no conflict, and no antagonism among the members of society.

"Absolute" justice in the realm of freedom is identical with the elimination of all justice in theory and practice. The economic content of this theory lies in the belief that the kingdom of freedom is economically identical with the concept of wealth, that is, such an organized adequacy of the means for life that neither in the production nor in the use of economic means could there be any competition that would make the cry for justice necessary. The abolition of justice is thus the abolition of its critical function. It lives by the concept of the identity of the social being of men and women with the economic process. That is, however, the characteristic of absolute theories of justice, which are not related to an active process but to a state beyond such activity. The moral "ought" that is expressed therein can therefore not be transformed into any specific action. It would correspond only to total revolutionary activity. An economic process of tradition that is the carrying out of a historically determined law or that is to be superceded by another order has no need of the critical mediation of the concept of justice.

On Marx, see R. Dahrendorf, *Die Idee des Gerechten im Denken von K. Marx*, 2d ed., 1971; D. Christoff and H. Sauer, eds., *Gerechtigkeit in der komplexen Gesellschaft*, 1979, especially the two chapters by A. Kunzli, "'Gerechtigkeit' als Ideologie und Eschatologie im Denken von K. Marx," pp. 49–79, and V. Siegrist, "Entfremdung und Gerechtigkeit," pp. 81–100.

John Rawls, on the other hand, has undertaken in his theory of justice to formulate a concept of justice that is radical in another manner. Its systematic presupposition is the freedom of the individual, the unconditioned value of which is said to appear in all relationships of material or functional inequality (economic and political). The freedom of individuals in their relationship to one another implies equality in principle. Freedom as equality defines a situation in which the problem of justice is unknown. But since this is a hypothetical situation and not a real one, Rawls has chosen a path according to which the construction of the concept of justice itself is the place at which the nature of justice, even in material aspects, is to be determined. The concept of justice is to come to full expression in the discovery and definition of material justice so that the formation of a world view, of a just world, should occur in a proper manner, that is, under the consideration of the principle that all are equally free (see pp. 201–5). Thus he established two principles of justice in which the content of distributive justice is put forth as the structure of discovery of justice in relationship to freedom as equality:

1. Everyone should have the same right to the most extensive system of equal basic freedoms that is compatible with the same system for all others.

2. Social and economic inequalities are to be so structured that (a) it is reasonable to expect that they will be to everyone's advantage and (b) that they will involve positions and offices that are open to all.

It is clear that Rawls gives precedence to the political organization of justice over the attempt to establish a material definition of justice. Here we see formulated a concept that in the current wide discussion of justice, above all in the context of world economic problems, is encountered wherever the contention is advanced that the central problem of justice is in the last analysis the problem of the distribution of power. Only control over the organization of economic activity can open the door to the demands for justice. This means more precisely that control over the control of economic goods is the place where the socially and politically relevant definition of justice makes it possible to conceive of absolute or complete justice. In this respect, however, justice, through the act of participation, becomes in meaning identical with self-determination. Thus at last the concept of justice takes on an unequivocal meaning, and it is understandable that in this way the political line of argument appears extraordinarily attractive.

We can find another correspondence to the line of argument developed by Rawls in the ecumenical discussion that is documented in the activities of the World Council of Churches. There the concept of justice is essentially interpreted through the political and social concept of participation. This has been expressed most recently in the formula of the "just and participatory society," extended in significance by the still-disputed expression "justainable" and its implied relationship to the ecological problem. See Philip Potter, "Science and Technology: Why are the Churches Concerned?" in *Faith and Science in an Unjust World*, ed. R. L. Shinn, 1980, pp. 21–29.

Both the orientation to a condition of economic wealth after the class struggle is overcome and the orientation to a similar political mastery of the possibilities of commerce move the problem to a place other than that of economic activity. Economics is subject to conditions imposed by the shortage of goods and their production and to conditions of interdependence in economic activity. Even so, Rawls's theory casts considerable light on the structure of the concept of justice, and this must be taken into account here.

In order to express concretely the significance of justice as an evaluative device, we may consider ideas of what constitutes injustice. Peter Berger advanced the thesis that injustice is only another name for dependence (*The Rich and the Poor*, 1976). Speaking in economic terms and in reference to the means of life, a state of dependence is of absolute importance; that is to say, the alternative of freedom or dependence is irrelevant, because economic activity involves dependence by virtue of the necessity of obtaining the means for preserving life. Through economic activity we become aware of this dependence. The thesis that injustice is merely another name for dependence cannot be taken to mean that justice is equal to independence. The argument must be carried forward by saying that injustice is a specifically qualified dependence, but justice involves an ethically appropriate expression of dependence. The problem of justice is the problem of the manner in which dependence is structured economically. The universality of dependence is called interdependence, mutual dependence. And the critical function of the concept of justice is to make us aware of the nature of interdependence as an all-embracing economic dependence in contrast to relationships of dependence that are one-sided in nature.

B. Moore clearly defined the material nature of injustice through the image of exploitation—"nonreciprocal social relationship" (*Injustice*, 1978, p. 455). The absence of reciprocity is the negation of interdependence in economic relationships to the advantage of one side. Injustice occurs when the actually existing interdependence of the economic process is not acknowledged or is used for the benefit of one side only. Injustice occurs wherever the fact that economic activity provides the reciprocal means of life plays little or no adequate role in providing orientation for the way economic activity is organized. But mutual dependence, interdependence, is the theme of justice. Thus justice, sets the theme for the task of acknowledging interdependence, not only its description and analysis. The analysis of the problem can only show where effort is still needed in order to establish justice. In the process of production and the conditions essential to it, in the provision of raw materials and their industrial use, in economic exchange, in labor relations and their social consequences, and so forth—that is to say, in the actual reality of economic activity—the responsibility to perceive economic activity as the expression of mutual dependence is always present.

If today injustice is primarily seen as the lack of recognition of reciprocity in the world economy between "rich" and "poor" countries, in most cases this involves the question of acknowledging this interdependence. Seen in this way, the concept of justice is not an absolute norm that holds sway over actual economic relationships, and in principle it cannot be adequate for any specific economic activity. On the contrary, the critical function of the concept of justice is relevant to actually existing relationships of interdependence in their concrete economic and social dimensions. The task of overcoming injustice *here* means therefore that the economically "rich" must vicariously assume the problems and unhappy dependence of the economically "weak." That does not simply mean equality. Equality, when it appears as a demand, cannot eliminate the economic dependence of people nor can it find expression in the negation of the economic task—productivity, capacity for producing and distributing goods, and so forth. It is much easier to imagine a more just world in which economic problems no longer play a role. As an explicit orientation to problems, justice affects the relationships among widely differing persons who are involved in economic activity and serves as a correction and critique of self-righteousness. Justice provides the context in which relationships of interdependence that have not yet been identified, especially in international economic activities, can become apparent.

The system of economic activity has the tendency to produce a state of universal equality. By contrast, justice, by calling attention to the differences among the nations and groups involved in the economic process, brings into play differing needs and differing interests in shaping how life should be lived, even when all are interdependent in a common economic process. Justice means that here we are not all to be subjugated to a single economic goal established, for example, by the developed countries, but that it is possible to realize differing goals. When the demand is made that the wealthy countries provide for greater justice, this inevitably means that in relation to other lands they are to give more than they take and thus let their actions be shaped by the dependence of the others in concrete ways. Since interdependence is in reality highly asymmetrical, it places demands on the wealthy countries. In this situation we can then say that the other nations can achieve justice only through participation in the worldwide economic process. It is this interdependence, or commonality, in which justice must be a criterion for economic activity.

4) Cultural Freedom and the Criticism of Culture

Cultural traditions must, for the sake of their authenticity, be open to criticism. Cultural freedom must take concrete form in the explicit recognition of reflection on culture as a critique of culture.

What distinguishes living cultural traditions from mere traditionalism or conventionalism is that they are open to a critique that functions as the criterion for their faithfulness to truth. Such a critique identifies a culture's own constructive character and applies it to those values or ideas of the good that are generally acknowledged as distinctive. We use here the expression "value" in the sense of that which experience has shown to be of value, because the only reason cultural traditions are handed on is that they represent forms of expression that have been tested by experience in mastering the tasks set for us by a culture.

The differentiation found in a highly developed culture cannot be expressed in a specific formula by which the sum of its experienced values could be determined. The identity of a living culture ranges from the values of socialization in the nuclear family to the global forms of expression of a cultural realm. Phenomenology of culture is not the task of ethics. If the present state of a culture is to be understood as the sum total of cultural history, we can speak only of an open identity. Ethics is interested in this openness in terms of truth in relationship to the process by which tradition is formed. This question cannot be dealt with through a general philosophy of culture but by a specific study of culture that is oriented to its activities, or better, to the ways it expresses itself through the graphic arts and the fine arts, in literature, music, and so forth.

To sum up the cultural task, it sets the theme explicitly and specifically for the process through which cultural tradition is formed in ever new and varying ways, and it makes visible the "constructive nature of human culture." In this sense, culture is relevant when it is not an image of trite cultural generalities, well-known points of view, and common ways of thinking, but where it makes itself known in altering perspectives, in dissolving and reforming the ways we see, portray, and hear the contingent nature of culture. Thus culture, with the explicit and independent formation of verbal and symbolic images, can be seen in the general sense as a critique of culture; indeed it is a critique of culture through cultural productions. Distancing oneself from the practical values of a culture, however varied these may be, brings into play the original sense of freedom in the activities that shape culture in relation to the practical values established through the process by which culture is formed. It makes explicit the way in which a culture can reflect on its component features.

Here a problem arises that is relevant not only esthetically but also ethically: it is the freedom to criticize culture, to live in a culture that can bring a critique against itself. What are the factors that play a role in establishing this freedom? Providing the freedom for cultural expression is a responsibility that follows of necessity from the humane and thus constructive nature of culture. To forbid free, innovative, and critical cultural expression in relation to an existing culture would mean the end of the process of cultural formation itself and the denial of its own preconditions. Such a prohibition could only be based on the belief that a specific cultural identity is the only correct one, and that it is essential to protect it from criticism or to establish it in preference to all others. Such a prohibition is usually based on political intentions that use the forms of cultural expression to preserve and enforce the will of those in power and makes those forms the servants of that will.

Much the same can be said of the reversal of the prohibition of cultural freedom in the form of the demand for a cultural revolution. A permanent, universally obligatory, root-and-branch transformation of cultural traditions could be required only on the basis of the political conviction that the power to change people through culture was totally at the disposal of the political will.

Cultural freedom as the freedom of a culture to bring a critique against itself is subject to the condition that this freedom must be expressed in forms that can be distinguished from popular culture and its practices. Here we find the ethical authority of the specifically esthetic forms of expression of "culture," as distinct from the direct moral or political will of the artist. It is only the form of the esthetic expression which mediates between the individual—at times moral and political—feelings of the artist and the general cultural effects of a work of art. Artistic freedom in all its forms is conditioned on a factor that is indissolubly tied to its ethical independence. This independence of cultural expression is particularly necessary when "culture" is not affirmative of but critical toward the existing culture and thus raises the question of the adequacy or the authenticity of that culture. The problem that arises here can lead to the discussion of what constitutes the moral relevance of explicitly cultural productions and whether there is such a thing as a direct ethical or political responsibility of art and literature. It is not the direct moral or political intention of the artist, but the intention mediated esthetically, that can and must be the sole object of cultural freedom. The form in which the critique is presented, that is, the form in which the content of a culture is portrayed symbolically in a specific aspect, demonstrates the freedom of the culture in that it does not prescribe the consequences for the actual culture but leaves that to the impact of the esthetic expression. The goal of such cultural freedom can therefore not be the direct action that produces specific consequences, but the stimulus to reflect on the culture in relationship to its traditional content and to view historically conditioned traditions in the light of the process by which they were formed. To this extent there is only an indirect ethic of cultural expression, which leads to direct ethical demands only where the freedom of culture, for whatever reason, is denied; but there the demands are unconditional.

There is a similar connection between scientific freedom and the threat to that freedom when science is politicized.

The more varied a culture is, the greater the awareness that even the traditions that are relevant and binding for everyday life belong to esthetic or scientific categories, so that the general impression may arise that there is a permanent cultural war going on. In such circumstances, where a culture is highly differentiated, the temptation may arise to subject the entire culture and its manifestations to a specific way of thinking. This occurs when an ideology is imposed. The only concrete way I know of to oppose this temptation is to identify clearly the ways and means of activity and the various competencies involved in them.

Freedom for cultural and scientific activity does not provide answers for all areas of life but is itself connected with the essential forms of expression and activity in all areas. In their presuppositions and their potential consequences, esthetics and scientific methodology are and must be clearly distinguishable from the modes of action in other dimensions of life, such as politics and economics. The goal of this ethical line of argument is to clarify the question of truth by means of a critique that is concerned with the preservation of the free and open conditions under which the question of truth can be posed in an unhampered manner for the cultural condition.

5) Truth and Religious Freedom

The church must test its own worthiness of the tradition by measuring its traditions by the truth of its confessional statements.

Religious and ecclesiastical traditions are not automatically preserved from traditionalism and conventionalism. In the context of the religious life and its institutional form, the question of truth is encountered in the specific question of confessing the faith. Ethical discussion must not only perceive the meaning of religious freedom as the question of truth in religion in a legal sense, but it must also consider it in relation to the content and structure of its confessional statements.

At this point only brief reference can be made to religious freedom as one of the basic elements in contemporary constitutions and in discussions of human rights. In the context of the state and political life, religious freedom has the clear meaning that the quality of a citizen's relationship to the political community may not be made dependent on any religious profession. That is the first meaning of religious neutrality under law. But this legal meaning of religious freedom owes its existence to a specific understanding of the content of religious profession and means not simply neutrality but a neutrality defined by a religious principle.

The historical and theological presupposition of the concept of religious freedom is that any confessional document itself raises the question of truth in reference to the traditions of religious awareness of the church. The specific feature of the Reformation confessions that is relevant for the ethical discussion is that they make clear the difference between "human traditions," in which the religious experience of the church is found, and the truth to which those traditions refer. If it is the case, as the Augsburg Confession teaches (CA VII), that human traditions can have a positive significance that promotes the order of church life but are not theologically binding, then the distinction between the content of the confession and the religious and ecclesiastical traditions of the practice of religion is the place at which the content of the confession addresses the church concerning its openness to the question of truth. Thus in this respect the confession always contains a critique of tradition. This is also true of the historical fact that the churches, separated as they are by their confessions, seek to be assured of their identity precisely through their confessional nature. One point of view sees in denominational differences nothing but scandal, but for the ethical argument it is important that the differing orientations of Christian churches to their confessions at least make it explicit in an objective manner that their ecclesiastical traditions are open to the truth that they affirm.

Any church that takes its orientation from a confessional standard is again and again challenged to apply the confession to itself and therefore to reject any equating of church traditions with the truth from which the church lives. The problem that confronts churches based on a confessional position is thus quite different from the guarantee of general religious freedom by the state. A consideration of the plurality of the mutually differing churches from the point of view of sociology of religion tends to see them as mutually complementary to one another or as possessing unity in their diversity, which makes it desirable in principle to strive for actual unity. But the guiding principle cannot be the abrogation of dependence on a confessional standard in order to achieve an undifferentiated church unity. We must not allow the goal of unity to be the disappearance of that distinction established by reliance on confessions—the distinction between the formation of religious traditions in the churches and the truth that has been committed to them. The ethically relevant question is oriented to a different goal, the achieving of clarity over the extent to which the nature and the content of our confessions themselves require this distinction. Obviously there are differences in the content of the confessions so that the distinction between the church and its truth is not expressed in the same way everywhere. For the sake of the truth, it is not possible simply and directly to reduce them to uniformity. According to the Protestant view, the process of forming religious and ecclesiastical tradition is an example of the differences in the self-understanding of the church, oriented to the doctrine of justification solely through trust in God's justifying grace, without any works on our part. Ecclesiologically, this leads automatically to the application to the church itself of the distinction between church tradition and the truth of the faith. Religious freedom applies then not only to the church's external relationships but also within the church. In the interests of truth, however, such an understanding of the church cannot simply be merged with another concept of the church, according to which the church by its ecclesial power in its dealings with people simply lays absolute claim to the truth through its own religious juridical form. In the context of an ethical discussion, and that is all that is involved here, the question must be raised as to how far an ecumenical movement whose goal is the unity of the process of religious tradition in a pan-Christian context can at the same time ward off the tendency to restrict the question of truth at the decisive point, that is, where it must be decided by the truthfulness of a church's own organization. The ecumenical movement encounters unavoidable difficulties in its fundamentally appealing concept of unity when it shows itself uncomfortable with the critical force of the question of truth for an understanding of ecumenism. At the same time other features of the ecumenical movement indicate that it has set in motion a process of mutual relativizing through which the adherents of the differing churches become aware of their common relativity in respect to a truth that none of them have at their disposal, but for the sake of which they must reaffirm their loyalty to confessions that are distinct from each other.

Empirical uniformity of the process of forming religious tradition is in any case not of value in itself and is no condition for the credibility of the church in an absolute sense. The theological reasons (in this sense, the reasons oriented to truth) that support an openness for a common formation of tradition are not in any case the same for all the separated churches. For the Roman Catholic Church or the Orthodox Church they are different from what they are for the churches of the Reformation. Thus it is not good to postulate as the goal of the process of forming tradition an identity of the empirical churches with the truth that they serve. The ethical authority of the question of truth for the process of religious tradition must also be accepted as relevant for the theological desire for unity and must remain open for religious freedom.

For a discussion of unity and confessional identity, see in particular the penetrating contributions of W. Pannenberg, *Ethik und Ekklesiologie*, ET *The Church*, 1983, pp. 59–83, 84–98, 99–115; J. Baur, "Kirchliches Bekenntnis und neuzeitliches Bewusstsein," in *Einsicht und Glaube*, 1978, pp. 269–88; H. Fischer, "Bekenntnis und Argumentation. Hermeneutische Probleme heutigen Umgangs mit dem Augsburger Bekenntnis," in *Das "Augsburger Bekenntnis" von 1530 damals und heute*, eds. B. Lohse and O. H. Pesch, 1980, pp. 237–52.

3. Dealing with Conflict: Applications of Reflection on Life

The applications of ethics are not exhausted by the doctrine of the basic structures and the tasks of the active life. Reflective thought about the realities of life, by virtue of which the ethical task always does and must become our theme anew, has its own place as a dimension of ethical discussion. It becomes an explicit topic in the face of conflicting differences among people. Life situations in which reflection on the realities of our lives becomes inescapable are to be found everywhere that the pros and cons of ethical issues are found. Ethics is not the study of problems that have been solved, of ready answers, of ethical successes. It is the basic way of dealing with the problem of how to live our lives. An openness to dealing with conflicts provides entry for ethical discussion in problem areas. They belong to the reality of life through which ethical discussion is handed on (vol. 1, pp. 26ff.). It is necessary to emphasize this once again because the positions that are formulated here in detail invite disagreement. Conflicts make it necessary for us to formulate our own arguments in order to bring the basic principles of ethics to bear on them in a specific way, but also in order to conduct ourselves properly and to contribute to the reformulation of ethical questions.

When we are dealing with conflicts, it is not possible for us to adopt any position we please. Reflective thought about life's realities involves a specific direction—the acknowledgment and affirmation of life. The first aspect of the argument to be developed here deals with the necessity of acknowledging the ways in which people differ from one another and in their relationship to their environment. This must always be taken into account in our activities. The revision, alteration, and expansion of our activity finds concrete expression in the various realms of life, in a manner analogous to our first two explorations of concrete ethical issues. Second, if we are to act responsibly in situations of conflict, we must express our affirmation of life and therefore must take a stand in the ambiguity of the situation of conflict. Third, in our search for ethical orientation on the boundaries of what is available to us for action, we must once again explore the justification of actions that even in conflict maintain the basic meaning of the ethical task. These three aspects of our reflections on life can be summed up in a maxim that may be expressed as follows: Act in such a way that what you do is always open to the recognition of the differences among human beings, in conflicts always expresses an affirmation of life, and at the boundaries of your activities is led by your experiences of the good.

a. The Necessity of Recognizing Differences

The positions represented here in reflective thought about life first find expression in concrete examples involving the recognition of differences in our common life. The social nature of life does not eliminate differences; freedom does not exclude dependence but includes it. Readiness to deal explicitly with reflection on life therefore provides new impulses to ethical insight.

1) Equality of Men and Women:
Emancipation as the Extension of the Family Ethos?

The demand for equality of men and women is a concrete example of reflection on the reality of life. Recognizing the differences among persons is the way to make our common life productive.

The demand for the equality of women and men is today (still?) primarily a demand for emancipation of women from social norms and traditional ways of life that make women subordinate to men.

In the history of Christianity we can see at this point the effects of the "dogmatizing" of Paul's statement "the women should keep silence in the churches" (1 Cor. 14:34) and the prohibition of marriage for priests and members of religious orders as *status perfectionis*. Today we can observe the revival for our Christian point of view of the use of Gal. 3:28, "There is neither male nor female, for you are all one in Christ Jesus."

Equality means that women be accorded in society a position comparable to that of men through equal treatment, as, for example, through legislation. Neither in history nor in individual lives is "man" an asexual being. But sexual polarity or social position is not free of quasi-natural ambiguity, so that it could serve as a universal validation of social differences.

The social history of the relation between men and women does not provide us with any unconditional obligation that would exclude the possibility of changing traditional regulations. The same is true of the sexual history contained in everyone's biography. Gender is a condition of life into which a person grows, a process in which one becomes a man or a woman. In the maturation process of young people this plays a prominent role. But each person grows beyond the immediate influence of this situation, and sexuality is integrated into the totality of the way we live. Therefore, in respect to one's life history, sexual identity is not an absolute or universal identification of a human being.

The emancipation of women as the demand for equal treatment therefore affects the relationship between men and women as a dependence that is not defined the same way for both. To a large extent emancipation means a clarification of relationships of dependence, the identification of direct or indirect effects, and thus the elimination of claims that are only seemingly unalterable. Therefore the research into the influence on the position of women in society exerted by social history and by the history of individual lives occupies a prominent place in the discussion of liberation. This work of clarification will not be reviewed here.

A prominent starting point for establishing in concrete ways the equality of women in relation to men is the question of employment and career opportunities for women. The historical movement developed from a period when any occupational activity by women was undervalued and emphasis was placed solely on women's work as mother, wife, and housekeeper, to a reversal in which those callings were deprecated in favor of professional activities for women. In this respect liberation is oriented around the dominant position of men in the various occupations. Thus the problem of dependence and liberation has merely taken on a new social orientation, because all professional activity, no matter how freely it is chosen, is subject to the conditions of social dependence, which create new and different problems. This is clearly seen today when it is said that the liberation of women, which comes through taking up an occupation, is a "male" answer and reinforces the characteristics of society that are defined in terms of a person's work and achievements. That is by no means an argument against the role of women in the workplace, but it does relativize the expectations of liberation that this involves. Belittling the tasks of mothers, wives, and housekeepers is the involuntary price paid for liberation from the "male" image. The opposite case of a man undertaking the responsibilities of the household is (still?) infrequent but is a likely consequence. The activities defined by the terms *home* and *family* must not be shoved aside by the tasks at which we are employed and thus end up at the bottom of the scale of values as objects of contempt. They have their own proper rank in life as tasks that are common to us all. A women's liberation that fed on criticism of the tasks of the home would fall far short and be poorly defined in its social meaning.

Women's liberation can therefore have still another meaning: A specific feminine life style in relation to a "man's world" can play for our life in society in all its dimensions a new role that will transform our standards. In this respect what we can have is not liberation of women from that which distinguished them as women from men, but a liberation in which women's distinctive characteristics come to a development and effectiveness that transcends the domestic scene.

Any catalog of "feminine" virtues, attitudes, ways of behavior, and impulses can be easily exposed as historical prejudices. There are, of course, good reasons for criticizing public life for the lack of those traits which historically, especially in the history of Christianity, have been primarily associated with women: patience, readiness for sacrifice, compassion, love, and so forth. But these virtues are not gender-specific, as if every woman and every man had specific virtues merely on the basis of sex. They are situation-specific. In this respect women's liberation means the opportunity in the reality of social life, especially in its public relationships, to expand the scope of peaceful, considerate orientation of our actions in reaching out to others, virtues that have their place in individual situations and in situations in the family or in the neighborhood.

Women's liberation, equality of women with men, does not then mean uniformity, abstract equality, but a mutually considerate recognition of the differences that arise from the uniqueness of each person. It means acceptance of community in our life together with persons who differ from one another but who in these differences are in relationship with one another. Far beyond sexuality in the strict sense, the sexual nature of persons is the theme of the independence and the inalienable individuality of men and women, expressed in our belonging together, our life in community, which as such is not at the direct disposal of any of us.

For the discussion of equality of women and men and sex roles, see E. Hahn, *Partnerschaft. Ein Beitrag zum Problem der Gleichberechtigung von Mann und Frau*, 1953; H. Ringeling, *Die Frau zwischen gestern und morgen. Der socialtheologische Aspekt ihrer Gleichberechtigung*, 1962; R. Nave-Hertz, "Über die gewandelte Rolle der Frau in unserer Gesellschaft," in *Theol. Quart.*

Schr. 156 (1076): 100ff.; E. Moltmann-Wendel, *Freiheit, Gleichheit, Schwesterlichkeit. Zur Emanzipation der Frau,* 1977; H. Schenk, *Geschlechtsrollenwandel und Sexismus,* 1979; A. Allemann-Tschopp, *Geschlechtsrollen,* 1979; A. Degenhardt and H. M. Trautner, eds., *Geschlechtstypisches Verhalten,* 1979.

To provide scope for this relationship of the sexes to each other beyond marriage and family, to include the social tasks that transcend individualism, this is the other ethically relevant aspect of the equality of women and men. The structure and content of equality in this sense can therefore be further clarified by looking at the family.

The family is the specific social structure, membership in which has been previously determined. Therefore all concrete goals and expectations, but also conflicts and arguments, are related to this elementary relationship. The ethos of the family consists in accepting this relationship with all its consequences for the life of the individual in the family, including adapting one's way of life to it. Family life is characterized by a basic expectation of trust, which each child gives to the father and mother, but also to brothers and sisters, and without which the child is not able to live his or her own life.

The response to this fundamental expectation of trust requires tolerance. It must be expressed in a multiplicity of individual acts performed in relation to the children and in response to this expectation. It must also go beyond specific expectations of care and devotion in a general spirit of toleration. The family's tolerance is called upon every day throughout the life of the family to an ever-increasing degree and in an atmosphere of mutuality. In this way it is an ever new affirmation that the members of the family belong together. Tolerance is required in the totality of the individual actions and attitudes in which the unity of the family is realized through the years. However varied the life of the family may be in age differences, changing external relationships to society, to school, and to community, in friendships and relations to other groups, it is a history of continuous attempts to be tolerant of one another.

A family's practice of tolerance includes the differences among those who as husband, wife, children, and brothers and sisters, comprise the family. This is the distinctive point of view that is decisive here. In the family no one is simply a "human being," but all are human beings in individually differing ways, ways that are determined by the social nature of the family. The family, to be sure, is not the only or the exclusive definition of social relationships. But it is, in relationships to those outside the family such as children to their peers and friends, the specific social form in which tolerance is expressed as the recognition of a community that does not negate the differences among its members but integrates them and is patient with them.

From what we have said here it follows that the family cannot without further thought simply be made an instrument for other purposes, be they social, political, or religious.

Totalitarian societies tend to view families as important agents in socialization and thus as forcefully as possible press them into serving the political purposes of the total society. Such societies fail to acknowledge the individual nature of life at the level of its primary social form.

Such tendencies to use people as instruments for political goals appear wherever pedagogical theories of socialization single out a specific goal of socialization from the total reality of the family. If, for example, the meaning of the socialization process is seen exclusively in the achieving of independence and identity for the person reaching maturity, it may easily appear as if family relationships with their demands for tolerance are only means toward the goal of socialization or, in cases of conflict, hindrances that must be overcome by transferring them into other forms of socialization. But the ability to take part in the life of a family is also an essential part of the maturity of the young adult, for that is the primary and decisive manifestation of our social nature.

While it is important to provide help for families in specific cases of need and while it is right to do so through advice, counsel, and financial assistance (especially in the many instances where the empirical reality of the family is in a precarious situation), it would be wrong to minimize the specific meaning of the social nature of the family, including its elementary need for mutual tolerance, by playing down that meaning in favor of the purposes of the larger society or abstract requirements for autonomy. Therefore political activity in all its forms in reference to the family must not have as its goal a "better" equivalent for the families that are actually in existence. That would not be wise because no one understands or can be certain how the establishment of other social institutions could be successful in correcting the failures of family life, much less in negating it altogether. Programs of social organizations outside family life can be appropriate only if oriented to the basic structure of the family.

On the historical and sociological aspects of research on the family, see R. König, *Materialen zur Soziologie der Familie*, 1974; D. Schwab, "Familie," in

Geschichtliche Grundbegriffe. Historisches Lexikon zur politische-soziale Sprache in Deutschland, eds. O. Brunner, W. Conze, and R. Koselleck, vol. 2, 1975; D. Claessens, *Familie und Wertsystem,* 2d ed., 1967; F. Eilser, *Einführung in die Familien Soziologie,* 1978; E. Shorter, *Die Geburt der modernen Familie,* 1977.

For works that are evaluative and take positions, see *Die Frau in Familie, Kirche und Gesellschaft, Eine Studie zum gemeinsamen Leben von Frau und Mann,* ed. Evangelical Church of Germany, 1979; *Familie in Wandel,* ed. H. Ringeling and M. Svilar, 1979.

Women's liberation, equality of women and men, is now, seen against this background, a formula for the "extension of the ethos of the family," for the extension of the meaning of the family for ethics and for the world in which we live. Arnold Gehlen, who coined this phrase (*Moral und Hypermoral,* 1969, pp. 83ff.) did so, to be sure, from aversion and contempt for the humanitarian ethos that it represents. Nonetheless, the observations and historical and sociological analyses that have been produced are illuminating and describe the state of affairs precisely. It is a situation that we can and should view positively.

Against this background we may also speak of the limits of the family. Just as the family is worthy of recognition by the whole of society, so too is the family under obligation to be open to society. In this respect as well as others, the family is a place for processing the requirements and claims of society. That an individual belongs to "society" is not as obvious to the individual as is our belonging to the family. For example, the family is a place of ongoing dialogue where our attitudes toward and our orientation to life in society are clarified and tested in the relatively safe climate of approval and belonging. But even so, society does not offer, nor do its groups, parties, and activities, anything of equal value to the family. The family can prepare persons for life in society and, if necessary, for opposition to it. It is not the final, ultimate value of community. It can be regarded as a distinct harbinger of the "family of man," of the "people of God," and so forth. Thus moving beyond the specific, individual family, independence from that family does not mean a breach with the elementary obligations that constitute the ethical significance of the family. It is not a stage of a movement that ultimately leads to the disappearance of the family. It is only a single step on the way to the formation of new nuclear or extended families.

In this process women's liberation, as a program for achieving independence from traditional roles in the family and in society, is the bringer of a new consciousness for the task of expansion of the ethical significance of the family.

2) Parties as the Political Form of Freedom

As structural features of political life, political parties represent reflective thought on the realities of life in the accomplishment of the political task. In the recognition of the role of parties, the differences within the commonwealth are made productive.

Political parties are an answer to the question of how, under a democratic constitution, the reflective thought of the body politic can be brought to bear publicly in the form of recognized differences, and thus how the social nature of liberty can find concrete expression for political activity, for its structure, and for its application.

The ethical problematic of this task can be perceived first of all against the background of the negative image that the concept of party has had throughout its history. Seen in historical terms, parties have not been regarded as having a very high moral worth. "Party spirit" carries with it the idea that truth is subordinated to partisan interests. A "party politician" is thought of as one who does not work for the common good but for the advantage of his or her party. "Party conflict" carries the connotation that the matter in question is subordinated to the desire to assert the will of that particular party. The concept of party thus "belongs to those few political concepts that for a long time indeed have had negative connotations, seemingly independent of the political points of view involved." A positive evaluation of the concept of political party is the result "of the distinction between the political subsystem and the total system of a society"; that is, "in correlation to the state of development of parliamentarian systems." This development took place largely after the Second World War. The historic development of the concept of parties is largely a history of a concept that draws distinctions. (The quotations in this paragraph on the history of the concept of party are taken from page 677 of the article of Klaus von Beyme, "Partei, Faktion," in *Geschichtliche Grundbegriffe*, vol. 4, pp. 677–733.)

A frequently encountered negative view of parties—characterized by a moralistic tone—is based on the position that the political task of the state is basically unambiguous and that through the involvement or interference of parties a basically superfluous conflict is stirred up, a conflict that wherever possible should be suppressed or avoided. But the features of empirical party life that are in this way condemned as negative are themselves expressions of reflective thought on life within political reality. The concrete nature of political freedom is encountered here in the equivocal nature of the current political task. It involves the effort to put forward alternatives, to struggle over priorities. The formation of parties is the manner in which this task is given shape. The recognition of parties, in contrast to the assumption of an unequivocal nature of the political task independent of parties, is a given of democracy. The ethical debate must therefore concentrate on the structure of the parties as concrete expressions of the reflective nature of political freedom.

Political parties are functions of a living democratic constitution. Therefore their plurality is a necessary criterion for their existence. This pluralism of parties is not something arbitrary but is based on a common life by which and for the sake of which parties always remain parties. The structure of a democratic party system works against the equating of a single party with the common good. This is because the plurality of parties that compete for the exercise of power in public life keeps open for all citizens the possibility of political alternatives, and thus the distinction between the will of those holding political power and the will of the public. By means of parties, citizen participation in the formation of the public will has a concrete base where the express acknowledgment of differences and alternatives plays a role. It is not an individual party in itself, but the reciprocal and shared relationship of parties to the common good, that is, the structure of the party system, that contains and renews the meaning of the political party system for a free society.

The totalitarian nature of a one-party system thus always presents us with an absolute claim to political authority that makes impossible the political task for the sake of which parties are formed, and thus subordinates the objective structure of freedom of the commonwealth to the will of a specific party.

The ethical issue here involves primarily the political form that the party system assumes. To define the issue more precisely, the task of political parties involves taking into account the necessity of their being acknowledged by the citizenry. This takes place as the parties regularly seek the support of the people in elections. In this way both parties and people are under the requirement (in a party spirit as organizations for promoting special interests) not merely to pursue mere party interests but to be oriented to the total interests of the party system. The necessity of having parties is not absolute in either a historic or a systematic sense. It is, rather, due to the appropriateness of parties in a representative democracy, that is, the appropriateness of an organization of political affairs in which an individual citizen is not directly involved in political activities in the narrow sense—legislation and the exercise of power. Thus representative democracy can be regarded as pragmatic, because the size and the internal differentiation of a community involves grounds for doing politics through representation.

This representative function of the parties is also full of consequences for the citizens. The parties have the task of communicating to the state the individual interests that are alive in a community. If these interests were not expressed politically at all, the state would have no defense against an autocratic exercise of absolute power and would be unable to fulfill its inherent responsibilities in a manner that would respect freedom.

If, on the other hand, these individual interests had direct influence on the exercise of power, the state would be threatened with permanent destruction and would be unable to carry out its political tasks in the basic sense. In respect to the citizens, parties have the responsibility to transform special individual interests into political tasks. Not everything that is of interest to the citizens of a state is of significant political interest. This work of transformation is necessary to prevent the direct influence of individual interests from disrupting the political life of the community. It is also important to postulate a relative independence of the parties from the direct will of the voters. In concrete terms that means that a democratic party system, in contrast to a one-party system, is recognized by its citizens as performing through its parties the task of mediating between them and the government.

In respect to both the public good and the citizens, political parties perform a key function for the achievement of a political order oriented to making freedom a reality. They are a basic element in the efforts of the political organization to think reflectively on political life.

On the systematic structure and sociology of political parties, see E. W. Böckenförde, *Die Verfassungstheoretische Unterscheidung von Staat und Gesellschaft als Bedingung der individuellen Freiheit*, 1973; U. von Alemann, *Parteiensysteme und Parlamentarismus*, 1973; J. Dittberner and R. Ebbighausen, eds., *Parteiensystem in der Legitimationskrise. Studien und Materialien zur Soziologie der Parteien in der BDR*, 1973; U. von Alemann, ed., *Partizipation—Demokratisierung—Mitbestimmung*, 2d ed., 1978; H. Kaack and R. Roth, eds., *Handbuch des deutschen Parteiensystems*, 2 vols., 1980; E. Wiesendahl, *Parteien und Demokratie*, 1980.

A specific problem in this context is the question of the ideological orientation of parties, as expressed in their programs or in the setting of general goals. Under the premises stated above, the ideology that defines a party should be one that distinguishes it from other parties. But the ideologies of parties are also to be measured by whether their content corresponds to the tasks defined by the common good. They should not formulate any total claims that in all respects, including their political form itself, could be achieved only by this one party. The limits of a party's ideology are encountered when it defines itself as the exclusive possibility for achieving the common good defined by the constitution. A party's ideological orientation must always be related to the existing life of the community and be capable of being interpreted in harmony with it.

The question of the meaning and purpose of a "Christian" party must also be subject to these premises. In both historic and systematic terms, a party can define its orientation in such a way that it measures itself by existing Christian traditions. In political terms, this must be an orientation to which the party does not have exclusive claim but whose content involves a shared obligation to political activity that transcends the party. In specific historical contexts, this can find expression in that "Christian" parties take on the nature of a group of like-minded persons, a partisan coterie, as was the case in the early postwar period, and thus set themselves off in sharp distinction to parties that are defined by a distinctive ideology.

The critical demands to which a party subjects itself find concrete expression in the conflict over normative orientation, in particular the political orientation that acknowledges responsibility for and the limits of political action in issues where human dignity and freedom are involved. Thereby political activity submits to the authority implicit in human liberty, authority that in some cases can also be brought into play in a critique of such activity. The claim expressed in the designation of a party as "Christian" can therefore never be identical with political claims of the party.

In this sense the term *Christian* defines for a party a self-limitation of its ideological claims, a limitation that can and must apply to all parties that in the interest of the common good are subject to the constitution and to law. In order to make clear what is meant here, we might formulate a model of the consequences as follows: Parties that explicitly serve the fundamental meaning of the political constitution of the life of the community can by virtue of this function, if they correctly understand what is involved, be designated as Christian parties. As a consequence we can conceive of a situation in which, alongside a Christian-Democratic Union, there could also be a "Christian" Socialdemocratic Party, and a "Christian" Free Democratic Party. See T. Rendtorff, *Politische Ethik und Christentum,* 1978, pp. 33ff.

This discussion leads to a third way in which a Christian party is related to "Christianity outside the party." One feature of the structure of Christianity is that it cannot and may not exercise any institutional force that would equate membership in a Christian church with the requirement or the preference that one belong to a specific "Christian" party. The independence of the churches in relation to politics is expressed in their recognition that political parties are independent. The authority of the churches can therefore not be expressed in terms of direct political intentions but must be open to and supportive of the structure of a democratic party system. Granted this presupposition, it is essential for the way we understand the content of the political task that through the existence of "Christian" parties the question be held open as to what are the political responsibilities of the Christian community as a result of the open nature of political activity, in contrast to political movements that have as their goal the elimination or restriction of relevant religious traditions. In respect to this issue, the existence of "Christian" parties in politics signifies that parties and the agencies of the state are not the only concrete expressions of the ethical realities of life, and that they do not control these realities but are in their service.

3) Participation in the Economy

Participatory management is a concrete expression of the cooperation of all those involved in the process of industrial production.

Participatory management is a program for the solution of issues that are inherent in a specific manner in modern industrial production. They involve the form in which reflective thought about economic activity takes place. When we speak of such reflective thought in this context we mean the problems that arise from the mutual dependence of capital and labor in the production process itself. Problems arise in all the necessary decisions, the interdependence, and the consequences for those involved, especially for those in the workforce. They involve problems within the industry itself as well as conflicts that arise in the total economic process. The structural problem is how to carry out this reflective thought without giving advantage to only one party in the participatory management. Therefore economic activity must be given a form that is open to the processes of reflective thought.

The following books are basic for an orientation in terms of social ethics: A. Rich, *Mitbestimmung in der Industrie*, 1973; W. Sohn, *Der soziale Konflikt als ethisches Problem,* 1971; and a number of the chapters in the Festschrift for A. Rich, ed. Th. Strohm, *Christliche Wirtschaftsethik vor neuen Aufgaben,* 1980. See also the positions taken by the EKD, *Sozialethische Erwägungen zur Mitbestimmung in der Wirtschaft in der Bundesrepublik Deutschland,* 1968, found in *Die Denkschriften der EKD,* vol. 2, 1978, pp. 85–111.

The legal and social form that participatory management takes may vary, but its basic goal is to make it possible for the conflicts determined by economic factors and by situations of dependence to be dealt with in a common context. Seen from the point of view of history, participatory management has derived its most enduring impulse from the "social question," that is, from the efforts to strengthen the position of the workforce as subjects rather than objects. But participatory management includes more than the individual problems of working men and women and their self-determination. The status of the workers as autonomous subjects in relation to the power of management should come into play in a manner that helps determine economic activity.

We shall examine here two aspects of the ethically relevant structure of the concept of participatory management, first in reference to the internal structure of the organization, and second in reference to the relationship of the economy to democracy. As for the first aspect, we can say, "The idea of the participation of the workforce in management is the German workers movement's alternative to class struggle" (H. Koch, "Die Mitbestimmungsidee in der evangelisch-sozialen Tradition," *ZEE* 20 (1976): 114). As an alternative it deals with the same problem as the theory of class struggle. The latter places the contrast between capital and labor in the perspective of a historical struggle, at the end of which stands the inevitable victory of the working class over capital and by which the workers take over complete control of the means of production. Participatory management seeks to give to the problem of freedom and dependence a form that is viable in the present day. Expressed very abstractly, this is the problem under the conditions of mutual dependence: As they are, capital and labor can exist only in a mutual relationship, capital only by means of labor and labor only by means of capital. This situation of mutual dependence can then be taken as a challenge if the social aspects of the situation are recognized. "Participatory management instead of class struggle" means expressly structuring the mutual dependence as a social relationship. Thus if we seek to organize the economy on the basis of participatory management, our goal will be to translate abstract, structural opposition into forms of real and concrete participation in a common task. This task does not directly involve the position of managers or that of workers, but their relationship to each other, because it involves "internal reflection" on the economic process.

Therefore the ethical significance of participatory management points us in the direction of providing for the economy an order that is appropriate to its proper tasks and thus moves out of the turmoil of an unjust division of power into a system of cooperation (A. Rich).

For further discussion, see F. Wagner, "Sozialethik als Theorie des Geistes," *ZEE* 19 (1975): 197–214.

Thus the success of participatory management is to be measured by whether it does not disrupt the productivity and the capacity of the economic process but instead enhances them. Above and beyond its legal form, participatory management derives its content through the task set by the economic process, the structure and specific form of which is at issue here. A program of participatory management is not a supplementary ethical requirement lying outside economic activity, but a program that makes the ethical task of structuring dependence in a manner commensurate with social freedom, making it concrete and attainable.

In its second aspect, the idea and practice of participatory management, both in its legal form and in its political motivation, is related to the structure of the life of the body politic, that is, to political democracy, even though it serves another purpose as well.

Early demands for a "constitutional structure for major industrial concerns," as, for example, in the idea of a "constitutional factory," were formulated by individual entrepreneurs and political scientists who were concerned that the organization of the economy should be seen in the context of the political system as an element of the social-political order. Thus from a point of view that takes the realities into account, economic activities are a constituent part of the common life. The overarching political structure leads to the requirement that the economy be structured in a manner analogous to the political order of the common life. The demand for a convergence of the economic order with the political structure of the community can become radicalized if participatory management in business also pursues political goals such as a new system of property and a redistribution of income, goals that tend to eliminate the difference between economic and political activity, the goal of total state control. Then participatory management would no longer be directed toward economic activities but would be a goal in itself. The concept of participation in the economy does not abolish the difference between clear and specific economic responsibility and comprehensive political responsibility. In any case, it is not possible to take the same reasons for reflective thought on economic activity, which are valid for a system of participation within an industrial or business concern, and use them to require a general, comprehensive participation that would eliminate the difference between the content of political and economic activity.

In this respect it is important to define the analogous role played by labor unions and by leaders in industry. The unions can appropriately regard their task as that of representing the interests of the workers as long as this is not thought of as identical with political duty (a state controlled by unions).

By the same token the managerial class, or those who control capital, cannot on the basis of their economic responsibility lay claim to the state (a state controlled by entrepreneurs). Thus participatory management in the economic world has a clearly defined significance only in a clearly limited relationship to the production process. It is not a way of subsuming political reflection on the reality of life under a specific economic determinism.

By means of participatory management the task of humanizing the workplace can become obligatory for economic activity, especially as participation in the internal life of a company. In such situations it always involves concrete relationships.

It is important to recall the well-known Hawthorne Experiment of 1927, from which dates the rise of modern industrial sociology. The experiment was conducted in Chicago by the General Electric Company. Its goal involved a purely internal matter at that company. It was designed to measure the results of changes in the immediate workplace on the productivity of the workers. Of special interest were various forms of illumination. The outcome of the experiment astonished the industrial engineers, because the group of men and women increased their productivity independent of the various changes in illumination and other conditions of the workplace. The first changes were improvements, but they were gradually reversed. Elton Mayo hit upon the idea that the decisive factor was not the technical changes in the workplace but the group itself. The special attention which they received and the special intensity of the concern shown by the members of the informal group for one another brought to light the importance of the human factor and human relationships. This discovery of the importance of informal groups was, in other words, the discovery that the experience of the meaningfulness of one's task is a social experience and is closely connected to the human relationships in the narrow context of the enterprise.

The evaluation of this discovery in terms of increasing productivity was highly ambivalent. Still it is the decisive starting point for the connection between a "humanizing of the workplace" and the demand for participation in decision making. The workers should themselves be involved in the structuring of human relations in the company, especially in the everyday organization of work, and thus in the concrete details of the manufacturing process. This involved and still involves such questions as were raised at one time among the followers of Taylorism.

F. W. Taylor (1856–1919) was the founder of so-called scientific management. The basis of this system for organizing work was the clear separation between those who planned work and those who carried it out (the distinction between white collar and blue collar workers). The goal was the strict organization of the manufacturing process in order to adapt the workers to new technical processes and means of production. Rational organization meant dividing the process into the smallest possible units in order to manage it more effectively, in organizational terms a completely rational division of work. Through increasingly fine division of the work units it was thought possible to simplify the activities of those involved in order to achieve maximum utilization of the work time and maximum efficiency in the work processes.

Participation of workers in decision making is a concrete application of humanizing the world of work, because humanization is not achieved at a specific time but constitutes a permanent task. In this sense participation can be regarded as an explicit form of reflective ethical thought within the economic process.

4) The Environment as the Relationship of Culture to Nature: The Possibility of Correcting the Consequences of Our Actions

Culture includes a reflective relationship to nature. Today such reflective thought requires new attention to the cultural shaping of our relation to nature as the environment of humankind.

The present state of development of our scientific and technological culture is determined by an increasingly intensive appropriation and exploitation of nature. In this the control of nature dominates over the care and protection of nature as a major component of the world in which we live. The consequences of our control of nature lead today to the critical question of whether human freedom over against nature must not be confronted by an awareness of our dependence on nature, and in this nature plays its own independent role. This leads to the very serious question of whether the relationship of humans to nature does not demand a dependence and a limitation of our freedom that corresponds to the social relationships of human beings to one another. In order to express the reflective thought of culture on our relationship to nature, we can attempt to regard nature as an autonomous "partner" of humans, with the demand that nature must be recognized as being such a partner. Criticism of the present system of human adaptation of nature to our own uses seeks therefore to develop from the dependence of humankind on nature the idea of the autonomy of nature over against humans, in the sense of Barry Commoner's law "Nature knows best." In a radicalizing of ecological consciousness we find attempts to formulate the binding quality of our relation to nature in a manner that integrates humanity as a part of nature and advances the idea of an ethical duty of humankind to find our place in the order of nature.

This critique of the human assumption of a position of superiority to nature rightly reminds us that in the past our relation to nature was regarded as an aspect of human culture. But such critics have neither theoretical nor practical grounds for claiming that nature has a comparable and independent position in which it is subject and the human race is object. The new awareness of the environment makes the valid point that human science and technology, though dominant over nature, is not a communication with nature but is a one-sided dominance and exploitation of nature. It would not be sensible to demand "communication" with nature on the same level as communication of persons with one another. Critics of the one-sided relation to nature through science and technology can point out that a culture dominated by technology alone no longer pays sufficient attention to reflective thought about its relation to nature. Human culture includes a relationship to nature and is dependent on it as the world in which it exists. Technology itself arose in relationship to nature, both in respect to the activities of culture in relation to nature and in the perception of basic physical ideas and concepts. The reduction of our relation to nature to the single aspect of its value, of domination and transformation, has largely resulted in the loss of a sense of nature as the world in which we must live. Seen in this way the problem reveals not only our present relation to nature but also a conflict within our culture that has arisen through the ever-increasing dominance of the scientific and technological dimensions of our culture. Thus it is highly appropriate to give concrete definition to the reflective thought in our culture that is found in discussions of environmental problems involving our culture in relation to nature, and to examine the consequences of our scientific and technological activities.

The problem confronted here can be formulated in general terms as follows: Human dominance of nature, in the form of use and exploitation, could throughout long periods of human history be described as serving the needs of human life, because the conditions under which nature always presented the possibility of its continuing use as a source of value to humankind were never considered to be in question. But the moment the awareness dawned that human dominance and exploitation of nature affected reproduction in the natural world itself so that in the long run the world of nature as the realm of human habitation could be destroyed by our domination, it was then no longer possible to avoid the question of how the relationship of human beings to nature, beyond our immediate interests in the current exploitation of nature, could be preserved or renewed.

In this extremely complex question we do not yet have completely reliable estimates of the condition of the natural world in which we live or of the possibilities of technological and scientific developments. Thus the field is open to interdisciplinary debate concerning wide-ranging speculations and complex moral demands. What they have in common is their orientation to the harmful or problematic consequences of developments in technology and science and their attempts to oppose those developments in every way possible.

For the relationship of our technological and scientific culture to nature, see the discussions in H.-R. Müller-Schwefe, *Technik und Glaube*, 1971; A. M. K. Müller, *Die präparierte Zeit. Der Mensch in der Krise seiner eigenen Zielsetzungen*, 1972; J. B. Cobb, Jr., and C. Amery, *Das Ende der Vorsehung. Die gnadenlosen Folgen des Christentums*, 1972; K. Scholder, *Grenzen der Vernunft*, 1973; G. Altner, *Schöpfung am Abgrund*, 1974; K. M. Meyer-Abich, "Zum Begriff einer Praktischen Theologie der Natur," *Evangelische Theologie* 37 (1977): 3–20; O. Jensen, *Unter dem Zwang des Wachstums. Ökologie und Religion*, 1977; and "Schöpfungstheologischer Materialismus. Zum Naturverständnis angesichts der ökologischen Krise," *NZsyst Th* 19 (1977): 247–60; G. Altner, et al., *Sind wir noch zu retten? Schöpfungsglaube und Verantwortung für unsere Erde*, 1978; K. M. Meyer-Abich, "Die Zukunft des Menschen in der Geschichte der Natur," in *Frieden mit der Natur*, ed. K. M. Meyer-Abich, 1979, pp. 11–37.

The problems of scientific and technological culture become concrete for our ethical discussion when and where they are relevant to our actions. We will not make progress by a stereotyped critique of that culture in general, nor by the demand for a totally different way of life, such as a sort of natural symbiosis of humankind and nature. It is only the consequences of our scientific and technological culture that provide a basis on which we can formulate our criticisms.

It is first of all necessary to distinguish between the intended and the unintended consequences of our actions. The intended consequences include victory over specific diseases, increased agricultural productivity, and the reduction of certain threats to life. The unintended consequences result from the means employed to bring about the intended consequences. As a rule there is consensus about the intended results. This is the side of progress about which consensus can be reached, because it is manifest in recognizable and obvious improvements in the world in which we live, improvements that can be experienced by everyone. The unintended results are those that no one wants but which appear or can appear under certain circumstances. These include such things as environmental pollution and destruction of the environment in ways that are obvious to everyone. There is no program that explicitly intends to produce these results. But both types of consequences result from the interaction of human activities with nature, that is to say, through our relationship with nature that is a part of our culture. Thus this relationship plays a decisive role in our critique.

A conflict necessarily arises when the unintended results wipe out the gain produced by the intended results or when they no longer permit any correction in the course we have chosen. Here we see the importance of the requirement that the intended activity through science and technology in relation to nature must be such that its results can be corrected, so that it can serve its long-range goals, those far beyond its immediate goals. This requirement can be expressed in the ethical maxim, So act that you will be able to correct what you do by means of the results of your actions. This maxim is applicable not merely to one's attitude but to the actual activity in the context of the results that the agent has sent in motion. The maxim cannot read, So act that you can correct the consequences of your actions in every individual instance. Such a maxim would require us to refrain from any action at all. Rather, the goal of the maxim is that the actual consequences of the actions seen in the difference between intended and unintended consequences would influence us in such a manner as to provide a corrective and to lead to a new definition of the intentions of the actions and of the instruments used to achieve them. The results of actions here represent the reflective thought of a technological and scientific culture and contrast with the realm in whose service the activities of that culture are carried out.

The question that must be posed today and discussed with all urgency is whether there are unknown consequences of the technological activity whose aim is the domination of nature, consequences that can never be altered. If, for example, it is true that in the production of energy results are set in motion that, according to our present state of knowledge, involve processes that are absolutely impossible to alter (either because of their duration or because of technical factors, for example, certain processes of radiation that last for ten thousand or more years, or processes of mutation that involve qualitatively unknown results), then it is our duty to turn scientific and technological research in a direction where there is still a possibility of correcting the consequences of that research.

Here only a few titles will be mentioned from the extensive literature on ecology: H. Westmüller, "Die Umweltkrise—eine Anfrage an Theologie und Christen," in *Umweltstrategie. Materialen und Analysen zu einer Umweltethik der Industriegesellschaft*, ed. H. D. Engelhardt, 1975, pp. 314–48; K. Oeser and H. Zillessen, eds., *Kernenergie—Mensch—Umwelt*, 1976; U. Kleinert, "Öko- logie und Theologie am Beispiel der Auseinandersetzung um die Kernenergie," *WuPKG* 68 (1979): 46–58; D. Birnbacher, *Ökologie und Ethik*, 1980; E. F. Schumacher, *Die Rückkehr zum menschlichen Mass*, 1977, 5th ed., 1980; E. F. Schumacher, *Das Ende unserer Epoche*, 1980; B. Frey, *Umweltökonomie*, 1972; Th. Strohm, "Ziele der Menschheit—Ethische Urteilsfindung im Horizont des Club of Rome," *ZEE* 22 (1978): 214–28.

The consequences of progress not only involve moral issues but are also the responsibility of scientists and technologists. They would not have carried out their responsibilities if progress produced consequences for which there was no possibility of correction. In such cases it would be irresponsible morally as well as scientifically and technologically, and therefore ethically, not to seek progress in another direction, because it would be irresponsible to shut our eyes to irreversible consequences. This criticism does not surrender the human relation to nature as subject to object without confronting the drive for progress at any price as a matter of course. The demand that our activities be subject to correction involves the relationship to nature that is a part of our culture.

Between scientific progress on the one hand and the use made of that progress by technology for economic purposes on the other, there is no inevitable, compelling, essential connection. The possibility of correcting the results of scientific and technological activity involves, quite apart from other aspects, the insight that the freedom of scientific research does not require a one-dimensional drive to produce something practical but instead involves the necessity of a critical evaluation of its own activities. To say "of its own activities" means also its relationship to nature. Reflective thought in a scientific and technological culture finds its application in that science and technology, along with their economic applications, involve a living world whose ethical significance is not the result of scientific and technological progress but is the precondition for any identifiable meaning that science and technology can have for us. It is an essential feature of the formation of a scientific and technological culture that is capable of accepting correction that it not be oriented solely to a domination of nature, but that it recognize that it is a part of a living world which makes science and technology possible and from which it must therefore accept correction. It is therefore not merely a question of individual problems that must be solved, such as cadmium in the soil, poison in the atmosphere, genetic engineering, though each of these is extremely dangerous. Such problems as these are indications of the basic problem whose structure we are exploring here.

In the development of reflective thought about our scientific and technological culture, it is essential that the experts in progress in these areas be willing to acknowledge that their activities need to be subject to correction and that they demonstrate this willingness by joining the discussion concerning the present crisis in our orientation to nature. The conflict between those who possess the expert knowledge but permit no criticism and those who are concerned with the problems resulting from scientific progress but can contribute only a moral awareness is evidence of this crisis. This division can be overcome only if the concept of the possibility and the necessity of correction is accepted as an integral part of the scientific and technological endeavor itself.

On the discussion of technology, technocracy, and responsibility, see, in addition to the sources mentioned above, the following: C.-H. Ratschow, "Die Technik als technologisches Problem," *Th. Gegw.* 15 (1972): 19–31; H. Lübbe, *Fortschritt als Orientierungsproblem. Aufklärung in der Gegenwart,* 1975; M. Buhr and G. Kröber, eds., *Mensch—Wissenschaft—Technik. Analyse der wissenschaftlich-technischen Revolution,* 1977; W. Ch. Zimmerli, ed., *Technik oder: wissen wir, was wir tun?* 1976; H. Beck, "Thesen zur Kulturphilosophie der

Technik," *Phil. Jb.* 86 (1979): 262–71; S. Wollgast and G. Banse, *Philosophie und Technik,* 1979; F. Rapp, *Analytische Technikphilosophie,* 1978; F. Vonessen, *Die Herrschaft des Leviathan,* 1978.

5) Spontaneity and Service:
The Ethical Significance of Diaconia

"Through love be servants of one another" (Gal. 5:13). The Christian ministry of service to those in need is a concrete example of the openness to the ethical task in areas beyond the formal regulations of our relationships in life.

Reflective thought on the ethical realities of life, as discussed in the preceding sections through specific examples, requires an ongoing alertness that concerns itself with more than the specific examples. There is no known rule for our dealings with the reality of human life by which the tasks that confront us in daily life can be brought together in an all-inclusive sense and ranked according to their importance. This realization makes clear how much the life that is given to us transcends our attempts to control it and give it shape. Human society must be ready under all circumstances to fill with new life all the institutions and social relationships that have been handed on to us. Any attempt to deny the need for such readiness by reducing life to the observation of social functions, rules, and arrangements would blot out the vision of a world that is worthy of our trust and capable of renewal. But it is not possible to imagine some supplementary formal competence that would once again make this individual and concrete reflection on the reality of life attainable. We need to direct our attention to the spontaneity of approach to such problems, which because it does not follow any formal rules corresponds to the individual situations of life and, between the lines of our general and well-defined activities, fills our activities with life.

Thus if we wish to renew the concrete ethical significance of religion, we must consider the concrete aspects of an attitude that is appropriate to and adequate for continuous reflective thought on the realities of life. In a sense that defines and also transcends all specific actions, the Christian life takes its orientation from the command "Through love be servants of one another" (Gal. 5:13). Love cannot be forced, and therefore it cannot be commanded "from outside." Love becomes concrete in service to others, which cannot mean satisfying a demand for obedience. Love is the concept of a spontaneity which in its openness to others "in, through, and under" the structures of the social world "does not insist on its own way" (1 Cor. 13:5). Therefore in concrete cases love breaks through the rules of society and, instead of mutual recognition and reciprocal relationships, arises from a one-sided relationship. Love is the productive renewal of the meaning of the creation of the world, expressed in an individual way (see vol. 1, pp. 72–73). Service is the concrete expression of love, not love as a general concept but love that is directed toward individual possibilities and gifts. "As each has received a gift, employ it for one another" (1 Pet. 4:10). Love is the context in which we can discover the relationship between receiving life and giving life, for in the context of Christianity love is passing on to others the possibilities for life that we have received. Service is the context in which we discover the concrete expressions of love in individual ways. An example of how these observations come together is found in what is called in church language "diaconia."

Service as diaconia makes no appeal to obedience and subordination. Its purpose is to help others better to succeed in life. It has no fixed dogmatic place in the teaching of the church. It stands in a certain tension with the formal truth claims of Christian doctrine and with the definition of the unchangeable identity of the church. In its empirical application it is quite variable. Its distinctive characteristic is not the propriety of its confession but the secondary place of such interest behind each commitment to do what love commands. The theoretical and theological lack of clarity found in diaconia is tied to the reality that serving is here the application of open reflective thought on the realities of life in the form of specific, individual needs; it is the fulfilling of expectations, not requirements.

Historically this is documented by the fact that Christian diaconia from the first has again and again been concerned with those who in the formal structures and relationships of society found no place of their own and who in their fate were dependent on the spontaneous help provided by others; they were the sick, the sorrowing, the poor, the helpless. Diaconia made of these situations in human existence a theme for social action. Thus diaconia and "charity" are closely connected and share a common history.

The special nature of diaconia becomes clear in its relation to and its distinction from social policy. Diaconia is not primarily oriented to a formal and universally valid formation of social relationships. Its task and the way it is organized are based on individual cases of need and ways of giving help. These cases are always the expression of structural problems in society. This has been especially evident since the renewal of Protestant diaconia by J. H. Wichern. Moreover, the diaconia of the church can be carried out through organizations that have social and political significance. Still the real point of diaconia as service is that its intention is to meet concrete, individual needs that are not being met by the formal organizations and institutions of society. When, therefore, diaconia as an activity of the church becomes itself social policy or organizes itself on the principles of social work, the question always arises whether such responsibilities should not be left to the corresponding groups that are responsible for the total welfare of society. The church's permanent service of diaconia, which is always in need of renewal, consists in its openness to tasks and to individual cases that are not cared for or even perceived by the formal organizations that administer the social responsibilities of the state.

H. D. Wendland has said of diaconia that it is "the form of activity and movement of the whole church" (*Die Kirche in der modernen Gesellschaft*, 1956, p. 14). Going beyond the form of ecclesiastical diaconia, Wendland spoke also of "diaconia in society" (*Botschaft an die soziale Welt*, 1959, pp. 263ff.). In this expression he related the spontaneity of care for one's neighbor to the social nature of the whole of life which, beyond all questions of what is expedient, beyond all legal and institutional rules and regulations, needs to be filled with the fullness of life.

The lively discussion over this special aspect is represented by the code words *Wichern I* and *Wichern II*, which were coined by Eugen Gerstenmaier. The discussion is summarized in detail by O. Myer in *"Politische" und "gesellschaftliche" Diakonie in der neueren theologischen Diskussion*, 1974.

In view of the explicit organization of the church's diaconia, it is important to formulate once again the ethical meaning of service. To serve, to serve one another, signifies in ethical discourse that there are many situations in which the goal and the possibility of success are anything but clear, in which the total context cannot be fully grasped, the interdependencies and the possible consequences are hard to perceive. In short, the fullness of life can be documented in an overpowering need for reflective thought about the world in which we live. Service, as a substitute for specific possibilities for charity, is often the way we first begin to find clarity about the path we should follow. In situations of uncertainty and multiple possibilities, service is the emergency measure we must use, whether in dealing with individuals to give them light in the darkness or in the larger context of society. A readiness to serve is not dependent on any formal church organization. As expressions of good will and spontaneity, service is always necessary wherever we enter new realms in the concrete experiences of life.

The church's diaconia thus continues to bear testimony to the dimension of diaconia in society.

b. Responsibility as the Affirmation of Life in Conflict

Taking a position in reflective thought about life becomes specific, in the second respect, in our dealings with life-threatening conflicts by requiring that we affirm life.

1) Abortion and the Prohibition of Killing

The affirmation of life becomes a concrete problem in the conflict between the preservation of the life of the mother or the life of the child. There is no complete solution to the conflict to be found either through abortion or through its prohibition. The issue of abortion requires that our understanding of responsibility be expanded in order to take into account the affirmation of the mother's life as well as that of the unborn child.

If as an example of dealing with conflicts we consider the issue of abortion, our ethical discussion must make specific the grounds that lead to ethical consultation in which there can be a place for ethical decisions. The following description of the problem is guided by the nature of this task.

In West Germany the public discussion of abortion was stimulated anew by the legal regulation of the disruption of a pregnancy (paragraph 218 of the StGB as amended in 1972). But ethical decisions must include the entire scope of the problem, the complexity of which is made clear by the distinctions among the different levels of discussion that are relevant here: the legal questions that include the regulating by law of the practice of abortion, especially the competence with which it is performed; the medical questions concerning the basis on which a doctor decides that an abortion should be performed; the biological questions, which are concerned with determining the beginning of and the possible dangers to the human life in the mother's womb; the questions of ethical norms, which are concentrated on the meaning of the prohibition of killing (the sixth commandment) in relation to abortion; and wide-ranging sociological questions concerning the social conditions under which an alternative to abortion can be found. The interrelationships among these various dimensions involved in an abortion confront us with extremely difficult problems when we seek to find as unambiguous a statement of the facts as possible and to reach a clear-cut decision. It is possible to try to avoid these difficulties by reducing them to a single aspect of the problem, whether it be the prohibition of killing, or the Hippocratic oath, or social conditions. But the unambiguous answer that might be won in this way would not do justice to the conflict.

Therefore the ethical discussion must be concerned with defining the nature of the conflict over abortion in the context of the ethical realities of life. The purpose of such discussion cannot be to arrive at a simple yes or no to abortion that would support an illusion of simplicity and clarity, when in reality a profound conflict over a life situation is involved.

The termination of a pregnancy involves in every case a serious conflict, because it is the negation of conception in a multiplicity of aspects. Usually the most prominent of these is the killing of the fruit of the womb, which is what happens here. For the woman this means both the negation of the pregnancy and the conscious rejection of a readiness to affirm the new life that has resulted from the union of the wife and the husband. Thus the conflict involves not simply the killing of the fetus but has an added dimension in the relationship between the wife and the husband.

In any case it is a far-reaching conflict, and in no case should the goal of the ethical discussion be to elevate the abortion to the rank of a normal act or of one that could be taken as a norm. In this sense there is no "positive" position on abortion, whose goal would be to bring about a situation in which the express purpose would be an abortion. Abortion cannot be a way of life that is freely chosen and affirmed as a basic practice. But on the other hand it must also be said that it would not be dealing adequately with the conflict over abortion to subsume it without any differentiation under the biblical prohibition of killing and to make that position our norm. Categorically classifying abortion as "murder" is not an adequate way of dealing with the ethical task that confronts us.

Thus there are two extreme solutions proposed for the question of abortion that do not call for a clarification of the ethical issues. First, it is not dealing with the issues to subsume abortion under the freedom of a woman to control her own body and to postulate a supposedly unambiguous solution because the woman has an unlimited right to self-determination. Such an unlimited right cannot be assumed in any relevant relationship, because in every imaginable case such self-determination always turns out to be at the cost of someone else. In the case of abortion the postulate of the woman's unlimited right to self-determination denies the conflict that arises because conception results in a life that, in spite of all symbiotic relationships with the mother, is independent and is a participant in the conflict. Thus the mother's right to self-determination must always be seen in this relationship and accepted as requiring a sense of responsibility.

But the strict rejection of any sort of intervention, the radical prohibition of any termination of the pregnancy, also fails to deal adequately with the conflict. This unconditional prohibition is the official position of the Roman Catholic Church, as set down in the Encyclical *Casti connubii* of 1930 and which since then has not been modified or amended in any official statement. This standpoint is distinguished by its lack of ambiguity, and wherever it is accepted it eliminates in each individual case all problems and considerations, or at least places the burden on others. It is very close to being a position that makes women and men into instruments of nature and pushes aside ethical responsibility in favor of the self-fulfillment of a biological process. In both the above cases the conflict is not recognized as a conflict but is obscured by an abstract maxim. The area of conflict over abortion is defined by at least three differing relationships, each of which has different ethical relevance: the relationship between the life of the mother and the life of the unborn child; the relationship between the pregnant woman and the doctor who is to perform the intervention; the relationship of the woman to the man who made her pregnant. The three relationships together constitute the field of conflict, the general and individual life situations in which the conflict over abortion arises.

The reasons that lead a woman to desire to terminate a pregnancy often arise through a conflict in her relationship with the man who has made her pregnant. In that case the unwillingness of the woman to carry the child to full term is due to a life situation, an extreme example of which would be a case of rape. It could also be a conflict because the woman is unmarried or because of a large number of problems in a marriage, such as the social situation of the family. The wish to terminate the pregnancy, as a negation of the unborn child, is then due to the absence of a situation in which the woman would be ready to accept the developing life, or to a deep disruption in that situation. The dominant factor in such a situation is thus not the direct desire to kill the unborn child but the anxiety and grief over the responsibility that will result from the birth of the child and the anticipation of failure to carry out that responsibility. The knowledge of being unable to deal with the situation means that without consultation and without making a decision it will not be clear how to resolve the conflict. This is appropriate if the discussion and consideration of an abortion is not distorted by the demand for compliance with an indisputable norm, but the way is open to a process of consultation that substitutes for the disrupted capacity of the woman to make her own decisions and is undertaken together with her. The expression "social integration" represents first of all an openness to the conflict and to a way of resolving the conflict on one's own terms.

Reasons for an abortion may be found next in the relationship between the mother and the life of the unborn child. A conflict can arise in the somatic relationship in a medical sense if the pregnancy may result in extensive damage to the health of the mother or the child and may possibly result in death. The causes of such danger may be purely medical in nature, but they may also involve conflicts in the life of mother and child in a larger sense. There may be a conflict in the relationship of the mother to the unborn child that can be identified and diagnosed only with the help of others, primarily the help of a physician. In such cases, absolute certainty is not possible. The evaluation of the conflict is dependent on the nature of the doctor's diagnosis and prognosis. But in general medical factors alone do not produce such accurate information that in every case the life of the unborn child would have precedence over the life of the mother. In such conflicts we immediately confront the question of what "preservation of life" means in specific terms. This principle must apply to both mother and child and thus demands that we recognize the conflict, because the principle of the "preservation of life" is not an adequate basis for a decision. It should go without saying that it would be no adequate application of this principle if the continuation of the pregnancy were to protect the developing life but not protect the life of the mother.

Finally, in any assessment of the conflict the responsibility of the physician plays a role; that is, the question of whether the termination of the pregnancy, which belongs to the competence of the physician, is compatible with the ethical position of the physician. In this respect the physician is drawn into the conflict because ethical responsibility demands that an abortion should be undertaken solely on the basis of the standards and criteria of responsible medical practice. The legal norms established for abortion affect primarily the activity of the physician and determine whether the practice is permitted or not.

Among the widely divergent theological, medical, and legal discussions, the following are of particular interest: J. Gründel, ed., *Abtreibung—Pro und Contra*, 1971; E. W. Böckenförde, "Abschaffung des 218 StGB? Überlegungen zur gegenwartigen Diskussion um das strafrechtliche Abtreibungsverbot," *Stimmen der Zeit* 188 (1971): 147–67; E. Jüngel, J. Moltmann, and D. Rossler, in "Das Abtreibungsverbot des 218" ed. J. Bauman, 1972; E. Wilkins, ed. §218, *Dokumente und Meinungen zur Frage des Schwangerschaftsabbruchs*, 1973; D. Hofmann, ed., *Schwangerschaftsunterbrechung. Aktuelle Überlegungen zur Reform des 218*, 1974. Dealing particularly with abortion counseling, G. Struck and L. Loeffler, eds., *Einführung in die Eheberatung*, 1971; M. Korschorke and J. F. Sandberger, eds., *Schwangerschafts-Konflikt—Beratung. Ein Handbuch*, 1977.

To limit the participation of physicians to discussing only their professional integrity in terms of possible criminal liability in a field into which they are inevitably drawn will not be adequate in the present situation. The legal assessment of the activities of physicians in the abortion controversy must remain open to the contributions of others involved in this area.

The abortion problem has given rise to discussions of legal, ethical, sociological, and even historical-philosophical questions, including basic questions of the ultimate relationship of modern women and men to life itself. The ethical discourse must limit itself in such a way as to make possible a certain ordering of ethical orientation and a cooperation with all those who are concerned with this area of conflict. For this purpose it is helpful to begin with the role of the physician. The premise that the preservation of life has priority in every case means here that abortion presents a conflict that lies within the express area of competence of the physician. It would not be constructive to promote social or individual situations in which, because of a dominant negative assessment of this conflict, an occult, nonmedical practice could flourish beyond the publicly recognized medical competence that can be evaluated. This is one of the reasons that have led many to support a new clarification and amendment of the provisions for punishment under paragraph 218.

Establishing a differentiation among the legal standards governing abortion has the ethical significance of actually removing instances of abortion from the darkness of inappropriate and harmful interventions and making possible an open involvement in the conflict over abortion. Both specific definition of the limits within which the physician is authorized to decide whether to perform an abortion and an increase of the sense of responsibility and sensitivity for the abortion debate move in this direction. In the public debate about the differences recognized in the legal regulation of abortion we encounter the argument that a change in the present strict prohibition of abortion would lead to serious weakening of the forces protecting life, would be an expression of the results of an increasing readiness to take the life of unborn children, and would be interpreted as indirect approval of such taking of life. This line of argument, which is often expressed in highly polemical terms, turns the issue upside down. The large number of illegal abortions is a sign that there has long been a difference between the norm formulated by law and the actual practice, a situation that was not remedied by the new provisions of the legal code. In order to deal with this discrepancy it is first of all necessary to permit and make possible a fully public consideration of the conflict over abortion. And there is no reason for believing that a strict enforcement of the prohibition of abortion or an increase in its penalties would constitute a contribution to an increase in ethical responsibility in this conflict.

The ethical significance of differentiations in the legal provisions is to be seen as a clear definition of responsibility. An example of the new definition of responsibility would be permitting the physician a measure of discretion in determining the medical factors that indicate that an emergency exists in the light of the "social" factors in the case. In dealing with the problem it is not a help to close our eyes to the fact that it is the sum of conflicts described as "social factors" that actually carries the greatest weight in the desire to have an abortion. These conflicts in their totality cannot be dealt with by a blanket decision based on a general norm. Therefore it is important for them to be dealt with primarily in the well-defined realm of the physician's responsibility.

The conflicts are concentrated in the situation of the woman who experiences pregnancy as a life and death conflict. It follows from this that it is not ethically responsible to make the woman bear alone the sole responsibility and the entire guilt and to concentrate the whole burden of decision making on the woman. It is rather the case that the ethical relevance of the so-called social factors points us in the direction of identifying and publicizing the area of social responsibility involved in the prohibition of the possibility of having an abortion. The alternative to medical intervention requires a reconstruction and alteration of the realm of responsibility so that in the conflict over abortion a life-affirming policy might develop. Medical practice can offer us no absolute therapy for such a confused realm of responsibility. Therefore it cannot be within the competence of the physician absolutely to prohibit the performance of an abortion. Moreover, the physician's responsibility cannot exclude the emergency factors involved in an individual conflict over abortion. Therefore in such a conflict if the affirmation of life is to be encouraged and promoted, then in any medical consideration the social factors must also be taken into consideration. A disruption of the pregnant woman's social responsibility involves the joint responsibility of the man, the family, and the community. This opens up the further possibility that the conflict over abortion may be removed from an area of absolute rejection as an act that is in principle ethically impermissible, and brought into the light of a public debate over the chance for accepting a new life. Counseling is a concrete approach to solving the ethical task that arises in our attempts to deal with the abortion conflict. Against the background of the history of this conflict, it is, seen in empirical terms, still underdeveloped and underutilized. Its ethical standard must be the support of the affirmation of life. Counseling must bring to the area of conflict a greater degree of ethical and practical attention than has been the case thus far. On the other hand, to stress the use or abuse that is made possible through the changes in the legal situation would be to avoid the task once again. Any solution to the conflict over abortion that places the entire weight on the prohibition of terminating the unborn life must be identified as inauthentic and a sham. Such a solution would utilize moralistic arguments to interfere with the necessary ethical approach that seeks to strengthen social responsibility and thereby identify the boundaries within which the solution to the conflict is to be sought.

2) Peace as a Political Task in Dealing with Conflicts

Peace is the essence of the political task. Political policy that emphasizes peace as the affirmation of life, even in situations of conflict, is the concrete expression of political responsibility in contrast to war, which is the failure of politics. In dealing with conflicts it is essential therefore to strengthen and renew the emphasis on peace as the task of politics.

To define peace as the essence of the political task is to define in specific terms the basic meaning of politics as concern over the threat that war poses to the preservation of peace. In view of the extreme complexity of the problems to be considered here and the passion with which they are discussed, the ethical elements of our task demand that the concept of peace be defined clearly.

To preserve, foster, and renew peace is the sum of the political task and involves all the separate political tasks and goals. The concrete application of the affirmation of life in conflict must be in accord with the ethical basis of this task and be guided by a comprehensive concept of peace.

To say that the specific theme of peace is the affirmation of life in the midst of conflict can therefore not mean that the pursuit of peace is a task that is to be distinguished from other political tasks. A specific "peace ethic," or "peace doctrine," could easily lead us astray at this point. There is more at issue here than constantly repeated assurances of a readiness for peace, a will for peace, an openness for peace. If we are to speak in concrete terms of what peace really involves, we must speak of the political task in all its aspects.

Thus in terms of method and content it is misleading to make peace the theme of a particular research or ethic, as if this implied that "peace" was absent from all other aspects of the political task rather than being as it is its dominant and comprehensive theme. Such a particularizing understanding of peace is not in keeping with the theological and ethical tradition. To speak of the peace of God, the promise of peace, the exhortation to preserve the peace does not imply a specific undertaking but challenges us with "peace" as the essence of God's intention for the reality of life.

Making the theme of peace into a separate specialty can itself contain the seeds of conflict if by that we isolate peace as a specific achievement of political policy and make peace an issue of partisan politics. Recent discussions of the concept of the search for peace quickly made this evident. It became necessary to distinguish between a concept of peace in terms of a comprehensive and positive political ethic that could deal with all dimensions of political action and a specific concept of peace that dealt with problems of the threat to peace posed by war and with specific forms of conflict resolution. Thus it involved a specific case of conflict. The positive, ethical content of the concept of peace is not in any of its aspects a special matter but is the general content of all political activity.

For discussions of the search for peace, see G. Picht and W. Huber, eds., *Was heisst Friedensforschung?* 1971; E. O. Czempiel, *Schwerpunkte und Ziele der Friedensforschung*, 1972; G. Picht, H. E. Tödt, and H. T. Risse, eds., *Studien zur Friedensforschung*, 1969 ff.; *Veröffentlichungen der Deutschen Gesellschaft für Friedens- und Konfliktforschung*, vol. 1; E. O. Czempiel and J. Delbrück, *Forschung für den Frieden*, 1975; *Friedensanalysen. Für Theorie und Praxis, Vierteljahresschrift*, 1975—.

These premises must be explored methodically and their content examined if we are to comprehend the task of working for peace in the face of the threat of war. These premises are particularly relevant to the ethical evaluation of war in relation to peace. "War" and "peace" are not two equally valid formulas for political activity. The well-known statement of von Clausewitz declared that war "is the continuation of politics by other means." Any view is false that regards war as one of two possibilities for defining political activity. Politics cannot regard peace and war as equivalent choices. Von Clausewitz's formula can only mean that even war is to be subsumed under the political task of achieving peace. War is the case in which politics ceases to follow its proper path in the fulfillment of its proper task and instead acts in contradiction to its task. Seen in this way, war is not and cannot be the end and goal of politics. No use of force, including the force of war, can take the place of politics. War can never be the legitimate content and goal of political activity in the way that peace can. War and violence do not set standards for good political activity but constitute problems that a politics of peace must confront. In relation to instances of open warfare, the political task can still be defined only in relation to peace. Only when we have a clear picture of the inherent nature of the basic ethical meaning of the political task can we have a clear conception of the issues of war and peace.

The threat of war between nations and peoples is always an example of the failure of politics, a conflict that has its roots in the way the political task is handled. The failure of politics can lead to war, and the war documents that failure. This is an indication of a breakdown in the political community that exists among nations and peoples. In cases of military expansion, exploitation, oppression, and conquest, wars begin when the intention is to achieve with force something that cannot be achieved with political measures. Thus the desire for war is documented by the failure of politics. Politics must then rely on the chance of victory; that is, the political task is turned over to military force and the hope for victory. Thus it is not political responsibility but military force that determines the results of political policy. Any political policy that makes its success dependent on military force and the chances of war is always bad politics. It finds itself in conflict with its own ethical responsibility. Thus "affirmation of life in the midst of conflict" means concretely that where a political policy has no other means for success than to rely on war it must change. A different policy must be established. War is never unavoidable for political reasons, but only because the policy is inadequate or the politicians incapable of recognizing their own limits and their need to change. Peace does not mean that politics no longer has to deal with conflict and that therefore for the sake of peace we must postulate an absence of conflict. On the contrary, for political activity peace means giving absolute priority to finding ways of dealing with conflict that are appropriate to the desire for peace.

This description of the problem takes on a dramatic sharpness since the talk of the "chances of war" comes to sound cynical because the military potential that is brought into play in case of war cannot count on a happy outcome in terms of the human world in which we must live. This is the changed condition under which the problem must be faced today and which defines our dealing with conflict, because it signifies a differing way in which the conflict is defined and intensified.

Adopting a relevant ethical position cannot be limited to weapons control. We must ask about the political structure of conflicts that threaten peace, because it is not weapons that lead to war but failures of policy.

The next step in defining the task of working for peace is to speak, at least in broad terms, of the political conflicts that threaten peace. They can be summed up under two aspects.

First, the modern problem of war is closely connected with the claims to sovereignty raised by modern states. Sovereignty is the political concept of autonomy, independence, freedom. Sovereignty, when it is not closely united with the ethical task of working for peace, tends toward the claim to total power and brings to light the political problems of a radical concept of freedom, which approaches the theological concept of divine omnipotence. Defining the limits of the political sovereignty of the state, both in external and internal affairs, requires a political equivalent of the theological differentiation between God and man, and this is decisive for our understanding of our ethical task. This definition of limits becomes urgent when it involves the coexistence of different sovereign states and the competition or integration that exists in their relations to one another. National sovereignty is the political source of war whenever it negates or disturbs the existence of other sovereign states or seeks to increase, strengthen, or achieve its own sovereignty at the cost of others. War in the name of state sovereignty always involves the suppression of the sovereignty and freedom of others and the assertion of one's own sovereignty as domination of others. Thus the limits of sovereignty is the first theme to be considered in dealing with conflicts between various states, the theme of peace in times of conflict.

These limits can be defined on the basis of the fundamental political task. They are defined internally in reference to the legitimation of political sovereignty. If this legitimation is thought of as independent of the citizens who constitute the state, then the exercise of a state's sovereignty in war against other states is at the same time the disruption of the state's task of protecting its own citizens and preserving their peace, because it is these citizens who are drawn into the war and must fight its battles. But, as Kant argued, that is incompatible with the self-determination of a full citizen.

Externally, the limits of sovereignty are determined by the demand for noninterference, which is always a principle of the recognition of the sovereignty of others. Here the limits of one's own sovereignty are determined by the principle that one state's claim to the right to freedom must also be extended to other states. War in the name of asserting or increasing one's own sovereignty is thus the negation of political sovereignty and therefore a contradiction to one's own political task. In this sense war is the breakdown of national sovereignty. This ethical logic is not the least important reason that the history of war in contemporary times has moved from wars in the name of national sovereignty to the concept of a League of Nations or the United Nations.

Second, in addition to the conflicts inherent in the rivalry of sovereign states, the conflict between differing ideological systems constitutes a specifically modern threat to peace. The specific problem of the ideology of class struggle as a permanent latent state of war lies in the fact that the contrast between social-economic systems is not a part of a political and ethical concept of peace. The contrast of classes implies the absence of peace altogether, because here "peace" would only be identical with victory over the enemy class. The presupposition here is of an irreconcilable contrast on the basis of which the political task itself is defined as a necessary conflict. This undoubtedly most powerful form of legitimation of war through a specific concept of peace in the sense of a moral and ideological basis for a "just" war can also become the motive for the Western democracies to help the "right side" to victory or to punish the guilty, with the goal of correcting a false world view to agree with the only "right" world view. In contrast to such self-justification of the contrasts between rival ideological systems, it is essential to present anew the political meaning of peace.

The challenge to work for peace that is expressed in the term *co-existence* of differing systems derives from the logic that such ideological contrasts know of themselves no boundaries. This is because the central ideology makes such claims for universal validity that by definition the possibility of recognizing others besides itself is excluded.

Lenin described it as a "basic error of the proponents of disarmament" that the socialists could "be opposed to every war without ceasing to be socialists. We say that arming the proletariat for the purpose of defeating the bourgeoisie, to expropriate their property and to disarm them—that is the only possible tactic of

the revolutionary class, a tactic which the entire objective development of capitalistic militarism has prepared the way for, established, and taught. Only after
the proletariat has disarmed the bourgeoisie can it be possible without betraying
its own task in world history to throw away our weapons as scrap iron, which we
will certainly do then but no sooner." V. I. Lenin, *The Military Program of the
Proletarian Revolution*, 1916.

At this point the ethical argument needs to take into account the
insight that the ideological factor in political activity does not legitimize
or serve as a basis for that activity but is brought to that activity under
specific presuppositions. Thus in the case of a conflict of ideologies the
ethical basis of the political task must be clearly distinguished from its
ideological claims. The application of the contrasts of ideological systems
to the political relationship of sovereign states or groups of states does not
resolve this conflict, but it does show a way in which it can be integrated
into the more comprehensive political task of working for peace, and in
this way it relativizes the conflict. That is the political, ethical meaning of
the formula of coexistence of differing ideological systems that are in
conflict.

By considering the cases just discussed we can find a concrete role for
the churches in the struggle for peace. Both in the rivalries of sovereign
states and in the conflict between ideological systems the churches must
through their existence and through the words they speak bear testimony
to the basic ethical significance of the political task—that peace, as over
against the sovereignty of states and the claims of ideological systems, is
always the most important agenda of politics. The political efforts to
secure peace may not be reduced to a function of the self-assertiveness of
states or to the expansion of ideological systems and thus be subordinated
to those ends. In this conflict the churches represent the knowledge of the
vital difference between the basic meaning of the political task and the
specific political will that makes use of political means to serve the ends
of asserting sovereignty or ideology. This knowledge is not theirs to
present in an exclusive way, but they are to present it as churches in
specific situations in the service of an inclusive concept of peace. At this
point in history, that means openly working together with others.

Against the background of political structures whose conflicts threaten
peace, the next step is to examine the special problem of assuring peace
amid these conflicts. By this I mean the specific problem of war and
peace, which in ethical discussions as a rule involves these concepts.

Military security against hostile threats is one of the essential, indispensible means of securing peace. But peace can by no means be assured solely or even chiefly through armaments. It is not merely that this would restrict and narrow the political and ethical significance of peace; it would also mean that the success of the political task would be dependent on the existence of armaments. But that is not the case. Only on the condition that peace be recognized as the ethical core of all political activity, only in the framework of an inclusive concept of peace, can the distinctive task of peacemaking through assuring peace in the face of the danger of war find its place in ethics.

This eliminates from any meaningful ethic every glorification of war, including "military" virtues, and efforts by means of war to give reality to the strength or vitality of a nation or a people. Such features of an elite ethos are not compatible with an ethic of how human life should be led. On the other hand, the pacifist rejection of war is completely congruent with the basic intention of the political task of avoiding war. But the total rejection of conflicts would not be a responsible way of dealing with them.

It is therefore a questionable procedure to take the Beatitude in the words of Jesus in the Sermon on the Mount "Blessed are the peacemakers" (Matt. 5:9) as meaning the same thing as historical or modern pacifism. Jesus' message speaks of a readiness to work for peace in the midst of conflict and in reference to human conflicts in this world and to conflicts with God. It does not, however, speak of any specific religious capacity for peace under easier conditions, which would claim the message of peace only for one's self while leaving the actual conflicts and problems to others. Our dealings with conflicts should be guided by the knowledge that the promise is only for those with a peaceable disposition. But to juggle away the political responsibility for the preservation of peace in this way would be to confuse this promise with a political alternative.

The securing of peace is a precarious task that involves affirming life in the face of the reality of violent conflicts that occur between peoples and nations and, because they are real, threaten the political task and bring its validity into question.

In this sense the securing of peace is a continuation of the political task of protecting the life of the community from threats from without. This also means that the existence of weapons and armaments and their use are under no circumstances legitimate or ethically justified in themselves, but only in the context of this political task and exclusively through it. For this reason it is an inadmissible simplification of the ethical discussion of the rightness and limits of securing peace by military means to ask this question without reference to the political task of preserving peace. In the political context it must be emphasized that the use of weapons in conflicts is not a political method that could carry the same weight as political action or could justifiably be used. In reference to armaments, it must be said that their use is justified in defensive situations where there actually is a powerful military attack or a powerful attempt at subjugation from outside the country. Their use is not ever justified, however, in a calculated military and political defense which in the interests of securing peace becomes a preventive, that is, actually an offensive calculation.

Such arguments based on the superiority of political negotiations over the use of military force are the only legitimation for securing peace by military power in order to avoid the outbreak of violent conflict. To be sure, this defines the concrete tasks and problems of present-day efforts to secure peace only in general terms and not in detail. Reflective political thought in dealing with conflicts first comes fully into play when we begin to deal with concrete problems. Those who refuse to do so on the ground that that would be moving in the wrong direction must acknowledge that arguments dealing with basic positions are relatively impotent to come to terms with concrete situations. But those who take seriously the political importance of working for peace cannot avoid dealing with attempts to find political solutions wherever violent conflicts threaten to break out.

In the present day this is especially true in reference to the most important potential conflict, the relations between East and West. These relations are chiefly oriented toward avoiding military conflict by the maintenance of military parity. The political intention and lines of thought that are at work in the definition and the quantitative achievement of such an "equality of armaments" require careful attention. Actual or intended military parity cannot in itself count as a political or ethical argument. Since the political task cannot and may not anticipate subjugation by a potential enemy, the attempt to maintain military parity can be a rational means for achieving political goals in a conflict situation.

The debate concerning the appropriateness and the limits of this concept of parity as a doctrine of mutual terror raises the question of whether under these premises the concept of military security has become self-justifying, so that the political meaning of the task is no longer recognized and the military task has become independent of the political. Thus any critique of a "self-perpetuating" arms race and a self-justifying concept of military parity must be a political critique that reasserts the priority of political activity over purely military concepts. Military armaments as a competition between weapons systems become a threat to the political search for peace in a comprehensive sense if the quantitative and qualitative demands come to outweigh the attention given to other governmental tasks. If the level of the military expenditures of the nations deprives political causes their necessary means and efforts, then military security is purchased at the expense of the development of efforts toward peace, both internally and internationally. If the weapons systems designed to preserve peace become life threatening in a way that is difficult to control, as is the case with atomic weapons, then there is no way to legitimate their use in the framework of a political policy that is responsive to human values. In the multiplying of dangers and the absurdity of such developments we reach a point at which such perfection of the means of securing peace no longer makes sense either militarily or politically.

Mutual deterrence has an identifiable value only in the framework of political goals. Thus the debate must go beyond the discussion of the nature and quality of armaments. It is possible to argue that this political value could be achieved at a much lower level of armaments, both quantitatively and qualitatively. If there are valid political reasons for assuming this, then the continuation of the previous development and expansion of armaments represents a permanent declaration of the bankruptcy of our efforts to achieve peace by political means. We would be at the mercy of an automatic military and technological process. Such a situation may be the consequence of our visualizing the political task of securing the peace in terms of military parity. That would be to say that the conditions for peaceful coexistence can be defined only as a balance of power, realizable through weapons systems and other military means. If our critique begins here, say in the demand for disarmament, then another problem arises. The experts in research into and definition of technological and material equality have long been aware that such equality cannot be fully defined in a satisfactory manner. There have been and continue to be inequalities, and new inequalities can always be discovered. Increased precision over the criteria for equality again and again delays agreement about the point in time and the preconditions for mutual and equal disarmament. Increased knowledge of the complexity of the concept of arms equality ultimately fuels the arguments which hold that a continuation of the armaments race is unavoidable.

This vicious circle in the search for a formula for military equality can be broken, if at all, only if the political factors in the theory of a military balance of power are identified, that is, brought to bear anew and in an independent manner. The concept of disarmament itself, if it is to be accomplished equitably within the framework of existing conditions, is under these conditions practically unachievable since exact standards of equality cannot be established. Thus the chief task for the future of political ethics is to find political ways to recognize and reformulate those conflicts that are at the root of the present system of armaments. The problem with which we started thus does not lead, at least not primarily, to a call to disarm but to a demand for a new political definition of the tensions that lie between the nations of the Eastern block and those of the West.

To be sure, this does not mean that we need to develop a totally different, previously unknown political policy. The first concrete step in this future task, as far as an ethical line of argument applicable to politics is concerned, is to explore the political content in the theory of the balance of power and its military consequences. If such political content were totally absent, it is hard to see where it would suddenly come from. The ethical approach can quite well begin by giving further concrete application to its task. At the very least a knowledge of this complex task would be helped by a historical-political reconstruction.

It can be maintained that the United States after 1945 viewed the political challenge of the Soviet Union increasingly as a military rivalry. The process of making the military adjustments in the relationships between the two powers was therefore seen as a channeling of the conflict. The military relationships between them had political significance as a provisional solution. Thus there was the expectation that a lasting political solution could be achieved after a transitional period, which was to be bridged by a tentative deterrence. The rivalry was accepted by the Soviet Union with quite different political and strategic goals.

In the course of the military rivalry, both sides continued to pursue political goals and concepts of international order. It would therefore be false, an oversimplification, to speak of an armaments race that automatically increased the level of armaments. It is also important in the interests of clarity to say that the definition of goals and the political efforts to achieve them were largely identified with military preparations, and this represents a fundamental weakness in the whole development. The Soviet goals, at least in terms of Soviet orthodoxy, can be seen as the building up of military power in order to create or alter a political framework for political solutions. The view of the West, on the other hand, was that a stabilization of the military relationship would result in at least a provisional and stable relationship between the powers.

For the older, prenuclear discussion of war and peace, the work of Q. Wright, *A Study of War*, 2 vols., 1942, is still important. For a discussion of the modern problem, see R. Aaron, *Frieden und Krieg zwischen den Nationen*, 1964 (German trans.); R. Osgood and R. W. Rucker, *Force, Order and Justice*, 1967; U. Nerlich, ed., *Krieg und Frieden im industriellen Zeitalter*, 1966, and *Krieg und Frieden in der modernen Staatenwelt*, 1966. On the problems of disarmament and the control of armaments, see D. G. Brennan, *Strategie der Abrüstung*, 1962; R. Ranger, *Arms and Politics 1958–1978*, and *Arms Control in a Changing Context*, 1979; K. D. Schwarz, *Sicherheitspolitik*, 3d ed., 1978; J. J. Holst and U. Nerlich, eds., *Beyond Nuclear Deterrence. New Aims, New Arms*, 1977.

In this situation it is not possible without a change in politics to arrive at a clearly differentiated political view of the conflict, a view in which military stabilization would have no political value of its own except in the avoidance of strategic advantage (which is not the same as equilibrium).

That this critical point has been reached can now—still at this same level of discussion—be demonstrated in military terms. The theory of equilibrium, or of mutual deterrence, is at least in Western terms based on a concept of how to ensure peace, not on offensive warfare. Because of the technological development of weapons, both sides have built up unprecedented offensive capacity, which because of the insufficient stabilization of relations could easily be used in a preventive or surprise attack with unprecedented strategic advantage (a "disarmament strike"). Stabilization therefore consists in denying the other side such advantage, for example, through possession of a sufficiently large number of invulnerable weapons for retaliation. This means that we have a situation of reciprocal offensive capability. For military and technical reasons, offensive warfare has now entered into the calculations, although each side declares that it will not make the first strike. This makes it extremely urgent to clarify the political nature of the East-West conflict and to raise to the level of political consciousness the structures from which the political antagonism arises.

In the foreground of this task and in the direction it should take we find all the concerns of the general public and also of the church. The course of politics to this point is not a one-time decision but a political and ethical process. As a contribution to this process we may look at several examples.

1. In the public discussion there is concern to make clear and unmistakable the peaceful nature of intentions in conflict situations with the "others" (those with whom we are in conflict) and not always to assume the worst of them. The perception of those on the other side is an important element in the description of the conflict. Forming concepts and perceptions that at the very least do not define the "others" as absolutely evil is a step toward peace because it gives encouragement to take political action. But these perceptions must include the recognition of real conflicts that are not part of the attitude of the respective parties toward each other but in comparison are objective in nature. To have peaceful intentions does not mean denying real conflicts.

2. It is important to take measures that build mutual confidence. This can involve thinking about the need of the other side for security and letting this play a role in one's own political responsibility. To insist on one's own security without thinking about the needs of the other side is irresponsible. But this includes taking seriously one's own security as a political responsibility in the search for peace and not lightly dismissing it from consideration. For security can only be secured and preserved together. To this extent we discover a sort of "socialization" of the problems of conflict.

3. It is essential that the political opponents work for an atmosphere of openness between them. That can mean that "we ourselves" (whoever we are) make our motivation, intentions, acts, and concepts transparent. To increase this transparence we should support those who value political action much more highly than military action. In this effort we must take earnestly into account the limits beyond which our own position and style of life are not acceptable in other political systems. There is no such thing as total openness. Therefore all negotiating is also political activity in which the respective positions are clearly marked.

4. Then there is the matter of decreasing the expenditures for military defense. This can mean that we become aware that armaments are not an end in themselves and that there is no inherent necessity that they be produced. Serious discussion of disarmament is an urgent political necessity, but a willingness to share responsibility is a prerequisite. Only those are qualified to participate who do not deny the importance of defensive preparations. The responsibility must be equitably divided. The demand for disarmament cannot be justified as morally "pure" on the grounds

that it is removed from political responsibility and also from any concrete responsibility to provide for national defense.

To be sure, these are only limited steps toward a political solution, but they are steps that accord with the hopes of those who work for peace. Only those who have hope have time to work for solutions through consensus. Those who are fearful press for quick solutions that tend to result in violence. A particular area for discussing these applications of ethics has developed in the churches. It has been characterized by the formula "Working for peace, with and without weapons." Here I shall comment on this movement only in relation to the foregoing discussion. We must ask whether the formula "Working for peace, with and without weapons" is genuine and valid, or at least equitable. Its practical importance for the churches is in bringing together those who hold differing positions. That is quite significant and should not be called into question here. Still we cannot avoid the question of whether the elements of this formula are of equal importance in terms of their content. This question is not directed toward the attitudes and convictions of the participants but to the political relevance of the formula itself.

This is not the place for a historical analysis of the origin, function, and use of this formula. Nor can the history and goals of the "Heidelberger Theses," which preceded this formula, be explored here. "Working for peace with weapons" is a formula that can be based only in a general politics of peace. It cannot mean achieving the intentions found in the concept of peace by using weapons and engaging in acts of war. It has validity only in relation to a politics of peace, of negotiations, of the forming of alliances, of promoting development that is in the context in which the concept of peace has been developed above. Moreover, the second part of the formula, "without weapons," involves the renunciation of the use of weapons and in this connection means primarily the rejection of military armaments and participation in their manufacture. There are good reasons for this, for example, refusal to serve in combat for reasons of conscience, as is provided for in the constitution of the Federal Republic of Germany. But anyone who wishes to do more than this in the cause of peace and to go beyond a specific religious and ethical position and the demands of conscience must have political reasons for doing so and thus participate in the formation of a politics of peace. Consistent with this argument, refusal to serve in the military is increasingly based on political reasons, and conscientious objection to military service must also be supported by political reasons.

But the tension and the debate involved here cannot be adequately

dealt with by the slogan "Working for peace without weapons." Boiled
down to its essentials, the slogan implies a decision that is no decision at
all. This becomes clear in that in the present discussion the phrase
"Working for peace without weapons" calls attention to the quite different question of whether there are strategies for defense other than the
dominant doctrine of mutual terror. This question involves an area that is
not at all covered by the formula "without weapons." In this situation the
formula leads to misunderstanding and confusion. It leads to the false
assumption that the nature of the political search for peace implied in the
expression "working for peace" finds concrete expression in the intentions
of the Christians who are involved, some of whom are "for" weapons and
the others are "against" weapons. But that is a sham discussion.

It is essential to have a new discussion of how to work for peace
"without weapons" or of the more sharply worded slogan "living without
armaments." Taken in another sense than the negative connotation just
discussed, the slogan "living without armaments" is not utopian but
represents a quite realistic possibility and a chance for a political
approach to peace. It is not as if "living without armaments" had no place
in this world. On the contrary, it has a clearly recognizable place and a
distinct reality. Wherever covenants succeed, whether in the sense of the
legal order of a territorial state (internal peace) or in the case of successful
covenants between states, we see the well-known and highly desirable
reality that people and states can live with one another "without armaments." It is possible, not through good intentions or mere moralistic
decisions but by means of mutual political efforts, to produce situations in
which it is possible to live without armaments. In plain language, we do
not need to arm ourselves against good neighbors and partners. It all
depends on the situation in which the formula "living without armaments" is adopted and filled with meaning. It has only relative justification in any specific connection. It must be explained in terms of the
conditions that must be established and preserved if a situation of peace
without armaments can be preserved. It is not and cannot be an absolute
formula. It would be a misuse of the formula in the church if Christians
tried to act as if on Christian grounds it were "unconditionally" valid,
that is, valid apart from any participation that is open to us in the real
politics of peace. But with this understanding, it is a constructive and
significant formula for defining and renewing that task posed for us by
the issues of war and peace.

Only if the political and ethical content of the two positions expressed
by the formula are distinguished from each other can we expect that the

discussion of peace in the churches will deal with genuine problem areas in the search for peace and not end up split between two opposing positions. Working for peace does not excuse us from the task of finding new ways to promote peaceful resolution of conflicts through agreements and covenants. Wishing to live without armaments does not excuse us from the task of developing together new ways of establishing and preserving covenants.

For discussions in the churches, see G. Howe, ed., *Atomzeitalter, Krieg und Frieden*, 1959; "Die christliche Friedensbotschaft, die weltlichen Friedenspro-gramme und die politische Arbeit für den Frieden," 1962, in *Die Denkschriften der EKD*, vols. 1–2, 1978, pp. 8–14; "Der Friedensdienst der Christen. Eine Thesenreihe zur christlichen Friedensethik in der gegenwärtigen Weltsituation. Erarbeitet von der Kammer der EKD für öffentliche Verantwortung," 1969, in *Die Denkschriften der EKD*, vols. 1–2, 1978, pp. 35–60; H. E. Tödt, "Die Lehre vom gerechten Krieg und der Friedensauftrag der Korchen," *ZEE* 14 (1970): 159–73; U. Duchrow and G. Scharffenorth, eds., *Konflikte zwischen Wehrdienst und Friedensdienst. Ein Strukturproblem der Kirche*, 1970; Evangelisches Kir-chenamt für die Bundeswehr, eds., *Gewissen im Dialog*, 1980.

3) The Conflict between Rich Lands and Poor Lands: Responsibility for a New Economic Order

Justice as a criterion for economic activity finds application in an openness to the worldwide conflict between the poor lands and the rich lands. The call for justice centers here on the task of renewing and transforming the world economic order in a responsible manner.

Preserving, promoting, and renewing justice is a task that gives to the affirmation of life in conflict a specific direction, which can be illustrated by several examples involving economic activity. The worldwide conflict between the industrially developed and economically rich countries of the world and the countries that are struggling for existence while threatened by starvation is a situation dominated by injustice. This is a challenge that responsible ethical discussion must deal with. To deal with this task in the framework of an ethical line of argument means in precise terms to develop perspectives in which the basic ethical significance of the economic challenge can be related in concrete terms to the new situation of economic development. To affirm life in conflict in concrete terms means here to identify the ethical significance of economic conflict in its basic features. Injustice on a world scale is the gap between the development of rich countries and that of poor countries. To use a metaphor, it is the yawning chasm that separates the two. The plethora of analyses, research projects, appeals, and reproaches that have resulted is a sign of the complexity of the issue. In the tension between moralistic and political simplification on the one hand and the impossibility of surveying all the details as well as the total economic situation on the other, the ethical line of argument must formulate specific lines of approach. The formula "affirmation of life in conflict" means first of all simply acknowledging the conflict and ascribing to it not merely marginal significance but a central place in the economic enterprise. The elementary duty to affirm life applies in the first place to assuring the basis of material existence for those persons and countries threatened with starvation. A concrete approach that acknowledges the conflict and affirms life becomes entangled in extensive controversies as soon as we try to analyse and describe the conflict. In these controversies we can observe two conflicting approaches that find expression in competing lists of demands. The one approach tries to deal, in general terms, with acute hunger and poverty as the primary material problem of injustice by having the rich provide help for the poor. "Developmental aid" as the perception of the need for assistance includes the recognition and affirmation of the state of dependence that prevails in the relationship between the "poor" and the "rich." Aid as an activity performed by the rich is addressed to their sense of responsibility and formulates tasks for them to perform. In this sense, there is talk, for example, of the "new social question."

The other approach, again expressed in general terms, sees the dependence of the poor on the rich as the real problem. Instead of aid, the real need is to promote the achieving of independence. Not aid but freedom is the paradigm, the independence of an economically self-sufficient way of life.

Both approaches contain distinctive perspectives of the causes of the conflict, such as the history of colonialism and the ways of overcoming it. They are associated with a multiplicity of individual perspectives and analyses, the content of which on closer examination is not de facto eliminated but expanded and corrected. The aid that rich countries give to poor countries takes hold only if the affected countries take it up and integrate it into their life. For example, the aid must lead to the formation of effective economic production that goes beyond mere help in time of catastrophe. The means for creating independent economic, technical, and industrial capacity can be made effective and permanent only if the developed countries help to accomplish this, for example, through the transfer of capital and technology. Without going into the details of this discussion, it is clear that both approaches seem to explain the basic form of justice in differing ways, just as we have formulated the basic meaning of responsible economic activity: openness to and acknowledgment of interdependence.

Most analyses of the conflict agree that it arises from the lack of congruence between economic interdependence on the one hand and political independence on the other. This is the result of the chronologically different historical development of the nations and national economies of the world and is the consequence of the different pace of the development of economic and political structures. In this incongruent situation it would be easy to strengthen independence against dependence. But every deeper exploration of the material problems involved in the conflict inevitably brings the dimension of interdependence into the foreground.

The ethical line of argument that we are following here has as its goal the translation of the basic principle of the affirmation of life in conflict into an economic argument. The intention is to show that interdependence is a concrete expression of justice, which by virtue of its ethical and economic logic embraces both the independence of those involved and their mutual dependence.

Concrete application of economic interdependence on a world scale is also the goal of the general but at the same time complex formulation found in the preamble to the proclamation of a new world economic order issued by the United Nations: "We the members of the United Nations . . . solemnly proclaim our common determination to work vigorously for the establishment of a new world economic order based on justice, equal sovereignty, mutual dependence, common interests, and the cooperation of all nations regardless of their economic and social systems, in order to remove inequalities and eliminate the existing situations of injustice, end the deepening gap between developed nations and the developing nations and to ensure the steady acceleration of economic and social development in peace and justice for the present and future generations" (quoted in the volume published by the Stiftung Wissenschaft und Politik, *Polarität und Interdependenz*, 1978, p. 318).

Here in a pregnant sense "justice" is combined politically with the expression "equal sovereignty." It is identified with the hallmarks of "mutual dependence" in terms of content brought together with "common interests" and given concrete expression by the reference to the "cooperation of all nations" as the way to bring this all about. It is on this basis that the task of overcoming the conflicts produced by inequality and injustice is depicted.

In order to clarify the issue of ethical responsibility, we should avoid if at all possible two unfruitful lines of argument. The first involves the attempt to find theoretical formulas for harmonizing freedom and equality that would reinforce the consistency of both concepts, that is, a conceptual program. The other consists in basing demands for action on moral and historical themes and motifs, that is, a program of appeals to the past. The development and application of the theme of justice ought to reinforce the paradigms of interdependence. This has an advantage for ethical discussion because the paradigm of interdependence is open to the recognition of conflict and to the participation of all parties in the resolution of the conflict, without having to require changes based on theory or practical politics which lie outside the concrete possibilities for action that are open to those involved. If this assumption meets with at least basic acceptance, then two far-reaching applications of justice arise from it, applications to which concrete responsibilities can be brought into relationship.

1. Recognition of the conflict in terms of a demand for justice as interdependence implies undeniably that the developed countries, the "rich," are primarily the ones of whom action is required. This means that developmental aid, including economic and technical assistance as well as voluntary grants, are and will remain for some time to come, despite all demands for equality and independence, a necessary concrete means towards the establishment of a new just order. There is at present a politically motivated critique of developmental aid which, in the name of an anticipated independence in all programs of developmental assistance, is regarded as a continuing form of dependence. This critique is basically in error because in concrete terms, where demands for achievable goals are involved, it gets in the way of the activity which for good reason must be demanded of the developed countries for the benefit of the underdeveloped. Developmental assistance, not on the basis of programmatic theory but on the basis of a pragmatic perception of interdependence, remains an unavoidable ethical and economic requirement.

2. The recognition of interdependence as the way to solve conflicts implies unavoidably that the "poor" countries must enter into and participate in the economic development that receives its major impulses from the developed countries. For it is alone through access to economic productivity and through economic means that the developing countries will be able to participate in the existing international interdependence

in their own independent ways. Insofar as the material problems of independence, equality, and justice were the result for the poor countries of their relationship to the developed countries, they must be attacked and solved in this context.

In opposition to this perspective, the argument is advanced that this would subject the nations of the world to an enforced development going far beyond the economic sphere and involving compulsory adoption of "Western" ways of thinking and acting. One consequence would be pressure to accept the dominance of a Western life style. Economic development is thus seen as the forerunner of Western cultural and political dominance.

In terms of the empirical state of cultural and social history, this argument is by no means free of ambiguity. It has principally been advanced from a Western perspective. Not only the developments in Japan, for instance, but also those in other parts of the world speak against too quickly identifying economic development with Western cultural dominance. For the perspective of cultural theory, consult H. Röpke's *Interculturelle Differenzierung*, 1973.

But even where this argument is applicable it cannot mean that all aid must be rejected, because in concrete terms this would be rejecting contributions to preserving life itself in situations where poverty prevails. Cultural and political independence includes the possibility and capability of obtaining the means to preserve life and can therefore not be obtained without dependence.

The attempt to clothe poverty as such with religious respectability, as is the case in many interpretations of the "theology of poverty," leads to the negation of concrete responsibility in ethical and economic tasks. It is quite another matter if "theology of poverty" is an attempt to apply to oneself the issues of interdependence in such a way that the developed countries come to feel that they are involved in this interdependence and begin to think of themselves in the same role as the other countries. In this sense it can be a contribution to making openness to interdependence a concrete issue and to strengthening their willingness to acknowledge their responsibility for promoting it.

The extended discussion of the problems of development is documented in G. Bauer, "A Systematic Bibliography on Theology of Development," in *Theology Meets Progress*, ed. P. Land, 1971, pp. 289–346; Council of the EKD, *Der Entwicklungsdienst der Kirche—ein Beitrag für Frieden und Gerechtigkeit in der Welt. Eine Denkschrift*, 1973; K. von Bismark and H. Maier, eds., *Entwicklung, Gerechtigkeit, Frieden*, 1979; H.-G. Binder and P. Bocklet, eds., *Entwick-*

lung als internationale soziale Frage, 1980. See also K. Borchardt, *Europas Wirtschaftsgeschichte—ein Modell für Entwicklungsländer?* 1976; P. L. Berger, *Welt der Reichen, Welt der Armen,* 1976; M. Nitsch, "Zur Diskussion über die neue Wirtschaftsordnung," in the volume published by the Stiftung Wissenschaft und Politik, *Polarität und Interdependenz,* 1978, pp. 317–35. On the discussion of the politics of development, see also the articles by C. Elliot, L. A. Gomez de Souza, E. Eppler, and W. Schweitzer in the special issue of *ZEE, Entwicklungspolitik,* 1970, vol. 14, pp. 1–2, and the special issue *Neue Weltwirtschaftsordnung,* with articles by Th. Strohm, S. L. Parmar, H. J. Stryk, H. Linnemann, and J. de Hoogh. See also G. Linnenbrink, *ZEE* 21 (1977): 2. See also "Wissenschaftlicher Beirat beim Bundeswirtschaftsministerium," *Fragen einer neuen Weltwirtschaftsordnung,* 1976.

4) Sickness and Health

Health is the capability of dealing independently with the conflicts in one's life. Sickness is dependence on the help of others in the conflicts that constrict our life. The work of physicians involves responsibility for the independence of lives threatened by conflicts.

The World Health Organization has issued a definition of health that calls attention to the multidimensional relationship between sickness and health. According to this definition, health is "a condition of total physical, mental, and social well-being." This definition sums up an increasing sensitivity in the public consciousness for the complexity of human life. In contrast to an orientation limited to physical problems and bodily well-being, as found in medicine, which is dominated by the natural sciences, this definition includes the mental and social dimensions of life. With the expression "a condition of total well-being" it approaches a view according to which there is really no one who could say without reservation that he or she was healthy. This maximum definition of health does not correspond to the reality of human life. Everybody would always have reason for feeling that they were sick.

Dietrich Rössler has called our attention to the danger of this utopian understanding of health. He proposes a contrasting definition that points the way to an ethical orientation: "Health is not the absence of disorders; health is the strength to live with them" (*Der Arzt zwischen Technik und Humanität,* 1977, p. 63). The advantage of this definition is that it does not take one situation or another as its point of reference but relates to the way we lead our lives. At the center of its criterion it places our ability to deal with conflicts. It includes the requirement that "we must accept our own limits," "that we must be able to accept ourselves," together with the requirement that "we must recognize our own possibilities within our own limits."

This provides helpful orientation for the ethical question with which we are dealing here. It places in the foreground bodily ills as defined in the more narrow concept of sickness, so that it is possible to distinguish between a "healthy" life and an unhealthy, "sick" life. This distinction is manifest in physical disorders. But it is also oriented to the capacity of dealing with disorders, and thus includes the mental and social dimensions. In this way our ethical orientation is given definite direction: If health can be defined comprehensively as the capability of leading one's own, independent life, even in the face of disorders, then sickness is a situation where help is needed, and we are no longer able to deal independently with life's conflicts. The person needs the help provided by the work of others, in this case, that of the physician. The primary person who can perceive the individual's need for help is the physician. Thus the ethical task is to be expressed concretely as one of medical ethics.

Building on the classic formulation of the so-called Hippocratic oath, a typical formulation of the physician's ethical responsibility today is as follows: "In my reception into the medical profession I solemnly vow to place my life at the service of humanity; I will practice my profession conscientiously and with dignity. The preservation and restoration of the health of my patients shall be the supreme purpose of my activity. I will preserve all secrets entrusted to me. With all my powers I will uphold the honor and the noble tradition of the medical profession, and in carrying out my duties as a physician I will show no distinction on the basis of religion, nationality, race, membership in a party, or social position. I will treat all human life with respect from the time of conception, and even under threat of harm I will not use my skills as a physician contrary to the commandments of humanity. I will show to my teachers and to my colleagues the respect that is their due. All this I solemnly promise on my honor" (*Deutsches Ärzteblatt* 76 [1979]: 2442).

The passion and the seriousness of this oath underline the truth that the physician deals with other human beings precisely where they surrender their independence into the hands of another, the physician, in a manner that directly affects their person. Therefore the physician's involvement with the body of the one who is sick has both factual and metaphorical meaning, and the criteria by which the physician orients his or her practice must be determined by the specific quality inherent in a life that is concerned with its independence.

In the oath cited above it is striking that this dimension of the physician's work, that is, the relationship it bears to the independence of the one who is sick, is not explicitly expressed. But that is precisely the starting point for the debate over the formulation of the ethics of a profession. The extent and the limits of the physician's efforts in relation to the one who is sick are ethically defined by the independence which the patient expects to regain. Above all other possibilities, this is the definitive criterion. Both the extraordinary scientific and technological possibilities of medicine and the organization and administration of the health system have in this their critical boundary and receive from it their ethical task.

The distinction between sickness and health must therefore be preserved in principle so that in concrete individual cases the physician can act in a responsible manner. In real life there is no such thing as an absolutely sick or absolutely healthy person. Both sickness and health are relative to the possibility for leading an independent life. Medical ethics must be guided by this distinction between sickness and health. Only thereby can we defend ourselves against the claim of omnicompetence for the physician. The competence of the physician stands over against the independence of those who seek the physician's help. Only in the light of this relationship does it have meaning to speak of the ethics of the physician as more than rules for specific instances of involvement with the patient. The standard for the relationship of physician and patient is that health problems are not to be handled in somatic isolation. The help the physician gives must always have as its goal the patient's independent involvement with the illness. For the competence of the physician is not directly established by the presence of a bodily ailment or a somatic deviance. It is established by the lack of independence of the person seeking counsel. Only so does the physician's competence have an ethical basis on which to proceed. Likewise the independence of the one who is sick should not come into consideration only at the end of a process of healing, when the verdict "discharged and cured" can be pronounced. At the very beginning of the treatment of the illness it should be supported and strengthened.

This structure of medical ethics must deal with such elementary matters as the duty of the physician to explain what is taking place, the necessity for the patient to agree to the treatment, the limiting of the treatment to the medically necessary measures over against the temptation to undertake as many profitable procedures as possible. The special problems of the medical profession in ethics have become very complex through the extraordinary extension of the scientific and technical means of treatment, and the arguments are quite involved. Moreover, the relation of the patients to the health care system and their expectations of the medical procedures have changed in both extent and quality. Through the modern health care system medical care has attained such a normative status that it is regarded by many as a component part of the expenditures for social welfare. In this context the limits of health and sickness are no longer clearly discernible. If in this respect there is a crisis in the health care system, it is a crisis closely connected with an ambivalence between individual responsibility and the claims we have on others.

For medical ethics this ambivalence makes itself known in a characteristic manner. If the "affirmation of life" represents a picture of the strong and healthy individual who is completely self-sufficient, then medical care is obligated to respect this picture. If at the same time the only disturbance of this independence recognized by the medical profession is a clear, objectively discernible somatic disorder, that is, the dominant view of illness is a strictly medical view, then the following situation can easily arise. Many persons will accept the limits defined and will exercise their independence within these boundaries even in dealing with disorders in their lives. Every reduction in a person's capability for achievement becomes a sickness that has a claim on the services of the health care system. An integral, practical medical ethic, on the contrary, demands of those with whom it deals that they acknowledge that people lead independent lives and that this includes their dealing with the disruptions of life, thus requiring a "patient's ethic." The ethical problems of illness for the lives of those who are sick and those around them, especially their nearest of kin, appear in a different light. Those who are sick claim the consideration of others and are dependent on them. The compassion that is called for, beginning with the daily care and concern and including the extensive effects on the lives of those involved with the sick, makes of sickness a conflict in which the claims of the sick on the lives of others become intertwined with the claims and expectations of those others. Here the affirmation of life means accepting illness as a situation in which the recognition that people depend on one another becomes in a specific way a concrete expression of their interdependence. For Christians, sickness, one's own as well as that of others, is an exemplary illustration that life cannot be measured by carefully weighed reciprocity and equality. It is of greater importance that one's own interests in life must give way to the concrete needs of others. Love expresses itself in the ethical task of vicarious substitution for those whose independence is decreasing or has been lost. This is the positive expression, not merely something intellectual, but the highly practical case of living out an affirmation of life in instances of disability that call for empathy, that is, in cases of serious illnesses that narrow the scope of one's life. The task that confronts us here is to perceive the ethical significance of the helplessness of those who are sick. Helping means taking the place of the independence that has been lost, not to reinforce and intensify dependence, but to reduce it and make it easier to bear. This means for all those who are called upon to help the sick that they must deny themselves full self-realization and at the same time make a contribution by helping the one who is ill achieve an independence of life even under those conditions. The ethical task of dealing with illness is a specific and concrete example of that common humanity that is given us through reflective thought on the ethical reality of life.

For medical ethics, see especially the well-argued statement in the book by D. Rössler, *Der Arzt zwischen Technik und Humanität,* 1977; U. Eibach, "Gesundheit und Krankheit," *ZEE* 22 (1978): 162–80; G. A. Neuhaus, ed., *Pluralität in der Medizin,* 1980; D. Ritschl, "Menschenrechte und medizinische Ethik," *Wege zum Menschen* 28 (1976): 16–33.

5) Life Conflicts and Guilt: The Ethical Meaning of Pastoral Counseling

Where conflicts give shape to our life, the affirmation of life always involves the restoration of trust. In this respect, the ethical meaning of religious praxis finds concrete expression and is summed up in the concept of pastoral counseling.

Conflicts, even when they are unsolvable or seem so, do not relieve us of the responsibility to go on living. Responsibility here can mean a heavy burden of guilt. On the outside, guilt involves accountability, receiving reprimands, even punishment. Inwardly, in relation to the person involved, guilt involves a sense of inadequacy, failure, and even despair. Conflicts that not only affect one's life from without but directly affect one's way of living require that in our affirmation of life we maintain and renew our capability for living by coming to grips with guilt-producing actions and failures to act. We are required to come to terms with other persons, but coming to terms with oneself has a different significance. Who is the "other" with whom "I" must come to terms? Openly coming to terms with guilt and life conflicts must take into account two preconditions. First, it is possible only if the outcome for the person is not life threatening or even fatal. Confession of guilt lives in the hope of forgiveness (see vol. 1, pp. 59–63). Second, this can be experienced concretely if the individual can in some way confront him- or herself. These two preconditions, in content and in practice, define the ethical significance of the care of souls.

For this ethical discussion we are using the concept in a specific sense. In theology it has other meanings also, e.g., the care of souls as the proclamation of the gospel, presenting the good news to individuals in order to awaken faith; the care of souls as church discipline, exhorting individuals to live in a manner consistent with the principles of the church; the care of souls as giving advice and practical help. These aspects, which provide relevant orientation for the life of the church, are not excluded here even though we will not go more deeply into the discussion of "practical theology."

The care of souls is the application of religious practice as affirmation of life in conflict. The pastoral counselor is defined as a representative of the truth that life, even in the midst of conflicts, is acceptable. This is an affirmation of the Christian meaning of forgiveness. The counselor is also the representative of the individual in the attempt to come to terms with oneself. The relationship between these two roles provides the form and the content for the practice of the care of souls. In this it is of secondary importance whether the task of the care of souls is undertaken by an ordained minister or by one Christian for another.

Reestablishment of trust includes in this context the reestablishment of trust in oneself. This statement is subject to being questioned, because in the ears of theologians it has overtones of self-righteousness, triumphalism. Reestablishment of trust in oneself means in this context that the trust of others has been received. The care of souls deals primarily with individuals. In situations of conflict and guilt, individuals are not in control of the conditions under which they act or of their environment. Affecting or changing these conditions is not within their power. Politicians who experience conflicts of conscience find themselves in such situations because they are exposed to pressures they cannot control. The woman who decides to have an abortion sees herself as threatened by circumstances. The care of souls is directed to individuals in conflict with their world. This is not to say that the social realities, the sum total of interpersonal relationships that play a role in a conflict and determine its conditions, should not have a voice in the care of souls. But in counseling, the emphasis cannot be on influencing or changing these circumstances but on the person who is affected by them. Those who see the situation differently are either involved in the practice of a different discipline, or their care of souls loses its evangelical emphasis and becomes mere legalism.

Reestablishment of trust is the formula for that which in religious language can be expressed in the word *consolation*. Consolation is a highly individual matter. In general social or political usage it means something less than one had hoped for. But consolation as the reestablishment of trust is not mere resignation. When the "world" of conflict cannot be changed simply because there are reasons why no human being is capable of doing so, the strengthening of trust establishes a healing counterforce against that world and provides the strength for inner resistance. Each person is in need of this trust and confidence, even if only in certain cases is individual counseling needed to establish it.

In this respect counseling is the concrete expression of the distinction between the person and his or her work, between the person and the world, and is therefore the religious practice that brings about the reestablishment of the ability to be a responsible individual. The goal of counseling is to promote through the reestablishment of self-confidence a process that carries one beyond a situation of guilt and conflict. Counseling seeks to open up possibilities in life that the person could not find alone. The care of souls as the strengthening of the courage to live even amid seemingly hopeless conflicts draws its life from the trust and confidence on which it, as a religious practice, is based. The counselor is not a great, successful figure who shows others the way to success or provides them with the techniques that will take them to the top. Nor does counseling build on guilt and conflict; it strives to deal with them. It is not based on crises and the negation of life, because these forces produce guilt and conflict for men and women. Its starting point is in our experiences of what is good, in our finding acceptance in life. To point out for those who are hard beset concrete ways to these experiences and to cast new light on them is the way to enable individuals to find such acceptance. In this respect as well it is true that counseling and the counselor are concerned with individual human beings and that they represent for these men and women the affirmation of life.

c. The Search for Ethical Orientation
at the Boundaries of Successful Activity

The third respect in which we take a position in our reflective thought about life becomes concrete at the boundaries of that which we are commanded to do and which lies within our power to accomplish. Boundaries here do not mark the end of our practice of the way we should live but are the place where we must take specific account of the "good" by which our actions at the boundary should be led and determined.

1) At the Boundary of the Shared Life:
The Command to Love Our Enemies

Our ethical responsibility for the way we lead our lives is not exhausted in the specific relationships of social mutuality. The command to love our enemies is the concrete expression of the undefined nature of the ethical requirements.

The boundary of which we are speaking in this first section is present everywhere and in all situations of our lives. Even where there is mutual agreement, there is still a boundary where not everything is unanimously accepted. Reciprocal recognition includes differences that do not disappear. The balance of giving and receiving is asymmetric. Every step that we take in life includes at least an element of one-sidedness in which the one party gives without a corresponding response from the other. Gratitude is not expressed, the expected attitude not displayed. Reflective thought about the ethical reality of life cannot count on everything being equally weighed and balanced. It requires of us more than a rational reciprocity. In our social relationships there is always some loneliness, isolation, or lack of agreement. That is true of the most intimate relationships as well as of the larger, impersonal relationships in the society of which we are a part. It is at this boundary that the search for orientation of which we are now speaking has its place in the conduct of our lives. The way women and men lead their lives is never entirely comprehended in social relationships. This boundary is not the end of our life and activity, not a wall that bars our path. On the contrary, it is here that in more intensive and involved form the question arises of the context of the life that was given to us and that we now share with others. Questions such as how to proceed or where our actions will lead us cannot be answered by anticipation of future patterns of our shared life or by looking back to past norms. Our steps in life and the results of our acts are not already fully oriented by the comprehensive context of relationships from the past. But the demand that we go on leading our lives remains.

Knud E. Løgstrup depicted precisely this one-sidedness in his analysis of the ethical demands as "the radical demand." He said pointedly that this radical demand invalidates the point of view of mutuality; here the demand is encountered in all the concreteness of its basis in the life that we have received from others. We are not ourselves the basis of our own life. It only remains for us to accept it as we take on ourselves responsibility for what we are and what we have. We did not call ourselves into life. (*Die ethische Forderung*, 1959, p. 130.) Compare the various formulations he gave to the radical demand.

At this boundary reflective thought on the basis of the ethical task becomes alive in a manner that we can only accept and seek to follow. The solution to this demand provided in the past in interpersonal relations as they were required and were lived out (as expectation of trust and reciprocity) no longer gives adequate orientation at this boundary. But the demand remains. We cannot simply turn aside and say we can't go any further. Such words as *faithfulness, sacrifice, commitment* become relevant and displace the already defined social relations of life. The obligation to lead our lives aright is not dependent on the expectations and encouragement of others, nor on the absence thereof. It holds in any case. No one can release another human being from it.

Against the background of this discussion of the boundary of social ties and the unconditional nature of the demand, love for our neighbor as love for our enemies can be a specific example of dealing with this boundary. Love for the neighbor includes within it love for our enemies.

See A. Nygren, *Eros and Agape*, 1930, p. 83. Nygren speaks there of how love for the neighbor should be "spontaneous and creative" (p. 84), and intends with this expression the same thing that Løgstrup meant, namely, the absence of reciprocity as being part of the texture of life.

The enemy is the typical case of nonagreement, of the definite limit on being in accord, of a negative social context.

It is certainly possible to include the role of the enemy in the paradigm of social relationships and reciprocity. C. Schmitt, for example, essentially constructed his political theory on the foe/friend relationship and established the recognition, or rather the designation, of the foe as a necessary element in political sovereignty. But is it within my power to designate who my enemy is? Does it make sense to make enemies for the sake of my own identity? Can the basic significance of the political task be seen in terms of the foe/friend relationship? Compare this with the much more relevant theory of integration developed at the same period by R. Smend, *Staatsrechtliche Abhandlungen*, 2d ed., 1968, pp. 475ff., pp. 482ff., and also the *Handbuch der Christlichen Ethik*, vol. 2, 1978, pp. 223ff.

The identity of the enemy is contingent; it marks the limits of communication, the rupture and threatening reversal of communication. Love, which we are bidden to practice as love of our enemies, means dealing with these limits, making responsible decisions at these limits.

The command to love our enemies in Matt. 5:44 has its own problem-laden chapter in the history of exegesis. Two characteristic interpretations have appeared again and again. The one seeks to view the enemy as not an enemy, whether he or she is a personal or a political enemy. To love your enemy means to discover this fact. We must stop picturing others as our enemies and in the face of enmity establish and strengthen the basis for understanding, where possible, through taking the initiative in establishing trust. Love of our enemies means showing goodwill against those of ill will in order to reestablish communication. This line of interpretation, which is in its own way thoroughly constructive, has as its aim the reestablishing of mutual recognition and trust in order to overcome the enmity. This makes good sense, but in the exegesis of the command to love our enemies it leads to the assumption that basically we are not dealing with enemies whom we should love, but, when the matter is seen aright, with a misunderstanding that can be eliminated if we act in a loving manner. In such an ethical reckoning, the command to love our enemies is robbed of its sharpness. The other line of interpretation leads to the conclusion that it is impossible to fulfill the demand at all.

Thus we encounter again and again the view that this command requires the impossible "because it disputes and negates a basic condition of human life in community," as Ch. Dietzfelbinger puts it in defending a widely held view in *Die Antithesen der Bergpredigt*, 1975, p. 52. The command thus is held to play no real role in human life and is important only because it cannot be fulfilled and thus sets a limit to human self-assurance. The paradigm for this interpretation is thus the normal state of social relationships, not a situation at the boundaries of those relationships. The misleading outcome of this interpretation is that the demand is moved from its role in human life and placed far off at one side. "Cannot be fulfilled" means here that there is no empirical possibility of doing it justice. The command to love our enemies would then be a word of judgment, and thus in Christianity the command would carry with it its own breakdown.

Both the view of U. Luck (*Die Vollkommenheitsforderung der Bergpredigt,* 1968), which interprets the demand in the context of the law as understood in the Wisdom tradition, and the literary and sociological analyses of G. Theissen (*Wanderradikalismus. Literatursoziologische Aspekte der Überlieferung von Worten Jesu im Urchristentum* [1973] and his more recent *Studien zur Soziologie des Urchristentums,* 1979, pp. 79ff., and the discussion of the rejection of the use of force and of love for one's enemies, pp. 180ff.), which connect the demand with a radical nomadism, are illustrations of how exegetically it does not lead to an irrational situation that cannot be paraphrased in religious terms, but to a demand that cannot be concretely fulfilled and that can thus be shoved aside as irrelevant.

Løgstrup provides an important clue when he writes, "The radical nature of the demand consists in that care for the life of others is not simply required of me if their trust increases my courage in life, but also when it is quite uncomfortable for me and is a disruptive interference with my very being. . . . In no small degree others may also be victims of my mistrust of them. . . . The command also means that I must take into my care the lives of those others who are potentially at my mercy, regardless of whether they are among my neighbors, or are strangers, and regardless of whether they are dependent on me in a relation of trust that I am pleased with, or in an enmity that calls forth my self-assertion" (op. cit., pp. 46f.).

The command to love our enemies does not mean that we derive our guidance of how to deal with them from some "theory of the enemy," for instance. The enemy does not define the content of the commandment. The enemy constitutes the concrete example that confronts us in the unconditional nature of the command. This should not bring into question the structural correspondence between this commandment and the Golden Rule (vol. 1, p. 71), but at the limits of the Golden Rule the distinct, independent ethical meaning of the command to love others comes to prominence. Love for our enemies goes beyond both the positive and the negative meaning of reciprocity—and also beyond the principle of retribution—and brings into focus the unconditional nature of the command to love. But in this context, what does "unconditional" mean? The enemies, the others, do not prescribe what is to be done. The prevailing norms of conduct are not to be adopted in this situation. The command to love has unconditional validity. The way we live must not be determined by others, by our enemies. The meaning of doing what is good is not qualified by the social function in which it takes concrete

expression. It is the bearer of its own original claims. Not adopting a
position of opposition to our enemies is the preserving of these claims.
Therefore at this boundary situation, those to whom the demands are
addressed become "in the real sense of the term, alone" (Løgstrup), that
is, alone in distinction to relationships of reciprocal acknowledgment and
agreement. This boundary is not the end of the ethical task but the place
where it becomes unavoidable. The standards and pattern of social life,
however they are tested and experienced, must once again lead to
reflective thought about their original meaning. In Tillich's words, the
command to love our enemies is the claim of the "unconditioned" in the
"conditioned." What we are to do cannot be learned from any rule.

> The Sermon on the Mount speaks of "doing good," of "blessing." In Romans
> 12:20 this is connected in a highly effective manner with shaming our enemies.
> Love for our enemies is brought together with the concept from Wisdom
> literature that in this way we "heap burning coals" on the head of our enemy.
> This, however, is to expect an outcome that may not occur. But exegesis has
> always looked for such fine, utilitarian ways of dealing with our enemies. The text
> in Matt. 5:43–45 states the commandment in relation to God: "He makes his sun
> rise on the evil and on the good, and sends rain on the just and on the unjust." In
> this way the text stresses that the evil and the unrighteous do not determine the
> nature of the treatment they will receive. The "perfect" nature of the Father (v.
> 48) means that under no circumstances are we released from the elementary
> responsibility of giving life, because that responsibility is given to us with life
> itself.
> For a systematic view of the state of exegetical-historical interpretation, see J.
> Bekker, "Feindesliebe—Nächstenliebe—Bruderliebe," ZEE 25 (1981): 5–17.

When something is received as life itself is, it cannot be fulfilled in any
empirical sense; it cannot be measured out through any chain of actions
or any program of activity. It is in this direction that we must look if we
speak of this demand as "impossible." If "impossible" meant that no one
could possibly do it, it would also mean that we might as well not try. It
would only be useless effort. "Impossible" points rather to the meaning of
a demand that is received with life itself. Therefore this demand lays
claim to the way we live our lives even on the boundaries of our
agreements with others, on the boundaries of our influence on them. It
does not let us off, even where it is impossible to fulfill in terms of mutual
agreement. The demand does not derive its meaning only when it is
fulfilled or when it succeeds. Like the life itself that we have received, it
determines unconditionally the ethical meaning of our life. The boundary from which we set out becomes for each individual the place where

we experience that we are never freed from taking a stand but must lead our lives in every case as those who have taken a stand in reference to the life that has been given to us, even where this cannot be done in conformity with those actions that are expected and demanded of us.

It is not our success in dealing with our enemies that determines the content and the meaning of our love for them. This love is required because love means that the demand is unconditional, and this is the basis of all individual demands on the way we live our lives.

2) Resistance and Revolution:
The Problem of Violence

Rule by violence calls forth resistance because it does not recognize the boundaries of political action. The ethical problem of dealing with violence can be given concrete form in terms of the openness of the political structure for opposition.

In the problems characterized by the key words *resistance, revolution,* and *violence,* we find once again in equally acute form the themes and structures of the ethical task that have been already developed and discussed in terms of the basic significance of the political task in its various aspects. Assuming all this, the conflict that is to be discussed here is that violence cannot be the goal of political-ethical practice, and still violence is practiced. This is not the place to discuss the phenomenology of violence, resistance, and revolution in their historic and political causes and goals. The use of violence in political life has its basis in the problem of political activity and its rationale. It is not a strictly irrational phenomenon. It forces us to search for ethical orientation at the boundaries of that which we can control through our actions. Violence is the political case in which these boundaries are violated.

The ethical ambivalence of violence is found in its reciprocal nature: There is a correspondence between the use of violence and being the victim of violence. The simple question of whether it is "permissible" to use violence, and if so, under what circumstances, does not adequately come to terms with the ethical problem. It is not simply the use of violence but being victimized by it that constitutes the conflict. Violence is activity that affects others without their consent and contrary to their will, and which is nonetheless violently forced upon them in order to overcome their resistance. Violence arises at the boundaries of issues where the goal can be agreement among persons. The mere lack of consensus cannot be a significant factor here, because there can be other ways of dealing with a lack of consensus. The use of physical violence is the step that violates the boundary. In this first sense, seen in political terms, violence is domination through subjugation.

The ethical ambivalence of violence becomes immediately obvious when we consider the question of its justification. In the perspective of those who use force, it looks quite different from the way it looks to those who suffer from it.

Those who use violence against others, for instance a government which possesses the means for exerting physical coercive force, pursue their goals beyond the limits set by disapproval of the others. It uses violence against them. A specific, distinctive demand for justification of the use of violence arises from this conflict on the part of those who if necessary retreat in the face of violence. It is important to be clear about this, because the political practice of violence is always justified in one way or another; that is, the necessity of justifying violence is basically always acknowledged. But it always depends on who expresses the requirement for justification and from what point of view the violence must be justified. Violence takes the place of agreement that cannot be forcibly extracted from those who are affected by the actions in question. Wherever violence takes the place of agreement or nonagreement, the demand for justification from those who use it is from their perspective the necessity of manipulating this resistance, this nonagreement.

Such justification of violence usually is accompanied by the observation that those affected by the violence had no right to participate in the decision to take the actions in question. They are "incompetent" to judge the goals of the actions that have affected them. Therefore, unfortunately, they can experience the actions in question only as violence, as "naked" force, that is, violence without any good reason. They themselves must bear the blame for their violent subjugation because they lacked insight into the actions that met with general justification, general in the sense of those taking the actions. Thus violence was the only course open. Any special justification of violence for those affected by it is thus superfluous.

Justification of force, while leaving out of the discussion of the action those affected by it, is an example of political rule becoming rule by violence. It is a thoroughgoing denial of the task of justifying the use of force to those affected by it because it negates the conflict that issued in resistance. The need for such justification is ignored when in special conflicts unusual measures are taken and general legal procedures are suspended.

The problem of justifying violence becomes clear when seen in a comparison with the legal imposition of punishment. The legitimation of the state's imposition of punishment (for example, the loss of freedom) means for the lawbreaker the use of physical violence. In a constitutional state this is strictly regulated by a judicial action in which the specific justification of the punishment must always be related to the specific violation of the law. The accused thus receives an orderly and fair trial. The state cannot simply use violence but first requires specific reasons for justifying the punishment, which in the nature of the reasons and in the degree to which punishment is imposed must be presented according to law, that is, regulated by general principles and appropriately imposed.

This comparison shows that the use of force from above is never justified in itself, that is, in the name of the rulers. It can be used only in the name of general goals capable of general acceptance, such as the preservation of public order. These general goals lose the force of their justification as soon as they can simply be imposed by force. They can be accepted as justified only if they and the means used to attain them rest on violence-free consent.

Corresponding ethical arguments apply also to resistance to violent rule. Political resistance that can lead to the use of violence is not directed against the use of force as such, but as a rule against the suspension of reasons for action that are capable of general acceptance and of justification. Resistance is bound to occur wherever government for political or ideological motives violates with force its own boundaries that are established by the basic task of politics. It is along this line of argument that we are to view the resistance to the political regime of National Socialism. This resistance did not proceed from a general criticism of the state as preserver of the rule of law. It was directed against the abuse of the power of the state, against government by violence. The extended and scrupulous discussion within the German resistance that finally led to the assassination attempt against Adolf Hitler on July 20, 1944, was defined by the question of whether the general grounds for justification of a violent resistance against the government in power were adequate to justify fighting violence with violence.

According to our line of argument they were adequate, not solely because of the political convictions and goals of the resistance fighters, but because the Nazi regime completely prevented by violence the possibility of nonviolent political resistance, did not recognize the basic rights of the citizens, and openly interfered with the just functioning of the state. Even so it was not such a general line of argument that led to actual violent resistance. Personal convictions and immediate political engagement cannot be arrived at in that way. In the search for general grounds for justification, the resistance itself became involved in supporting the quality of that order on behalf of which it was fighting against the rule of violence.

Violent resistance at the limit of negotiations that can no longer be conducted by agreement among the parties involved can be justified as necessary resistance if there is no longer any way that this resistance can make itself heard by political means. A form of government or a governmental policy carried out by force that no longer permits the opposition room for disagreement with its policies and goals nor uses regular means such as elections to secure public and free agreement to its political mandate negates its own need to justify its actions and runs the danger of becoming a regime based solely on violence. It arouses, at least potentially, violent resistance. But in such situations resistance is not based on an absolute affirmation of violence and the use of force. Moreover, the history of the line of thought followed by the German resistance would be incorrectly interpreted if anyone concluded that its goal was violence. Violence as the ultimate means for overcoming a violent regime can never be justified solely on the basis of violence but only as a means toward establishing a political system that makes it possible to use nonviolent means toward reflective thought about the political order. To that end resistance is the means to set aside a state of affairs that theoretically and actually hinders such thought. Therefore we affirm that the problem of the right to resist can be solved in the long run only if the right to resist is itself incorporated into the structure of the political system. For example, this is the case in the union of a government based on law and a parliamentary democracy. Here resistance is accorded a status such that it does not need to resort to force in order to achieve its goals. It can be organized as a legal opposition and can therefore commit itself to the processes by which resistance as political opposition functions within the institutions of the commonwealth.

Against the background of this positive goal resistance can be justified, not generally to be sure, but through ethical argumentation in specific situations of oppression and of government by violence. It is necessary, however, that the specific factors involved in the issues and structures be taken into account so that the difference between resistance and a general justification of violence remains clear.

This difference becomes clear when compared with a political concept in which violence as revolution is a constitutive mark of the government and also an element in the structure of the government itself. If a political and social order is in every respect the product of violent class warfare, then in this respect "violence" is a constitutive mark of the political system itself. A political order that not only historically and in a contingent manner but by structural necessity is based on violent revolution must hold that in all cases of disagreement with the goals of the government's policies the use of violence is justified. Under this presupposition violence is inherently necessary in political activity and therefore requires no specific justification.

This revolutionary understanding of violence confronts a twofold problem. In what way shall reflective thought about the political order be expressed if it does not result from the existence of the political will of those who dissent? How can such a system bring about change in its own policies other than through the historic example of violence? For the necessity of political change coupled with the necessity of political struggle, if not provided for in nonviolent means in the political structure (e.g., by a change of government), could be brought about only by means of violence. Therefore a revolutionary political order must always understand itself as the result of violence, as in the class struggle or war of liberation out of which it arose. After the revolution the ethical task is confronted anew in the realization that the revolution did not produce a final political situation. The task involves not only how to deal with one's "enemies" but also with further internal political development. Ethics must here emphasize the insight that even the revolutionary will does not have absolutely at its disposal all the conditions necessary to political activity. Even an order established by a revolution is not in itself so perfectible that it can control the totality of its people's way of life and bring into subjection permanently and without limitation every aspect of political and individual life. Therefore such a political order must reckon with the fact that even revolutionary violence is not a way in which reflective thought on the ethical realities of life can be brought to a standstill.

It is not through denying the political and ethical problems posed by violence and the use of violence but through incorporating them by legitimating and acknowledging the right to resist that we find the only ethically justifiable way to confront them.

The clearest discussion of the place of resistance in a constitutional democracy has been provided by A. Rich in *Radikalität und Rechtsstaatlichkeit. Drei Beiträge zur politischen Ethik,* 1978. On the total content of this section, see also

T. Rendtorff and H. E. Tödt, *Theologie der Revolution. Analysen und Materialien*, 3d ed., 1969. A.-M. Thunberg, "Macht, Zwang und Gewalt—Notwendigkeit und Entartung," *ZEE* 15 (1971): 141–50; J. de Graaf, "Die Gewalt: Kritik ihrer Rechtfertigung," *ZEE* 15 (1971): 129–40; Th. Strohm, "Justitia et Pax—Erwägungen zu einer Grundformel politischer Ethik," *ZEE* 16 (1972): 193–207; Kirchenkanzlei der EKD, ed., *Gewalt und Gewaltanwendung in der Gesellschaft. Eine theologische Thesenreihe zu sozialen Konflikten. Erarbeitet von der Kammer der EKD für öffentliche Verantwortung*, 1973; Th. R. Weber, "Politische Autorität und Revolution," *ZEE* 20 (1976): 98–113; M. Ulrich, "Terroristische Gewalt und demokratischer Rechtsstaat," *Internationale Katholische Zeitschrift* 7 (1978): 123–34; Th. Strohm, "Aspekte des Terrorismus in sozialethischer Sicht," *ZEE* 23 (1979): 118–32.

3) Material Development and the Quality of Life

Those who have it good are not necessarily living a good life. The search for quality of life at the limits of growth must take concrete form in a new responsibility for the quality of human life.

"For what will it profit a man, if he gains the whole world and forfeits his life?" (Matt. 16:26). Making money and increasing the material goods of life are not necessarily identical with increasing and intensifying the quality of life. Therefore a separate emphasis must be given to the search for the quality of life. That search involves a critical attitude toward what we regard as the totality of material growth but is not simply opposed to it. Quality of life is not simply an alternative to or a negation of material well-being. That line of approach would lead us astray. We can't simply say that if we were worse off materially our quality of life would be better. Still, access to large quantities of goods and a strong rate of growth is not identical with access to the quality of life. The search for quality of life always takes place at the boundary of that which we can achieve through economic and technological activity. The experience that the search for success through such activity never ends but starts over again and is intensified must therefore be defined in terms of its ethical direction. And then reflection on our ethical task begins again.

Individuals as well as societies experience the incommensurability of material well-being and a full human life. This resumes an old theme of ethical theology. Compare the discussion of the relationship between happiness and ethical responsibility in vol. 1, pp. 137–46.

The present search for a new definition of the quality of life takes place against the background of an expansion of the material possibilities for enriching life that is without parallel in history. This search leads to the experience that the quantitative and qualitative increase of the possibilities for our lives seems to have become self-perpetuating, and that the search for quality of life has no independent place of its own. Our first question therefore is not how, over against systematic economic expansion, an independent ethical consciousness can be preserved and renewed, but why it seems necessary to do so. The heart of the argument that we find in "alternative" life styles or "alternative" ways of life, for example, is this: The expansion of material goods and services has been liberated from any conscious setting of human goals; it has become self-perpetuating. It becomes a problem when we become aware that the quantitative increase of material wealth in the present threatens to destroy the future of human life.

Erhard Eppler underlined the urgency of the search for quality of life when he wrote that "economic growth is no standard for the humanization of a society, the extrapolation of existing growth trends no longer promises a human future, and we are therefore forced to look for new standards and goals." This means, if we heed the warning, that we must seriously question the equating of a higher standard of living with the quality of life.

The new discussion of the quality of life increases our attentiveness to phenomena that we can already identify as having negative effect on material growth. Where there is a lack of clean air, pure water, uncontaminated food, there are also indications of a future decline in the quality of life. This leads to a different kind of calculation, in contrast with the calculation of economically successful growth. This counter-calculation finds expression in orientation to safety through human solidarity, success through the wise use of one's own powers in work, play, and social life, and the search for a concept of the quality of life that goes beyond merely consuming.

On the first level it may be asked whether on the basis of the concept of quality of life we can develop standards and time measurements that would enable us to compete with the quantifiable standards of the increase of material well-being. This is the discussion now going on about the measurements that can be applied to evaluate the welfare of society. There are attempts to develop new standards for determining the state of the welfare of society which, it is hoped, can as social standards compete with the economic standards of what a society produces.

On this question, see E. Eppler, *Massstäbe für eine humane Gesellschaft: Lebensstandard oder Lebensqualität?* 1974; W. Zapf, ed., *Lebensbedingungen*

in der Bundesrepublik. Sozialer Wandel und Wohlfahrtsentwicklung, 2d ed.,
1987. Here we find attempts to make it possible to measure the quality of life in a
manner that would be relevant for political planning and analysis. Multidimensional evaluation of welfare leads to other points of view for the evaluation of
the quality of the state of social development. But this still does not touch the
heart of the problem of ethical orientation. It leads us only to different orientation
for the requirement for alertness, which is oriented to a differently structured,
qualitatively formulated need.

On a second level the question must be raised regarding which way
and with what methods the quality of life can actually be defined and
then realized. This involves the independent formulation of ethical
judgments in relation to the current self-perpetuating trends.

Eppler formulates the problem as follows: "If we regard freedom and participation in decision-making as components of the quality of life, then the method
by which we define the quality of life is itself a component of that quality. The
democratic process for defining and achieving quality of life is a way of prac-
ticing that quality. Whenever quality of life is determined in an elitist manner
and imposed in an authoritarian manner it is corrupted from the start."

With this political formulation of the method by which quality of life
is achieved, the real problem is identified: The search for quality of life
cannot be separated from the search for human freedom and self-
determination. It is a precarious situation when the dominant impression
is that humans no longer play the leading roles in defining economic
development. Quality of life fundamentally has to do with human
freedom, with the question of whether we are still free in relation to the
condition of the world in which we lead our lives. The question of quality
of life thus comes more and more to be involved in the search for an order
of material life such that it is not only brought into being by human effort
but is also a present order that people freely affirm.

On a third level the search for quality of life becomes identical with an
affirmation of an ascetic life style. The tension between economic growth
and the search for a responsible quality of life can be identified in its
ethical structure if it is brought together with the concept of asceticism.
This was done, for example, by C. F. von Weizsäcker in his article
"Gehen wir einer asketischen Weltkultur entgegen?" *Deutlichkeit,* 1978.

Asceticism in its basic and elementary sense means renouncing possibilities offered to us by economic and technological development, and is
thus a negative definition in relation to the economic order. That can
simply mean limiting one's own consumption and developing a new and

simpler life style. The constructive meaning of such renunciation is self-determination, regaining control of the possibilities for one's own life in contrast to the process of self-perpetuating economic development.

For some years now, H. Schelsky has been pointing us in this direction, beginning with the first great debate about growth in the Federal Republic, involving the consequences of prosperity ("Der Mensch in der wissenschaftlichen Zivilisation," 1961, republished in *Auf der Suche nach Wirklichkeit,* 1965). For Schelsky the main question is, How can the individual maintain his or her moral, religious, and cultural identity, or independence, in the face of the pressures of a society based on ever-increasing consumption? Schelsky believed then that the only known way that we can follow is the way of asceticism, of refusal to follow the crowd.

Asceticism in its basic meaning is a negative form of autonomy. This is true of the old religious or moral meaning of asceticism as well as of its modern renaissance in the form of "alternative life styles." Asceticism as abstinence from fleshly pleasures, from sexuality, from the "way of the world," as its concrete expression has again and again shown us in manifold ways, is oriented toward keeping control of one's own life and determining one's destiny, and therefore identifying the dependencies from which by abstention we can gain or regain autonomy. The modern forms of alternative life styles are a reaction to the complex nature of our technological-economic culture. They are like a mirror of a growth-dominated society and have it as their goal to break out of the imminent interdependence and compulsive conformity of the "system." The guiding concepts of the nature of a "good" life are related to the way in which freedom as self-determination is placed in the service of the goals that the individual has chosen. This is also where C. F. von Weizsäcker's line of argument leads, if he would allow the question of an ascetic world culture to lead to the concept of self-determination, which then renewed itself in the cause of preserving the world, that is, self-determination as a path of service.

Hereby the decisive point of view is evoked. Max Weber, in his well-known analysis of the connection between the Protestant ethic and the spirit of capitalism, has shown that Protestant asceticism was adopted in a subsequent historical-economic context that had effects for the self-determination of asceticism far beyond the religious intention involved.

Max Weber, *The Protestant Ethic and the Spirit of Capitalism,* 1905. The consequences of asceticism, as Weber himself saw, are no longer determined by the will to asceticism itself. At the end of the process there stands the "steel casing" of the capitalistic society: "The Puritans wanted to be people with a vocation—we must be."

However we may judge in detail the historical and sociological connection of asceticism with modern society as Weber developed it, one thing is clear: If asceticism not only serves the goal of direct control of one's life and thus of directly attaining self-determination, but also brings consequences for the whole of society, then every program of asceticism must also take into account the larger consequence that would actually follow from a change in one's own conduct. The firm resolution of those who choose an ascetic or alternative life style is no substitute for responsibility for the consequences of their choice. The model of asceticism and the model of an alternative life style cannot be adequate alternatives to assuming responsibility in the realm where the problems have arisen that lead to the search for alternatives. A program for achieving quality of life cannot include an attempt to escape responsibility for the consequences that it will cause in society. If the search for quality of life could be conducted outside the existing realm of responsibility, it would be an ethically irrelevant and empty search.

In ethical terms, quality of life can only mean that in the face of the consequences for the whole of society adequate measures must be taken to ensure responsibility. Since, however, no one can assume concrete responsibility for the entire global, worldwide process, we must seek to find in the anonymity of global trends of development specific and limited individual areas of responsibility where it is possible to produce developments for which human beings can truly assume responsibility in the context of technological and economic development. The goal of "quality of life" is explicit organizational responsibility in a growth-oriented society where reflective thought confronts situations that are impenetrable and cannot be surveyed in their entirety. Only so will it be possible to establish in this world the idea that it is not the material goods of this world that are decisive for the quality of life but the participation of freedom-loving women and men in the activities of life.

The global definition of responsibility has been the primary concern of the "Club of Rome," which seeks to communicate its insights and theses to those in positions of responsibility. See D. Meadows, *The Limits of Growth,* Report of the Club of Rome on the Human Situation, 1972; M. Mesarovic and E. Pestel, *Menschheit am Wendepunkt,* 1974; D. Gabor and U. Colombo, *Das Ende der Verschwendung. Zur materiellen Lage der Menschheit,* 1976; The RIO Report to the Club of Rome, *Wir haben nur eine Zukunft. Reform der internationalen Ordnung, Leitung Tinbergen, J.*, 1977; Th. Strohm, "'Ziele der Menschheit'—Ethische Urteilsfindung im Horizont des Club of Rome," *ZEE* 22 (1978): 214–28; *Aufgabe Zukunft: Qualität des Lebens*, 10 vols., pp. 1973ff.

4) Growing Old and Facing Death

The experience of growing old and facing death provides concrete examples for an affirmation of life that goes beyond all our possible activities. Orientation at the boundary of life must therefore be explored as a distinct ethical task.

Growing old is a test of the independence of the way we live our lives before God and our fellow human beings. For those who are growing old, the affirmation of life at its boundary becomes a theme of the limits of life, of one's lifetime, of death. It is not the task of ethics to formulate new roles for the elderly or to appeal to their sense of responsibility. Ethics must deal with points of view in ethical orientation that support and promote the independence and the dignity of the elderly.

Growing old changes our view of the world. It brings with it a reduction in the size of the individual's world. This experience determines the way life is lived. Each one must deal with this. Withdrawal from active life; the end of one's career; decrease in communication and in many tasks in which the individual has participated in community life; the loss of responsibilities and competences; whatever name we may give to such experiences, all lead again and again to one point: In growing old the congruity between the individual and society is lessened and slips away. The older person thus receives in a new way that goes beyond his or her personal biography the task of coming to terms with the reality that a human being is more than the present life; one's own life and the environment are not identical. Society outlives the aging of an individual; the time of a society and a person's lifetime are not congruent. Old age becomes a specific time for confirming the independence of life, even in relationship to one's own active possibilities, which in old age are defined by the past, not by the future.

The dignity and independence of age must therefore be sought independent of success, in the conscious affirmation and a partial and gradual loosing of the connections between the individual and society, in acceptance of the fact that life is lived only once and cannot be repeated. The Christian tradition has always taken account of this fact. It has distinguished between an individual's expectation of the end and hope for the future, and an expectation of the end time in terms of the course of human history. The increasing loneliness of old age in relation to "this world" can be seen in the light of the hope for an individual religious role in the community of life on the other side of the activities of life.

The task that old age brings to our lives should therefore not be primarily measured by what an older person can still do, that is, by an expected or simulated extension of the active life. Day care for the elderly, which is organized as a mirror image of kindergarten for the young, can take on the aspect of a negation of the independence of the elderly. The elderly must come to terms with the envy and hate felt for the young, who still have their lives before them. In relation to old age, acceptance of life means, both for the elderly themselves and for those who deal with them, respect and consideration; but respect for past accomplishments must not crowd out confidence in one's ongoing life. An ethical orientation to old age thus has independence as its goal, not in terms of accomplishments but in terms of freedom for the life to come. The relevance that death has for life—a motif of Christian spirituality— does not lie in death itself but in a new openness that we receive for life. This is the bridge between earthly life and life itself. The consciousness of dependence, which becomes intensified in old age, should be taken as a predictive indication that life beyond its earthly span can be relied on because it has its safe shelter in God.

The ethical relevance of old age becomes especially clear if we ask the question of how society deals with old age. A society that evaluates old age and the elderly only in terms of their no longer contributing to society would be a society that would not even be able to acknowledge its own finite nature. The negation of old age is also the negation of the spirit of humanity. To recognize old age for its own worth and its relevance for independent living means for the whole of society an acknowledgment of the limits of our ability to control what is human. In terms of individual life stories, old age means distancing oneself from the current events of the day and from the immediate impact of the present in order to be open to the whole of life. Thus the shift in what we remember when we grow old from current events to memories of the past has symbolic significance. Attention to and patience for the elderly are always good examples of what our relation to life should be. The fragmentation of life's activities in old age is an occasion for specific reflection on the ethical reality of life.

These perspectives and orientations take on concrete significance in the special question of caring for others who are dying. The current discussion of this theme has been given lasting emphasis through the writings of Elisabeth Kübler-Ross. They have made a substantial contribution to overcoming the general silence in the face of suffering and death. Their basis is the principle that to talk about death and dying is the first essential step toward preparation for death while we are living, toward preparation for dying, and toward the humanizing of death. This task is in the foreground of the problem of helping the dying in the more restricted sense. It makes clear that preparation for dealing with death cannot and must not be left till the final phase of the death process. It was the discovery that there was absolutely no consciously structured perception of the final phase of dying when the physician's skills were exhausted and even beyond that point that led Kübler-Ross to direct her attention to caring for the dying. This led to the very helpful approach that emphasized the rationality of the belief that the human being who has begun life is not entirely comprehended in present reality and thus can freely and openly approach the problem of his or her death and can transfer this into attentiveness to the dying.

What does "death with dignity" mean? This is the most important question in dealing with the dying. Human dignity includes the ability to confront death and to understand it and shape it. Therefore death with dignity cannot without further ado be equated with an easy death, with camouflaging the death process. The task that is set for us by the question of death with dignity includes a full and open recognition that there can also be a "bad" death.

The denial of death that we encounter in today's society is the result of a one-sided understanding of human dignity, which values only the "strong" who are noted for accomplishments and success or those for whom the way to self-realization is open. Under the pressure of this concept of human dignity, which is basically lacking in compassion, every trace of human weakness and misery must be hidden away. Even the attitudes of physicians and the medical institutions are no better than the rest of society. By contrast the Christian attitude toward death takes death and dying seriously.

This attitude has consequences for the way we help the dying. Ethically responsible care cannot include the practice of euthanasia in which the physician hastens death. For euthanasia, as freely chosen death with the help of others, is nothing other than an avoidance of death in that it denies the humanity of the death process. The physician's activities may therefore not include taking the initiative in the death of a sick person.

There can also be no doubt that euthanasia cannot be combined with categories by which the value or lack of value of a life is determined. The decision of the physician cannot involve any general decision about classes or groups of persons who should be killed. Care for the dying must be clearly and unambiguously distinguished from any verdict about the worthiness of a person to go on living. Bringing about a death does not qualify as care for the dying. For the same reasons no other interests should be dominant in the process of dying, whether it be an acute situation in which a desirable organ transplant can be made from a dying patient to another person, or whether it be a situation of imminent death in a hospital.

But for our attitude toward death with dignity and especially for the actions of the physician, let it be said that it is not only permissible but also intimately connected with the worth of the patient to let him or her die. The newly articulated consciousness of human dignity in the face of death has called forth a countermovement to the further development of scientific clinical medicine, which with all its technological possibilities for prolonging life is often remarkably insensitive to the human element in the death process. This constitutes a present and acute problem, a task to be faced in our care for the dying.

The nature of the problem involved here can be made clear by the example of Paul Moor's book *Die Freiheit zum Tode,* 1973. He reports how the patient (his sister) raises with him the question of active care in dying and how he indicates his positive feeling about it. Then he continues, "Silence. A dead end. Neither of us wanted to take the next step in the conversation. I had endeavored to say that I would help her if she asked me to. But even in her painful condition she could not bring herself to speak openly and to place me in so dreadful a position."

The question that arises in the extreme situation of an anticipated active hastening of death might be phrased like this: Can the activities of a physician remain humane if they do other than lighten suffering and lessen pain? Beyond that Moor's silence, the "dead end," points to an objective problem: Given a case in which physician and patient had fully agreed to take steps to hasten death, when would be the right time to do so? By what criteria should that point be chosen? It is not a question of the time at which death occurs but of a point in the process of dying. The experience of physicians indicates that there are various phases in the process of dying: deep depression, specific experiences, new euphoria, and courage to go on living. Even the units by which we here measure time cannot be unambiguously defined. How are we to measure the meaning of such phases and experiences when they will never occur

again "in this life"? (See E. Wiesenhütter, *Blick nach drüben. Selbster-
fahrungen im Sterben*, 3d ed., 1976.)

Dying is and will remain a situation at the boundaries. The freedom to
die must also involve and affirm the ambiguity of this situation in all its
individual variations. It is impossible to produce here an accurate interpretation that would accord with the scientific and medical evidence.
Therefore an ethically responsible understanding of caring for those who
are dying must focus on the human process of accompanying the one
who is dying, an understanding that can take the place of the physician's
perplexity when he or she has done all that is possible, and that can give a
good name to the process of letting someone die.

The necessity of caring for the dying exists today because of the
problems that arise from death in a hospital setting. A hospital is an
entirely inappropriate place for caring for a person who is dying because
its whole structure is not adapted to this need. This is no reproach against
physicians but a problem of the organization of hospitals. They often
deny a person the meaningful and attainable basic right to die with
dignity. But still it is not beyond the realm of possibility that the
organization could be adapted so as to make it possible to accompany the
dying in a manner worthy of human dignity.

The seemingly passive care given to the dying is, properly understood,
in reality active care. The following points indicate that this is the case:
Care for the dying is an expression of solidarity, not care given by those
who are superior, healthy, with all five senses still acute, and who in spite
of all their impatience with this weak person still take a little time for him
or her. Care for the dying is care given out of deep solidarity by those
who can lay no claim to endless life, but only, like the sick, to a life that
will end, and in the light of the completion of life are just as dependent
on God's help as is the one who is dying. Care for the dying is in this way
vicarious care for a life in death.

Care for the dying means a consciously planned presence with the one
dying at the time of death. It is to be grounded in gratitude for the life
that has been given and is now about to be taken from the survivors. In
this way care for the dying is also the basis for successful mourning.

In this sense care for the dying is always also help for the living who are
accompanying them. Death brings a separation of person and work,
separation from the person whom God takes to himself and from the
active life that the person has led in this finite existence. In death this
separation becomes final. To perceive it aright is to see it as a distinction,
the basis of which is the validity of the assurance of life itself. Care for the

dying must therefore be seen as multidimensional. The cooperation of the persons and functions involved—physician, pastor, staff—without obliterating their separate competencies can help to prevent the death from becoming a one-sided and therefore an inhumane clinical death. Care for the dying means individualizing the process. Therefore the specific presence of significant individuals is the most important care that can be rendered. Seen in this way, care for the dying directs our attention back to life, to the position we take to life, to our attitude toward life. In the face of death we can affirm that we do not live by that which is present, and our entire lives are directed toward this truth. Thus the theme of care for the dying leads us directly to the tasks of how we are to lead our lives.

On the questions of care for the dying the following are particularly important. Elisabeth Kübler-Ross, *On Death and Dying*, 1969, and *Death, the Final Stage of Growth*, 1975; H. Mochel, *Milder Tod*, 1973; P. Moor, *Die Freiheit zum Tode*, 1973; P. Sporken, *Menschlich sterben*, 1972, and *Umgang mit Sterbenden*, 1978; U. Eibach, *Recht auf Leben, Recht auf Sterben*, 1977. The theme of euthanasia is dealt with in H. Ehrhardt, *Euthanasie und Vernichtung "Lebensunwerten" Lebens*, 1965; V. Eid, ed., *Euthanasie oder soll man auf Verlangen töten?* 1975; H.-D. Hiersche, ed., *Euthanasie*, 1975; A. Eser, ed., *Suizid und Euthanasie als human- und sozialwissenschaftliches Problem*, 1976; M. Büchner et al., *Zur Problematik der Euthanasie*, 1977. On the explicitly theological and ethical aspects of death, see K. Rahner, *Zur Theologie des Todes*, 1965; E. Jüngel, *Tod*, 1972; H. Ringeling, "Bemerkungen zur These vom natürlichen Tod," in the collection he edited, *Ethik vor der Sinnfrage*, 1980.

5) The Good and Salvation:
On Success in Living

Experiences of success in life point the way to how we should live. An approach to the ethical task that is oriented to such experiences serves to enhance the sense of hope in Christian ethics.

The applications of ethics lead us back to our starting point, and that is the topic of this last section. The applications of ethics in the context of ethical theology started from the success of the ethical task that is expressed in the symbol of the "kingdom of God" as our encouragement to serve the good, an abiding encouragement that transcends success (see vol. 1, p. 148). The basis of all ethics is reflected in the concept of the highest good; this realization is the liberating presupposition of the success of a specific life and activity and thus is the basis of our freedom to

act. At the end of our journey through the applications of ethics, this is
something more than and different from the assurance that they are only
examples, not exhaustive and not immune to correction. The end leads us
back to the beginning. Once again, but now in an awareness of the
differentiations and the complexities in the content and structure of this
ethical presentation as it is manifest in the applications, the question of
the relationship of our human lives to the ultimate success of life, to
salvation, is discussed. Thus our theme now is the application of the
applications to that which the symbol "kingdom of God" has to say for
ethics.

For reasons that have been mentioned again and again in the foregoing discussion, theology confronts the problem of determining the
difference between the task of leading our lives and that of serving the
kingdom of God in such a way that the orienting power of the Good is not
lost or distorted. Ethics and salvation, responsibility and hope, works and
faith, creation and the kingdom of God are not mutually exclusive.
Mediating between them is the all-pervading influence in the applications of ethics, not in the sense of their direct identification with each
other, but also not in the sense of their being closed to each other. The
creative context in which the differences are perceived gives its stamp to
the Christian nature of an ethic as a theory of how human life is to be
lived. Ethical theology must transcend the polarization that we encounter at this point. The criticism that a person is endeavoring to bring in the
kingdom of God by proposals for action often contains a warning that is
justified, both theologically and practically. But such a person must be
tested by how he or she draws on the orientation intended by the
"kingdom of God" in ethical theology rather than merely rejecting it.
Otherwise the criticism is unproductive. The criticism that a person is
willing to deal only with the given possibilities of human action in "this
world" and is closed to any radical change likewise often contains an
appropriate warning. But such a person must be tested by how he or she
applies to the conduct of life the ethical and theological intention implied
by that position. Otherwise the criticism is an empty slogan. In this
present discussion ethical theology defines this relationship as "application of the applications." This means a continuation of the path that has
been thus far followed in the ethical line of argumentation.

One of the givens of life as we live it actively is the experience of
success, not total success, but success in specific instances. It brings an
experience of fulfillment. Situations in our personal lives bear witness to
this: love that is fulfilled, enduring friendship, a community that broa-

dens our lives. Situations that reach beyond our individual lives can also bring us fulfillment: a constitution that gives us protection and freedom, enterprises that bring happiness, progress that improves the conditions under which we live. The experience of fulfillment always has something of immediacy about it, no matter how manifold the circumstances and factors that have brought it about. Immediacy means a situation in which we become aware that "This is it," this is what we mean by happiness, fulfillment, success. In this situation there is nothing more that we could desire. The psychology does not interest us here, but our attention is focused on the nature of what we have experienced. We never have a final experience of success in life. It is always specific in relation to time and to its content. When we say that we experience fulfillment, it would be more precise to say that the experience was given to us. We have such an experience, but we cannot create it for ourselves (unless it is by a manipulative process such as intoxication or drug use, an illusory experience). Experiences of fulfillment that come to us are points of orientation in our longing for the good. Through such experiences, whether from within or from without, we receive guidance for the living of our lives. What this comprises can be made clear through the immediacy of such experiences and the factors that make it up and into which it resolves itself again.

Those who against the background of such experiences can only lament that they are not enduring, that experiences of fulfillment are not always and everywhere the experiences of which life is made up; those who when they experience the good think only of the times when it is absent distort life's success into an unending "what ought to be." They suppress the experience of the good in that they do not let it be itself but always want to create it. Those who accept such experiences and even enjoy them, but while having the correct insight that they do not control these experiences believe that they have no lasting consequences, are equating success in life with chance. These experiences have then no role to play in the normal course of life and are therefore suppressed.

The critical point is how we are to define the relationship between ethics and salvation, between the way we lead our lives and success in life.

Theology has always approached this problem by raising the question of the unity of God's actions in the distinction between God's "secular" and God's "spiritual" rule, by the question of how God's coming to "this" world is related to the way people live in the world. This involves the relation between faith as anticipation of success in life on the one hand

and living in responsible fashion on the other. The relationship has been represented in various ways in the concrete applications of ethics. Theological ethics must explain it in terms of the hermeneutical and ontological precedence of the kingdom of God, the gospel, and faith over all the demands we face in leading our human lives. From that point of view ethics and salvation are interrelated and yet remain distinguishable from each other. If eschatology makes ethics possible (see vol. 1, pp. 186–88), then Christian ethics must make this relationship clear in its application to issues. Thus the structure that the line of argumentation has followed may once more be summarized.

We can state that the institutions of life, such as marriage, the political structure of our life in community, the processes of economic activity, the progress made by society, are the realms where this relationship may be observed, and they mediate this experience. Thus we could measure off these concrete applications and through them give examples of what the successful life is. But we cannot arrange these moments in life in such a way that they represent the unmediated nature of this experience. In this respect everything that can be cited concerning the differences among the applications can be accepted without reservation. Even so we can say that the thematic position we have taken on the conduct of life is the point at which ethics and salvation interact for us. To let this position be characterized by the experience of success in life is therefore the task that embraces and directs all other specific tasks; it is the real task of Christians and of the church, it is their proper undertaking.

Ethics as the theory of how to lead the Christian life means then taking a position toward life that gives full scope to the experiences of fulfillment and takes its guidance from them.

Instead of providing further analysis and structure of the text, here at the end I want to bring together a kind of "guidance for life." In the light of the fact that in all its aspects life is something that is given, the Christian life takes concrete shape in encouragement and not in discouragement, in enabling and not in demanding. In respect to the giving of life in all its concrete tasks, the Christian life brings renewal and not destruction, expansion and not constriction. In respect to reflective thought about life and persons, about its openness and lack of limits, the Christian life means growing together and not growing apart, encounter and not separation.

These statements must stand on their own. They represent the attitude with which the experience of the good, however limited and specific it may be, can through the way we lead our lives enter into our ethical tasks. Our attitudes, our practice of the faith, mediate between the ground of our hope and the need of the human world for hope and thereby reinforce the meaning of ethics for hope.

Ethics is not the final word in theology. It is the application of the ethical meaning of theology and undertakes the task of discerning how the conduct of our human lives participates in the reality by which all our actions live and toward which they move. Therefore constructive work is more important than criticism, or to put it more simply, the Yes is more important than the No.

Index of Subjects

Index of Authors